Who was the mysterious "Wonderman of Europe"?

The end of the 18th century marked the end of an old order in France. And one man was trying to make the transition as smooth as possible. He was the Count Saint Germain, known throughout Europe as the "Wonderman."

He dazzled the aristocracy and the royal courts with youth potions, jewels and magical feats to engage their attention for a more serious purpose: to warn them of the impending revolution and the bloodbath that would follow. At the same time, he used his powers to expand scientific knowledge.

In this century, Saint Germain continues to work for the freedom and enlightenment of mankind. And he has dictated to Mark L. Prophet and Elizabeth Clare Prophet formulas you can use to practice alchemy for your own liberation.

You will learn how to materialize objects from a universal source of energy. But the primary purpose of alchemy is not to create wealth or to change lead into gold.

Alchemy is a powerful method of transforming yourself. So powerful that the principles Saint Germain imparts make this the greatest of all self-help books.

The basic message: you are not powerless. You do not have to be a victim of circumstances. You can alter your destiny. You can change your life, your nation and your planet.

Saint Germain tells you *how* to do it. He reveals secrets he has used for centuries. Techniques you can use today to duplicate his achievements.

He tells you how Jesus used alchemy to walk on water, multiply loaves and fishes, change water into wine and perform other "miracles." And he explains how *you* can:

- Create mental pictures to materialize objects, including an amethyst Maltese cross
- Harness energy to alter matter
- Control your emotions
- Get rid of anxiety—for good
- Look younger and have more energy
- Create a cloud of infinite energy to change your life, fulfill your destiny and heal your planet

Saint Germain On Alchemy contains a 117-page handbook of essential alchemical and spiritual terms. It also includes illustrated sections on:

- Saint Germain as the Wonderman of Europe
- The Mystical Origins of the United States of America
- The Great Seal of the United States
- George Washington's Vision of America's Trials

Saint Germain On Alchemy illumines and inspires. And it gives you the keys to self-transformation.

But they won't do you any good unless you use the alchemical formula revealed in this book and encrypted in the acronym: TRY!

SAINT GERMAIN ON

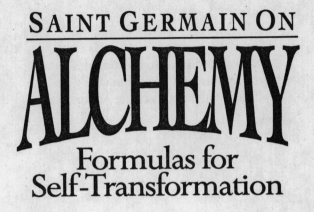

ALCHEMY

Formulas for
Self-Transformation

Recorded by

Mark L. Prophet
Elizabeth Clare Prophet

SUMMIT UNIVERSITY ◆ PRESS®

Dedicated to the disciples
of East and West who would be
the first alchemists of the Aquarian age

SAINT GERMAIN ON ALCHEMY
Formulas for Self-Transformation
Recorded by
Mark L. Prophet and Elizabeth Clare Prophet

Library of Congress Catalog Card Number: 85-61263
International Standard Book Number: 0-916766-68-3

This book is set in 11 point Electra with 1.5 points lead.
Printed in the United States of America
First Printing: 1985. Second Printing: 1986. Third Printing: 1987
Fourth Printing: 1993

SUMMIT UNIVERSITY 🌿 PRESS®

Contents

BOOK TWO
INTERMEDIATE STUDIES IN ALCHEMY
Alchemical Formulas for Self-Mastery

JESUS CHRIST AND SAINT GERMAIN
Wayshowers of the Aquarian Age

BOOK THREE
A TRILOGY ON THE THREEFOLD FLAME OF LIFE
The Alchemy of Power, Wisdom and Love

Contents ix

al·che·my \ˈalkəmē, -mi \ *n* -ES [ME *alkamie, alquemie,* fr. MF or ML; MF *alquemie,* fr. ML *alchymia,
alchimia,* fr. Ar *al-kīmiyā'* the philosopher's stone, the
alchemy, fr. *al* the + *kīmiyā',* fr. LGk *chēmeia,* prob.
alter. of *chymeia,* prob. fr. Gk *chyma* fluid, fr. *chein* to
pour—more at FOUND (to melt)] **1** : a medieval
chemical science and speculative philosophy aiming
to achieve the transmutation of the base metals into
gold, the discovery of a universal cure for disease,
the discovery of a means of indefinitely prolonging
life, and the great or magic power of transmutation
2 : a power or process of transforming something
common into something special **3** : an inexplicable
or mysterious transmuting **4 a** *archaic* : a golden-
colored alloy **b** *obs* : a golden-colored trumpet

SAINT GERMAIN AS THE WONDERMAN OF EUROPE

The Wonderman of Europe

"Will you have the kindness to tell me," said the Countess v. Georgy, "whether your father was in Venice about the year 1710?"

"No, Madame," replied the count quite unconcerned, "it is very much longer since I lost my father; but I myself was living in Venice at the end of the last and the beginning of this century; I had the honour to pay you court then. . . ."

"Forgive me, but that is impossible; the Comte de St. Germain I knew in those days was at least 45 years old, and you, at the outside, are that age at present."

"Madame," replied the count smiling, "I am very old."

"But then you must be nearly 100 years old."

"That is not impossible," Saint Germain replied.

He *was* the Wonderman of Europe—this we know. But was he the lost third son of Prince Ferenc Rakoczy II, the deposed Hungarian ruler? Or did he, as the Ascended Master Saint Germain, materialize a body to give the appearance that he had descended through the royal house of Hungary? His birth, death, and true identity are shrouded in mystery.

But one thing *is* certain: he was highly visible in the royal courts—and invisible! He was seen to 'disappear' as he left the private quarters of the king and queen at Versailles. Without a doubt, his feats as the Count Saint Germain are exclamation points across the diaries of the eighteenth-century greats.

In the court memoirs of Madame de Pompadour, Prince Karl of Hesse and Madame d'Adhémar, he is remembered as *l'homme extraordinaire*. Described as slim but well-proportioned, of medium height and with pleasant features, he had fascinating eyes which captivated the observing who chanced to study them. He wore diamonds on every finger—and on his shoe buckles. Even after his remarkable conversation with the Countess de Georgy in 1767, he did not age.

Madame d'Adhémar met him in 1789. "It was himself in person.... Yes! with the same countenance as in 1760, while mine was covered with furrows and marks of decrepitude."

Ageless, a mystery man. There is nothing, it seems, he could not do. He was admired as a great philosopher, diplomat, scientist, healer, artist and musician. He knew history so well that it would seem he had actually experienced the events he related. Madame de Pompadour recalled that "sometimes he recounted anecdotes of the court of the Valois [French royal house of 1328 to 1589] or of princes still more remote, with such precise accuracy in every detail as almost to create the illusion that he had been an eyewitness to what he narrated."

His knowledge extended not only back in time but also around the globe. "He had traveled the whole world over," de Pompadour wrote, "and the king lent a willing ear to the narratives of his voyages over Asia and Africa, and to his tales about the courts of Russia, Turkey and Austria."

He spoke at least twelve languages so fluently that everywhere he went he was accepted as a native. These included French, German, English, Italian, Spanish, Portuguese, Russian and Eastern languages. "The learned and the oriental scholars have proved the knowledge of the Count St. Germain," wrote a countess at Louis XV's court. "The former found him more apt in the languages of Homer and Virgil than themselves; with the latter he spoke Sanskrit, Chinese, Arabic in such a manner as to show them that he had made some lengthy stay in Asia."

He was with General Clive in India in 1755, where he said he learned to melt jewels. At the court of the Shah of Persia from 1737 to 1742, Monsieur de Saint Germain exhibited his skill at precipitating and perfecting precious gems, particularly diamonds.

He also traveled to Japan, as he told Madame d'Adhémar. There is no telling where else he visited, for he would appear and reappear unpredictably all over Europe. Yet there was a purpose behind all that the Wonderman did. And his wonders went far beyond mere genius.

He was skilled in healing and the use of medicinal herbs. Some have speculated that it was Saint Germain's use of herbs combined with his simple eating habits that prolonged his life. Prince Karl of Hesse wrote, "He thoroughly understood herbs and plants, and had invented the medicines of which he constantly made use, and which prolonged his life and health."

He gave an elixir to Madame v. Georgy which made her keep looking 25 for 25 years, according to contemporary accounts. She lived so long that she came to be called the old everlasting countess.

Saint Germain also prescribed an herb tea for the health of the Russian army and he offered to cure Jacques de Casanova of an acute disease in three days. But the rogue declined the drugs, not trusting anyone, not even the most trusty of alchemists, having himself swindled many.

The count was a virtuoso on both the piano and violin as well as an accomplished painter, poet and artisan. Wherever he traveled, he was welcomed as scholar, statesman and raconteur. He formed secret societies, was a leading figure in the Rosicrucians, Freemasons and Knights Templar of the period, and penned the occult classic *The Most Holy Trinosophia*, using a mixture of modern languages and ancient hieroglyphics.

Monsieur de Saint Germain never confirmed

or denied anything that was said about him. Instead, he would respond with a smile or a studied evasiveness. His skill as an alchemist was praised by Louis XV, who provided him a laboratory and residence at the royal castle of Chambord. And his alchemical demonstrations were nothing short of miraculous according to his chroniclers.

Madame du Hausset, who was *femme de chambre* to Madame de Pompadour, writes at some length of Saint Germain's marvels.

Her memoirs tell us that in 1757, "the King ordered a middling-sized diamond which had a flaw in it, to be brought to him. After having it weighed, his Majesty said to the Count: 'The value of this diamond as it is, and with the flaw in it, is six thousand livres; without the flaw it would be worth at least ten thousand. Will you undertake to make me a gainer of four thousand livres?' St. Germain examined it very attentively, and said, 'It is possible; it may be done. I will bring it to you again in a month.'

"At the time appointed the Comte de St. Germain brought back the diamond without a spot, and gave it to the King. It was wrapped in a cloth of amianthos, which he took off. The king had it weighed immediately, and found it very little diminished. His Majesty then sent it to his jeweller . . . without telling him of anything that had passed. The jeweller gave him nine thousand six hundred livres for it. The King, however, sent for the diamond back again, and said he would keep it as a curiosity."

At one European court, this eighteenth-century Merlin requested that several bones from a deer and boughs of a tree be brought to him. When presented with these "ingredients," he slipped into a large palace dining room. Several moments later he reappeared and invited the guests to follow him. When the doors were opened, all were astounded: inside the room was a forest with deer grazing around a lushly laden board of haute cuisine.

With similar ease, Saint Germain accomplished the alchemist's dream—the changing of base metals into gold.

In 1763, Count Karl Cobenzl wrote in a letter that Saint Germain perfected "under my own eyes . . . the transmutation of iron into a metal as beautiful as gold, and at least as good for all goldsmith's work." The Marquis de Valbelle reported seeing Saint Germain change a silver six-franc piece into gold.

Casanova wrote of a parallel experiment in which Saint Germain changed a twelve-sols piece into a gold coin. However, he thought it was a trick and hinted to Saint Germain that he had substituted one for the other. Saint Germain rebuked him: "Those who are capable of entertaining doubts of my work are not worthy to speak to me," and bowed the unbeliever out of his laboratory at once and for good.

The count was not only an alchemist, but an Eastern adept, displaying yogic behavior, meditating in the lotus posture and calming animals by his fiery spirit.

One Dutch admirer, J. van Sypesteyn, wrote, "Sometimes he fell into a trance, and when he again recovered, he said he had passed the time while he lay unconscious in far-off lands; sometimes he disappeared for a considerable time, then suddenly re-appeared, and let it be understood that he had been in another world in communication with the dead. Moreover, he prided himself on being able to tame bees, and to make snakes listen to music."

A Master of masters—*he was not a charlatan.* Nor was he a figment of the imagination. He is mentioned in the letters of Frederick the Great, Voltaire, Horace Walpole, Casanova and even appears in the newspapers of the day—*The London Chronicle* of June 1760, a Florentine paper, *Le notizie del Mondo*, in July of 1770, and also in the *Gazette of the Netherlands*.

He was entrusted with the state secrets of several countries, indicating that he enjoyed the long-standing trust of those he dealt with at court. He was sent on negotiating missions by Louis XV, one of the first to practice secret diplomacy. The archives of France contain evidence that English, Dutch, and Prussian statesmen of his time regarded the count as an authority in many fields.

"He appeared to be more intimately acquainted with the secrets of each court than the *chargé d'affaires* of the king," Madame de Pompadour wrote. Voltaire remarked that Saint Germain knew the secrets of the prime ministers of England, France and Austria.

Although many suspected him of being a rogue and swindler, it is clear that money was not his object. He was always well provided for, and Madame de Pompadour writes that the count gave the king beautiful paintings and passed out "diamonds and jewels with astonishing liberality." Clearly not the behavior of a treasure hunter.

Indeed, he was a philanthropist. Prince Karl of Hesse described him as "the friend of humanity, wishing for money only that he might give to the poor; a friend to animals, his heart was concerned only with the happiness of others."

"Wherever he was personally known he left a favourable impression behind, and the remembrance of many good and sometimes of many noble deeds. Many a poor father of a family, many a charitable institution, was helped by him in secret," van Sypesteyn wrote.

In *Studies in Alchemy* Saint Germain explains that he actually precipitated goods to give to the poor. "When serving in Europe to dissipate some of the poverty and confusion so prevalent there," he writes, "I did use universal alchemy to produce the substance which, although temporary in nature, supplied many human needs."

But why all of this extravaganza at court? What was he trying to prove? He was trying, precisely—with wit and humor and his prophetic, masterful presence—to galvanize an age in the face of the inevitable passing of the old order. His plan of action was to establish a United States of Europe—before the pulling of the ripcord of the bloody French Revolution should leave nothing bad or good of the royal houses of Europe.

Another of Saint Germain's aims was to accelerate the progress of science and technology to lift man into a capacity for greater spiritual awareness. At times he played the part of patron saint of the Industrial Revolution.

Count Karl Cobenzl witnessed his development of mass-production techniques. Among them were bleaching flax to look like Italian silk, dyeing and preparing skins "which surpassed all the moroccos in the world, and the most perfect tanning; the dyeing of silks, carried to a perfection hitherto unknown; the like dyeing of woollens; the dyeing of wood in the most brilliant colours penetrating through and through . . . with the commonest ingredients, and consequently at a very moderate price."

And believe it or not, Saint Germain actually set up a hat factory for Count Cobenzl! He also began mass producing his own various inventions while sponsoring other technological advancements. "I am much needed in Constantinople; then in England," he told one memoir writer, "there to prepare two inventions which you will have in the next century—trains and steamboats."

His object seemed to be to assist the rise of a middle class while convincing the monarchy to make a smooth transition into the modern age. While he accomplished the former, the apathy of the ruling classes and the intrigue of corrupt advisers thwarted his success in the latter.

The monarchs, while in admiration of his miraculous accomplishments, pronounced them "interesting." Always willing to be entertained by him, they were not easily prodded into action. When it came to taking his advice, they politely ignored him; and their ministers, jealous to the quick, despised him.

A case in point is Louis XV's aborted secret mission. He sent Saint Germain as his envoy to Amsterdam to negotiate a peace treaty ending the war between the French and Austrian alliance and the English and Prussians.

Too soon, the French ambassador in Amsterdam got wind of it, was offended that the king would employ an "obscure foreigner" in his stead, and complained to the foreign minister, the Duc de Choiseul, who immediately sent out orders for Saint Germain's arrest. The duke's desire was not for peace, at least not then, and especially not a peace for which he could not claim credit.

The next day before the King and his council, Choiseul exposed the mission, averring, "I am convinced that no one here would be bold enough to desire to negotiate a Treaty of Peace without the knowledge of Your Majesty's Minister for Foreign Affairs!"

The king, as usual, took the course of least resistance. He neither challenged his minister nor championed Saint Germain and remained silent as to his own part in the affair. However, discredited, his peace mission aborted, the count did manage to avoid arrest—perhaps by the warning of the king or, more likely, by his own foreknowledge.

The same treatment continued under Louis XVI, but this time Saint Germain was prepared. First, he sought audience with the queen. Madame d'Adhémar was present and recorded the scene. He spelled out for Marie Antoinette precise details of the terror to come and begged her to warn Louis.

He said, "Some years yet will pass by in a deceitful calm; then from all parts of the kingdom will spring up men greedy for vengeance, for power, and for money; they will overthrow all in their way. . . . Civil war will burst out with all its horrors; it will bring in its train murder, pillage, exile. Then it will be regretted that I was not listened to."

He told the queen that he wanted to see the king without the knowledge of Monsieur de Maurepas, saying of the king's chief adviser, "He is my enemy; besides, I rank him among those who will further the ruin of the kingdom, not from malice, but from incapacity." Stating his availability "at their Majesties' command,"

Monsieur de Saint Germain took his leave of the queen.

He left for Paris, heading out of the country, having told Madame d'Adhémar that he knew the king would speak to Maurepas and he had no wish to be thrown into the Bastille and have to resort to a miracle to get out. She protested that the king might not. In that case, he replied, he would be back in time.

Marie Antoinette went straight to the king, who then quizzed Madame d'Adhémar about the count, saying he had "seriously alarmed the queen." Sure enough, Louis asked the advice of Maurepas, who told him Saint Germain was a rogue, whereupon the self-serving adviser went immediately to the residence of Madame d'Adhémar to arrest the Wonderman. Saint Germain was nowhere to be found. No sooner had he declared his intent to lock up Saint Germain in the Bastille than the door to her room opened and the thaumaturgist entered. Approaching Maurepas, he said:

"M. le Comte de Maurepas, the King summoned you to give him good advice, and you think only of maintaining your own authority. In opposing yourself to my seeing the Monarch, you are losing the monarchy, for I have but a limited time to give to France and, this time over, I shall not be seen here again until after three consecutive generations have gone down to the grave. I told the Queen all that I was permitted to tell her; my revelations to the King would have been more complete; it is unfortunate that you should have intervened between His Majesty and me. I shall have nothing to reproach myself with when horrible anarchy devastates all France. As to these calamities, you will not see them, but to have prepared them will be sufficient memorial of you. . . . Expect no homage from posterity, frivolous and incapable Minister! You will be ranked among those who cause the ruin of empires."*

"M. de Saint-Germain, having spoken thus without taking breath, turned towards the door again, shut it, and disappeared," Madame d'Adhémar writes. "All efforts to find the Count failed!"

And the lesson is wisely and painfully learned: an alchemist of greatest mastery, even *the* adept of the centuries, having only the best of intentions and the solution to global problems and the rise and fall of nations, must bow to the free will of mortals. He may advise, but not command; and when ignored, he is obliged to withdraw.

Monsieur de Saint Germain continued to write letters to the queen, warning of impending debacle, but once the crisis had reached a certain point there was nothing he could do to turn back the revolution that had been building since the death of that master statesman, Louis XIV.

Several years later, just before the storm broke, Saint Germain met Madame d'Adhémar

---

*Monsieur de Maurepas died in 1781, seven and a half years before the storming of the Bastille, the symbolic end of the *ancien régime*. History remembers him as the one who dissuaded Louis XVI from instituting reforms which might have forestalled the Revolution and allowed France to avoid the Reign of Terror, passing smoothly from monarchy to republic.

again early one morning in a chapel in the *Récollets* in Paris. He predicted the doom of the king and queen and said that it was too late to save them. The following is her recording of the conversation:

"What did I tell you, and the Queen too? that M. de Maurepas would let everything be lost, because he compromised everything. I was Cassandra, or a prophet of evil, and now how do you stand?"

"Ah! Comte, your wisdom will be useless."

"Madame, he who sows the wind reaps the whirlwind. Jesus said so in the Gospel, perhaps not before me, but at any rate his words remain written, and people could only have profited by mine."

"Again!" I said, trying to smile, but he without replying to my exclamation said:—

"I have written it to you, *I can do nothing, my hands are tied by a stronger than myself.* There are periods of time when to retreat is impossible, others when *He* has pronounced and the decree will be executed. *Into this we are entering.*"

"Will you see the Queen?"

"No, she is doomed."

"Doomed! To what?"

"To death!"

Oh, this time I could not keep back a cry, I rose on my seat, my hands repulsed the Comte, and in a trembling voice I said:

"And you too! you! what, you too!"

"Yes, I——I, like Cazotte."

"You know...."

"What you do not even suspect. Return to the Palace, go and tell the Queen to take heed to herself, that this day will be fatal to her; there is a plot, murder is premeditated."

"You fill me with horror, but the Comte d'Estaing has promised."

"He will take fright, and will hide himself."

"But M. de Lafayette...."

"A balloon puffed out with wind! Even now they are settling what to do with him, whether he shall be instrument or victim; by noon all will be decided."

"Monsieur," I said, "you could render great services to our Sovereigns if you would."

"And if I cannot?"

"How?"

"Yes; if I cannot? I thought I should not be listened to. The hour of repose is past, and the decrees of Providence must be fulfilled."

"In plain words, what do they want?"

"The complete ruin of the Bourbons; they will expel them from all the thrones they occupy, and in less than a century they will return to the rank of simple private individuals in their different branches."

"And France?"

"Kingdom, Republic, Empire, mixed Governments, tormented, agitated, torn; from clever tyrants she will pass to others who are ambitious without merit. She will be divided, parcelled out, cut up; and these are no pleonasms that I use, the coming times will bring about the overthrow of the Empire; pride will sway or abolish distinctions, not from virtue but from vanity, and it is through vanity that they will come back to them. The French, like children playing with handcuffs and slings, will play with titles, honours, ribbons; everything will be a toy to them, even to the shoulder-belt of the National Guard; the greedy will devour the finances. Some fifty millions now form a deficit, in the name of which the Revolution is made. Well! under the dictatorship of the philanthropists, the rhetoricians, the fine talkers, the State debt will exceed several thousand millions!"

He took his leave of Madame d'Adhémar with these words, "I will take up my part again and leave you. I have a journey to take to Sweden; a great crime is brewing there, I am going to try to prevent it. His Majesty Gustavus III interests me, he is worth more than his renown."*

Departing the small chapel, the Wonderman disappeared! Madame d'Adhémar's confidential servant, who had been stationed at the door of the church, saw no one pass.

She herself, stunned by Saint Germain's words, remained in the chapel and decided not to warn the queen that day but to wait until the end of the week. By then it was too late.

---

*Gustav III of Sweden, a monarch whose reign was known as the Swedish Enlightenment, introduced reforms such as free trade and freedom of the press while strengthening the monarchy. In the atmosphere created by an aristocratic conspiracy against him, he was shot and mortally wounded in March 1792.

Saint Germain's prophecy came true in astonishing detail. The next time Madame d'Adhémar saw him was at the Place de la Révolution October 16, 1793, at the beheading of Marie Antoinette. The Master was with her in the end as he had been with her from the beginning, watching over her from the moment she had arrived in France from Austria to become the ill-fated French queen.*

Next, Saint Germain backed Napoleon in a final attempt to establish the United States of Europe; le Petit Caporal took Saint Germain's power, but not his advice, and sought to use it in self-gain, exceeding the Master's instructions—whereupon Saint Germain withdrew, as by now he was wont to do, leaving the ambitious and foolhardy Napoleon to his Waterloo.

For Saint Germain, this was the coup de grace. His opportunity to set aside the retribution due an age had passed. And so the "Mystic Messenger" departed Europe. Henceforth, until his return in 1981, the only voice of fate the continent would hear or heed would be Karma.

While Napoleon was still a child, Franz Gräffer recalls the count saying, ". . . One needs to have studied in the Pyramids as I have studied. Towards the end of this century I shall disappear out of Europe, and betake myself to the region of the Himalayas. I will rest; I must rest. Exactly in

---

*The sixteenth and last child of the Holy Roman Emperor Francis I and Maria Theresa, Marie Antoinette was married to Louis XVI in an expediently arranged marriage between the Hapsburgs and the Bourbons in 1770.

eighty-five years will people again set eyes on me. Farewell, I love you."*

The rejection of Saint Germain by the crowned heads of Europe caused him to depart the visible world. And the words of Jesus' lamentation might well have been his own: "O Jerusalem, Jerusalem, thou that killest the prophets, and stonest them which are sent unto thee, how often would I have gathered thy children together, even as a hen gathereth her chickens under her wings, and ye would not!"

As he himself said, "Thus it is ever with us truthful people; deceivers are welcomed, but fie upon whoever says that which will come to pass!"

In his devotion to the cause of world freedom, Saint Germain had been working diligently on many fronts. "Having failed in securing the attention of the Court of France and others of the crowned heads of Europe," he said through his twentieth-century Messenger Mark L. Prophet, "I turned myself to the perfectionment of mankind at large, and I recognized that there were many who, hungering and thirsting after righteousness, would indeed be filled with the concept of a perfect union which would inspire them to take dominion over the New World and create a Union among the sovereign states. Thus the United States was born as a child of my heart

*See I. Cooper-Oakley, *The Comte de St. Germain: The Secret of Kings* (London: The Theosophical Publishing House Limited, 1912), pp. 1, 27–29, 36–38, 42, 43, 50–52, 66–67, 72–73, 87–91, 99, 144–45. Available through Summit University Press.

and the American Revolution was the means of bringing freedom in all of its glory into manifestation from the East unto the West."

Even before the debacle in France, Saint Germain was busy forming a more perfect union out of the Thirteen Colonies. According to tradition, on July 4, 1776, he inspired upon one of the signers of the Declaration of Independence an impassioned speech urging the patriots to "Sign that document!"

In a meeting in Cambridge, Massachusetts, he, "the mysterious old professor," inspired the designing of the flag. Throughout the Revolution he overshadowed General George Washington and when the time came anointed the Master Mason the first president of the United States of America.

True to his word, Saint Germain reappeared in the latter nineteenth century to assist the Masters M. (El Morya), K.H. (Koot Hoomi), and Serapis Bey in the founding of the Theosophical Society. In the 1930s, Saint Germain contacted Guy and Edna Ballard and gave them the initiations and revelations they recorded in the books *Unveiled Mysteries*, *The Magic Presence*, and the *I AM Discourses*.

In 1958, the Ascended Master El Morya on Saint Germain's behalf founded The Summit Lighthouse in Washington, D.C., through Mark L. Prophet to continue the publishing of the Ascended Masters' Teachings and to maintain weekly contact with their chelas throughout the world through letters called Pearls of Wisdom.

Under the canopy of The Summit Lighthouse Saint Germain then sponsored the Keepers
of the Flame Fraternity, providing graded lessons
in cosmic law to those who would join him in
keeping the Flame of Life for mankind. He dictated *Studies in Alchemy* in 1962. *Intermediate
Studies in Alchemy* followed in 1970. *The Trilogy
on the Threefold Flame of Life* was delivered by
the Master as a transition between the two,
whereas *The Alchemy of the Word* represents his
tutoring of our souls by revelations and under-
standings communicated during the past twenty-
five years of our service together.

Saint Germain, by his own admission, has
never ceased his behind-the-scenes activity to
contact souls of light not only in Europe and
America but throughout the world. His has been
an unceasing effort to prevent World War III,
nuclear holocaust, the dire predictions of Nostra-
damus, the perils of the Fátima prophecy and a
host of ills knocking at the doors of the nations
whose rumblings recall Jesus' vision of these end
times recorded in the Gospels and Revelation.

If the captains and the kings, the powerful
and the weak-willed have ignored this world
spokesman for freedom—this alchemist of the
sacred fire par excellence—keepers of the flame of
liberty in every nation have not.

At one point in his career, having lost faith
in the ruling classes and any ability they might
have had to change the course of history, Saint
Germain was heard to exclaim, "O for ten

thousand scrubwomen who will faithfully give to the cause! With these I will show you how to change the world with Divine Truth."

And so it came to pass... Through the common people, whom the Lord and Abraham Lincoln also loved, Saint Germain's mission to bring individual freedom, peace and enlightenment to the earth continues unchecked and without parallel in the history of mankind. His is a message and a worldwide grass roots movement. He calls it his Coming Revolution in Higher Consciousness!

Every lover of freedom on earth, every spirit quickened by freedom's flame deserves to know his name, to make contact with his heart, to study his writings and to support his cause—which is the cause of all the people of planet earth.

To that end this little book: *Saint Germain On Alchemy*, is released to the world with greatest joy this Thanksgiving Day 1985.

Praise God who sent beloved Saint Germain to free our captive hearts in Jesus' name!

Elizabeth Clare Prophet

November 28, 1985
The Royal Teton Ranch
"where my heart is"
Montana, U.S.A.

MARK L. PROPHET

ELIZABETH CLARE PROPHET

*The inner meaning of alchemy is simply
all-composition, implying the relation of the all
of the creation to the parts which compose it.
Thus alchemy, when properly understood, deals
with the conscious power of controlling mutations and transmutations within Matter and
energy and even within life itself. It is the
science of the mystic and it is the forte of the
self-realized man who, having sought, has found
himself to be one with God and is willing to
play his part.*

SAINT GERMAIN

Book One

Studies in Alchemy

The Science of Self-Transformation

Saint Germain

Full many a glorious morning have I seen
Flatter the mountain-tops with sovereign eye,
Kissing with golden face the meadows green,
Gilding pale streams with heavenly alchemy.

SHAKESPEARE
Sonnet XXXIII

CHAPTER I

The Law of Transfer of Energy

Two thousand years ago when Christ walked upon the waters of the Sea of Galilee, his demonstration was a manifestation of the natural law of levitation operating within an energy framework of cohesion, adhesion, and magnetism—the very principles which make orbital flight possible. The light atoms composing the body of Christ absorbed at will an additional quantity of cosmic rays and spiritual substance whose kinship to physical light made his whole body light, thereby making it as easy for him to walk upon the sea as upon dry land.

His body was purely a ray of light shining upon the waters. The most dazzling conception of all was his ability to transfer this authority over energy to Peter through the power of Peter's own vision of the Christ in radiant, illumined manifestation.

By taking his eyes temporarily from the Christ, however, Peter entered a human fear vibration and vortex which immediately densified his body, causing it to sink partially beneath the raging seas. The comforting hand of Christ, extended in pure love, reunited the alchemical tie; and the flow of spiritual energy through his hand raised Peter once again to safety.

The further example of the Master Jesus releasing a flow of energy—as in the case of the woman who touched the hem of his garment without his knowledge aforehand—shows the impersonal love of God which responds equally to the call of faith from any of those creatures he has fashioned so wonderfully and so purely in the supreme hope of absolute cosmic freedom for all.

These two examples refer to aspects of the Great Cosmic Law which are not commonly known but which are commonly discussed or skirted about by religious groups. The law of transfer of energy is vital to the science of alchemy; for without it, it is impossible to "create" Matter. It is a law that nothing cannot create something.

True knowledge of the impersonal law of transfer of energy is also vital to the correct understanding of the Great Law. For it proves that God, who makes the sun to shine on both the just and the unjust,[1] does manifest through both

Jesus declared during his Palestinian mission that "the kingdom of heaven suffereth violence, and the violent take it by force."[2] It must be realized, then, that it is possible to wrest from the hand of God some of the secrets of governing the forces of nature and controlling Matter, even though the individual and motive be not absolutely pure.

But let none ever think that the one so doing shall escape from accountability, for he is fully responsible for each use or abuse of energy within his world.

The reason I am choosing to begin my exposition on alchemy with a note of warning and a sobering explanation is not to cause anyone fear, but rather to instill in all who read a deep and abiding reverence for God—which is the only fear permitted in our octave. It is in reality holy awe that engenders within all who love the Great Law of Love the fullest respect and adoration for the wisdom which so fearfully and wonderfully made all creation in the image of fearless freedom.

All those who misuse the powers of the universe for selfish ends find sooner or later that they must relinquish their hold upon their ill-gotten gains; and the penalty they pay is frightful indeed. To produce substance to feed the poor, to heal at a touch a withered hand, to raise the dead, and even to set aside natural law and perform, by the magic of alchemy, miracles of infinite wonder—this seems to mankind to be the ultimate in their use of heaven's grace.

Let me embrace the Spirit of freedom that makes it possible for a man made in the immortal, loving, God-free image of his Creator to do these things and many more to the benefit of society and to the happiness of his benefactors. But above all, let me praise the proper use of the blessed divine science of spiritual alchemy.

The ancient alchemist has ever been a colorful figure—even to his own contemporaries. But time has gilded his image with a glory far greater than that which he ever possessed, and it is ever thus when approaching the aspects of mystery.

It is in the simple graces of life that men will find their freedom, albeit the more complex aspects are progressive expressions of the laws of Life that shall enrich the well-being of this earth and of all its people, harnessing their total good on behalf of the most lovely world of freedom that could ever be conceived of, even in the mind of a New Atlantean!

So much for the moment regarding the world society. Let us now consider the individual and his role in the use of alchemy.

The inner meaning of alchemy is simply *all-composition,* implying the relation of the all of the creation to the parts which compose it. Thus alchemy, when properly understood, deals with the conscious power of controlling mutations and transmutations within Matter and energy and even within life itself. It is the science of the mystic and it is the forte of the self-realized man who, having sought, has found himself to be one with God and is willing to play his part.

Through the years men have attempted to glamorize me with the allure of distance in time and space, which always lends enchantment to the view. I do not sell myself short as the Father's handiwork, but in common with beloved Jesus and others among the great Masters of our Brotherhood, I am especially interested that each man obtain his rightful place and the proper understanding of how he ought to exercise authority in the universe and in his own world and affairs.

Let everyone who begins this study do so with the understanding that I have a purpose in speaking here and that that purpose is to make each one of you alchemists in the truest sense of the word. This means that you must become familiar at inner levels with the *all-chemistry* of God and how each facet of creation is brought into manifestation in Matter, in your consciousness, and in your daily life.

In order to do this properly, you will need to meditate and reread these lessons many times, calling to me and to your own God Self, your I AM Presence, for illumination on any point that is not immediately clear to you. When you have the inner degree of Alchemist of the Sacred Fire conferred upon you by your own Christ Self, you immediately become a candidate for admission to the outer court of the Great White Brotherhood. This factor alone is a great incentive for you to become proficient in genuine spiritual alchemy.

It has ever been a fallacy of human thought to deny the so-called miracles in the life of the great avatar Jesus. Nonetheless, he, as a son of God, revealed to all these mighty formulas which, if understood and practiced, would long ago have transformed the planet into a paradise of perfection.

Enough, then, of human nonsense and human creation! As Shakespeare would have said it:

Off then with the old,
The decay, and the mouldering mustiness
Of this shapeless mass:
On then with the eternal vastness
Of an unfettered spirit—
A being of such freedom
As moving seems apart
Even from Reality
And projects the image
Of eternal hope
Into the tiniest gem or dewdrop
Cupped within a blossom rare.

I AM for the freedom of all,
Lovingly,

Saint Germain

CHAPTER 2

The Purpose of Your Alchemical Experiment

Void is unfruitful energy. The alchemist must develop a sense of the value of time and space and the opportunity to manipulate both. Freedom is won by quest and conquest, but mainly by the conquest of the finite self. True mastery of the finite comes through the indrawing love, the compelling, almost magnetic heart call of the soul to its Divine Source.

Only the great inflow of the cosmic light of God can release the soul from the imprisoning shadows of its human creation. Summon, then, the purity of purpose which will make your creative design good; relentlessly challenge the base elements which arise like hobgoblins to disturb and try the plan you have begun; then patiently evolve your God-design—the purpose of your alchemical experiment.

The true science of the Spirit is more exact than mundane measures can yet determine. Therefore, know thy Self as the white stone or elixir from whence all thy creation must proceed in orderly fashion. If the key ideas are not created from within thee who art the alchemist, then the whole act is either hapless or an imitation of the work of another.

Now, if it be God thou wouldst imitate, then "Well done!" may truly be spoken of thee; but if the vanity of mankind, then piteous let thy consciousness remain. The True Self of man, from whence cometh every goodly design, is worthy to be consulted as to what it is desirable to create. Therefore, the true alchemist begins his experiment by communing with himself in order to perceive the inspiring thoughts of the radiant mind of his Creator.

It is in imitation of lesser qualities and lesser states of consciousness that society has molded many of its erroneous concepts. To correct these concepts, to forge an ennobling culture, to draw the lines of good character, man and society must look to lofty examples.

Let men who would practice alchemy learn first to mirror the great examples of all ages who have used heaven as their design, and then let them learn to select the best qualities of their lives so that alchemy can be used as it was divinely intended, as the most noble method of achieving the desires of the heart right here and now.

I strongly suspect that many of my auditors, but few, if any, of the most sincere students, are anxious to have imparted unto them at once the philosophers' stone or the magical properties that will make them at will a combination of

Aladdin and Midas with a trace of benevolence sprinkled in.

I here declare for those who think thusly that while I shall impart tremendous knowledge concerning the science of alchemy in the whole of this nine-part study, I doubt very much that unless they absorb the secrets of the first lessons with utter humility, allowing me as the instructor the privilege of preparing the teachings as God would have me do, they will not at the very end find themselves wanting. And it will not be the fault of either teaching or teacher!

I do not intend to give a lengthy discourse on the vanities of worldly life, but I would like to point out that it is the hope of the Brotherhood in releasing these teachings at this time to avoid for our students the mistakes of some of the early alchemists whose sole purpose seemed to be the acquirement of riches and honor and the ability to produce from universal substance the energies to change base metals into gold.

Let me hasten to say that not all of the early alchemists confined their goals to temporary gain. Indeed many stalwart souls pursued alchemy with the same reverence they would a quest for the Holy Grail, seeing it as a divine art and the origin of the Christian mysteries, as when Christ changed the water into wine at the marriage in Cana of Galilee.[1]

We desire to see the original concepts about alchemy given new meaning, and we desire to see the meaning it acquired in the mystery schools brought to the fore. For the uses to which this science is presently put must be translated to a higher dimension if mankind are to reap the full benefits thereof.

Unless this spiritual science is applied to the freeing of individuals and society from drudgery, confusion, and compromise with the densities of human thought—as is our wish—the purposes to which God ordained it will remain unfulfilled. We who pursue the high calling of the alchemist aspire to see all attain a place where they can both teach and extol the basic purposes of life to the youth of the world as having far greater than mere temporal pleasures, which in reality serve a lesser purpose to a divine alchemist than does a pacifier to a suckling child.

Let no one think because I spend this time in introducing the heart of the subject to you that my discussion is not pertinent to the facts at hand. Unless each one understands that he individually must exercise his God-given right to use power wisely and lovingly, he cannot help but fall into pits of self-delusion and rationalization.

Now, it is God's plan that everyone on earth pursue the understanding of himself and his destiny. Conceit born of intellectual pride has caused many a sincere student, and even a number of worldly masters of one science or another, to fall into traps of their own creation; and in many cases they never knew when the snare was sprung.

Therefore, if any subject be included here, let no one think he can omit it simply because he may seem to know it already or because he has considered it before. We place many gems of thought in the most unlikely sentences, which, though plain enough of speech and easily seen, may require more than the diligence of even an honest heart's scanning.

Saint Peter voiced the query "And if the righteous scarcely be saved, where shall the ungodly and the sinner appear?"[2] It is well for the would-be alchemist to realize that this is an exact and true science whose illumination is conferred upon man by God himself. Its purpose is to teach mankind how to obtain for themselves every gracious gift and virtue which their lifestreams might require in finding the way back Home to God's heart.

I do not say that you cannot learn to materialize every wish of your being—and this aspect of alchemy is for some the easiest part of the whole, while for others it remains the most difficult. I do say that the design of those wishes ought to be contemplated more than the wondrous science of bringing them into manifestation from the invisible. For to create a worthy design is a most noble endeavor, worthy of the God in man, which alone can set him free to fulfill his immortal destiny.

We have labored below and waited above for the children of this world to cease the plunder and pillage of war, to cultivate the education of the underprivileged, to relinquish the desire for class distinction, and to offer themselves as would princes of the realm to serve effectively the needs of their impoverished yet noble kin. We are presently determined to seek out the faithful of all nations and to empower them with the means whereby they can individually escape from the self-imposed bondage of the times and obtain their own priceless inheritance.

Naturally, this heritage is neither temporal nor ephemeral. However, when serving in Europe to dissipate some of the poverty and confusion so prevalent there, I did use universal alchemy to produce the substance which, although temporary in nature, supplied many human needs and was both comforting and helpful to the world and to the personal lives of my beneficiaries.

I conceive nothing wrong in the idea, nor do I look with disfavor upon your having a divine source of supply to meet all your needs. I do feel it is needful for you to keep constantly humble and grateful as God places within your hands the key to the control of natural forces.

Again, and second to no idea contained herein, is the constant need to understand the universal scheme or plan of creation so that all that you design and do will be harmonious with eternal Law and cosmic principles.

I hope that I shall have neither affrighted nor discouraged any of the students of alchemy from pursuing this marvelous divine study. I am, however, now free to proceed with more relish, for I have magnified the eternally manifest principle of the immortal intelligence of God which some call inspiration, while others call it simply the mind of God.

Whatever men may call a quality, it is its possession that counts the whole nine points of the Law. Therefore, love the emanation of divine wisdom contained herein, which, like sunlight shimmering through the trees, touches with its fingers of Light all through which it passes. For only by love can you truly possess.

I AM the resurrection and the life of cosmic purpose within you.

In the name of Freedom, I remain

Saint Germain

CHAPTER 3

The Sacred Science

The domain of individual destiny is controlled by an interplay of many cosmic forces, mainly benign; but in the present world society, due to mankind's misunderstanding of both earthly and heavenly purposes, these forces have been turned to other uses, frequently chaotic and disintegrating.

Alchemy was originally intended to be a means of enriching individual destiny by making available the technique of changing base metals into gold, thereby producing opulence in the affairs of the successful practitioner. The dedication of the early alchemists to the cause of ferreting out its secrets was complete, and it was sanctified by the coordination of their minds with the works of their hands.

These alchemists pursued their experiments under the duress of persecution led by the entrenched reactionary forces of their day, and it is a tribute to their lives and honor that they persisted in the search. Thus they brought forth and bequeathed to humanity the bona fide results of their efforts as acknowledged scientific achievement and annotated philosophic knowledge to bless the culture and archives of the world order.

It ought to become increasingly clear to the students of this course that I am determined to bring to your minds and feelings a new sense of freedom. The wholesome concepts presented herein must indicate to your total being that the key to alchemy that must precede the acquisition of all other keys is the mastery of yourself, to a greater or lesser degree.

This key must be recognized for what it is, for self-mastery is the key to all self-knowledge. It must then be understood and used, at least in part. And you must acknowledge without question that you yourself are the alchemist who shall determine the design of your creation. Furthermore, you must know your self as the Real Self and your creation as coming forth from that Self.

It may surprise some to learn that seething vortices of humanly discordant thoughts and feelings daily impose a hypnotic effect upon almost everyone on earth. These tend to nullify the great concentration of intelligent, creative power that is the birthright of every man, woman, and child on this planet, though it is consciously employed by far too few.

While increasing numbers among mankind seek after freedom, the reactionary elements, either with or without purpose, attempt to burden the race with new shackles each time deliverance from one form or another of human bondage is secured.

The alchemist, to be successful, must be consciously aware of his God-given freedom to create. Those restrictions and restraints imposed upon the soul as forms of human bondage must be shunned. Yet in every case these must be distinguished from the necessary laws which structure society. Beauty and righteousness must be emblazoned upon the left and right hand to remind the would-be alchemist of his responsibility to God and man to behold his works before releasing them to see that they are indeed good, and good for all men.

I am releasing in these studies in alchemy methods of visualization which will give to the students who will apply them as I did the ability to perform for God and man a service of the first magnitude.

I trust that the myth of human equality will be dispelled and that in the dignity of equal opportunity the evolutions of this planetary home will come to know and love the expansive potential of the Christ in all. Thus the forging-ahead of humanity will be marked by a greater malleability of the soul and less ignorance of man's universal purpose to develop his individual talents than has heretofore existed on earth.

As the early alchemists attained a measure of success in probing the secrets of the universe, they became acutely aware of the need to band together and to withhold from the public eye certain discoveries which they made. A number of religious orders and secret societies grew out of this need, and the remnants thereof have survived to the present day.

The need to repress as well as to express was recognized, just as enlightened men of today realize that harmony in the social order and among the nations and the eradication of the causes of war and civil strife would remove all reasons for withholding any knowledge that would prove to be universally beneficial.

Let me declare—because I can speak in the light of true knowledge—that the early alchemists were not nearly so unsuccessful as history would have men believe. Their discoveries were legion and they included knowledge both secular and religious, scientific and philosophic. Above all, they unlocked many truths which at a later date were made general knowledge.

Let not the world discount all of the stories that have been recounted of the suppression of invention and new ideas for economic and political reasons. When it suited their purposes, men in high places have ever so often instructed their hirelings to keep secret the very knowledge which belongs to the ages and which is the heritage of the people of all nations.

Regardless of such dishonorable dealings, the Masters of Wisdom will never transfer this knowledge to mankind until the alchemy of reason heals the internal breach of selfishness within enough of the race that the torch of knowledge may be everlastingly held in the selfless hand of Justice.

I am preparing your minds in these first three lessons to better assimilate the full release of wisdom's flame that has been made a part of this course. It is frequently the despair of men that they did not have a certain choice bit of knowledge long before it came into their hands. This feeling is certainly understandable, but no lamentation that is without constructive leadings is ever desirable.

It is preferable that men perceive the now of the present as God's hour rather than the folded parchments of past ages. The fading hieroglyphs of yesterday's errors can neither confute the present truth nor act as a panacea to heal their unfortunate sowings; they serve only as media of contrast to amplify the present sense of gratitude that glories in such progress as now manifests to dispel the ignorance of former times.

A determined dedication to use the energies of today to open the doorway into the domain of the future is expected of the student of alchemy. Therefore, let him see to it that his present expansion of the science of alchemy is sufficient to transform the base qualities of the human nature into an altar on which the flame of living Reality will fire the grandeur of the golden age now emerging within the Christ mind.

Let his endeavors likewise be sufficient to balance the travails of world injustice. And let him work to secure for posterity eras of increasingly abundant progress, enlightenment, happiness, and universal spirituality.

When used by the alchemist, symbols and symbology properly understood are literally charged with meaning. For example, mercury is the symbol of speed and interprets to the consciousness the thought of wakeful, reverent alertness, which swiftly endows the chemistry of action with the intensity of application.

Salt equates with the idea of selfhood and reminds mankind of the need to have the self retain the savor[1] of its Divine Source in preference to the crystallization of identity within the Sodom and Gomorrah of materiality indicated in the historical figure of Lot's wife.[2]

Fire, as Life, is the catalyst which can be increased from the cosmic light within the cosmic rays in order to intensify and purify the radiance of Life in the contemplated design. Moreover, the conscious invocation of Life makes all of the alchemist's manifestations doubly secure.

Earth symbolizes the natural crystalline densities created out of Spirit's energies and sustained by the beings of the elemental kingdom. These tiny creators, in their mimicry of human discord, have transferred to nature mankind's inharmonious patterns.

Thus the convergence of human error upon the planetary body came forth as thorn, thistle, insect, and beast of prey. And the Pandora's box of astral forms was opened by laggard civilizations whose misguided free will and selfishness have perverted Life's energies even on other systems of worlds. It is this discord imposed upon the very atoms of substance which the alchemist must remove from his laboratory before he can create. It is this dross which the alchemist will purify by fire.

I do not expect that every reader will immediately understand all of the concepts that are included in this course. While it is true that I advocate simplicity in the phrasing of the basic laws of God, I am also aware that thoughtforms worded in the higher order will be productive of greater good as the world is able to accept them.

I therefore include herein elements designed to challenge those of every level of awareness to study to show themselves approved unto the God flame within.[3] Thus individual alchemical advances will be achieved by all who faithfully apply the teachings.

The most insidious type of bondage is that in which the prisoner is not aware of his chains. I am certain that the real science of alchemy can serve to set free everyone on earth who will accept it. Therefore, out of respect for its supreme purpose, I consider it to be the sacred science.

Remember, blessed children of men, that the purpose of true science should be to increase happiness and to free the race from every outer condition that does not serve to exalt man into the pristine greatness of his original cosmic purpose.

All postulations—whether of a social, economic, religious, or scientific nature—should be infused with the freedom which allows men to progress. All who attempt to lead mankind progressively forward in these fields should admit to the possibility of change without in any way challenging those infallible pinions of the human spirit referred to as "life, liberty, and the pursuit of happiness."

Certainly the opportunity for progress and the freedom to innovate cannot affect the immutability of divine truth or the integrity of the Logos, whose power uttereth speech from those untrammeled heights to which we jointly aspire.

I AM progressively yours in the holy science,

Saint Germain

✠

CHAPTER 4

Dare to Do!

Versatility! I am eternally grateful for that many-splendored quality of creation! The universe is fragmented; it is spread apart from a center of oneness to a diversity of light, color, tone, and density. Each partaker of a scene, whether pastoral or of transitory ugliness, ought to remember that the splintered shafts of light rays that compose the swaddling garments of all of creation connect directly with the Great Source and Fountainhead of cosmic unity.

In my historical experiences preceding my ascension—which was identical in its raising action to the elevation of Jesus the Christ—I was in a constant state of listening grace whereby my inner ears and eyes were fixed upon a lovely realm of light and perfection which served to remove the sting of earthly life from my consciousness, producing a comfort that my friends did not perceive. They often pondered the cause of my inner serenity without understanding its origin.

The contacts with my earthly brethren and the appearances that I have made since my ascension have not always been under circumstances where those I met were aware of either my identity or my power. May I humbly state that as in other similar cases where one of the ascended host has elected to part the veil of Matter and maya to contact directly unascended humanity, the latter have entertained "angels unawares."[1]

I am well aware that some of my readers may opine, inasmuch as I am one who has passed through the veil, that this release of my words is of a psychic or spiritualistic nature. Let me quickly affirm that it is neither. God be praised that my own lifestream need not subscribe to such limiting forms.

The fact that we are expressing or "vibrating" our life in higher dimensions where ordinary human faculties of seeing and hearing do not function renders neither our service nor our reality of any less effect, nor does it force me to subscribe to the above-named methods of communication. Blessed ones, you do not by ordinary means perceive radio waves, for they remain inaudible until detected in the miracle of the electronic tube; therefore, trust in heaven's capacity to communicate with man directly.

Because of my dedication to the holy cause of freedom, I have since my ascension consistently maintained a contact with one or more lifestreams embodied upon earth—and that by cosmic decree and with the approval of the heavenly hierarchy. Beloved Jesus and other great luminaries who have descended in the fullness of the divine plan have likewise appeared to their disciples down through the ages and do occasionally manifest to men and women of today with no more effort than that employed to dial a radio or television.

My purpose in discussing the subject of heaven's winged messages from the great cloud of witnesses[2] is not as foreign to alchemy as might at first appear; for it portrays to you a necessary part of my program in the cause of freedom, of which the current series in alchemy is an integral part.

You see, blessed ones, the creation of the visible is wholly dependent upon those essences which are not visible to the unaided eye. Yet the central ideas occupying the minds of most people —originating as they do in the transient effects of human causation—are not of enough consequence to deserve comment or to be ordained with permanent reality.

I am certain you will agree that even as the range of ordinary human experience becomes monotonous for souls both great and small, so it is a wonderful blessing to them to be able to see into the higher octaves of creation by means of an adjusted consciousness and thus draw inspiration directly from the mind of nature and nature's God.

Ignorance with its defilement of the Law deprives the individual and society of enlightenment. The only cure is illumined obedience, together with scientific attentiveness to the detail of the Law.

The benefits of divine wisdom remain unknown to many who suppose that the old familiar theories are adequate to meet the demands of the hour and that nothing beyond empiricism or the empirical method is required. Actually, the accepted tenets of modern science, being but partially true, are incomplete and therefore provide an inadequate foundation upon which to base advanced research and the control of the elements.

An attitude of complacency does not allow for progress in any endeavor, human or divine. Thus, where grace might abound it does not. Complacency remains a bulwark of reactive ignorance, preventing mankind from sharing in the abundance which all heaven stands waiting to shower upon those free souls whose purity of heart and guileless nature make most receptive to our thoughts.

Before conferring alchemical knowledge of any depth upon you, I wish to exalt you into that divine nobility which is as real as the light of the day and your greatest strength in meeting the challenges of the morrow! To do this may require some examination of the spirit of those sincere alchemists whose excursions into the unknown were productive in more ways than one.

Even the souls who failed completely to discover a method of changing base metals into gold were benefited beyond their farthest dreams by the blessings which came to them as a result of their search. Even the persecutions served to band them together in singleness of purpose, which, midst human diversity with its unfortunate tendencies toward greed and selfishness, is an achievement in itself.

I am in the hope that you will prepare yourself to succeed in your endeavors. Above all, stand ready to make the necessary changes in your thoughts and preconceived ideas that will make it possible for you to be victorious. If man expects to succeed in alchemy, which is in truth dependent on the higher laws of spiritual science, he must nurture the faith on which the strength of his invocation and concentration will rest.

The fusion of metal, the control of atomic forces, and the direction of electronic energy by the mind of man acting in higher dimensions are easy enough once the grasp is acquired. However, after years of dependence upon the five senses and the attendant acceptance of mortal limitation, I am certain you can see how utterly important it is that your thinking become geared to new possibilities in order to function free of human restrictions and the dampening of a divine ardor by those who say because they do not know, "Impossible!" Let me say to all in freedom's name, *try!*

While you are preparing your consciousness for the reception of the knowledge of tomorrow, be aware, then, of the need to ponder the origin of concepts involving limitation.

Beloved ones, you must be sane and balanced in all you do, but realize that true science borders on the miraculous to those who do not understand its formulas. You approach a solid wall with the idea that you cannot walk through it; yet it is not solid at all, but as full of holes as the wire of a chicken coop. You cannot walk upon hot coals without burning your feet, and yet medicine men of a less illumined culture than your own do so with impunity.

Countless miracles of Christ have been duplicated by men and women of various times and climes since his wondrous advent, and yet because of human skepticism and forgetfulness, the wonder of it all has been relegated to the realm of myth or the imaginings of gullible minds. Let me plead for a renewal of faith in the power of God, for this is a requirement of everyone who would be a wonderman of spiritual accomplishment on behalf of the holy purposes of the universal law itself.

Without faith it is not only impossible to please God,[3] but I declare unto you, it is impossible to manifest the perfection of his laws. As faith is so great a requirement, would it not pay well for each one to reexamine his reasons for doubt?

Note well that most doubts arise from patterns of self-deception and the practice of deceit and the failures of the human mind to fulfill its professed integrity. Seeing, then, that such negative conditions stem from the consciousness of error, would it not be ever so wise for all to look unto Me (the Presence of Almighty God) and live?[4]

With God all things are possible,[5] but as in every science, proficiency does not usually come about without knowledge and its persistent application. The few who are exceptions to this rule may be called geniuses, but when the whole law is understood, it will be proven that even they had their hours of diligent study and practice.

I particularly want to point out that the purpose of our release of alchemical secrets in this course is to place in your hands and in the laboratory of your consciousness the knowledge of the law which we ourselves have used for centuries with the greatest of success and with the reverence for life which is of prime necessity to an inquiring mind poised on the loving intent of an honest heart.

Here idle curiosity is exchanged for that moral grandeur which so lifts a man above his fellows as to make of him a divine star in the firmament of his contemporaries. Lifted, then, by no false pride or intellectual misinterpretations, the true alchemist stands with humble mien, gazing expectantly at the teacher who will impart to him, if the attitude and the application be correct, the priceless knowledge of the ages.

May I fondly hope that you will reread the early lessons and assimilate therefrom a new sense of progress and of new possibilities? I am determined that many in this class shall succeed, and I shall continue to do my part above and below in your octave that this prove true and that great illumination, hope, peace, and understanding be born and renewed within you all.

I AM faithfully yours,

Saint Germain

✠

CHAPTER 5

The Need, Power, and Motive to Change

The now of the present hour must be utilized as a chalice of spiritual opportunity. Life must be indulged by its highest objectives, honored by the adoration of exalting principles, and merited by selfless service. Beloved people, the power to change is within every man. Prefer this power and venerate it above every limiting condition, and watch the alchemy of Self expand!

Transmute the lies of shadowed substance that arrest your spirit's upward soaring. Realize that conditions of human limitation are but ghosts that parade upon the stage of mortal existence, only to be laid to rest forever by eternal Reality.

Each man must become aware of his choices and select either freedom or fetters as he explores the chemistry of his present state, brings it into focus upon the mirror of truth, and then determines to alter each base condition, constructing within the crucible of the hour that hallowed progress which is born of eternal perception.

Destruct, then, the base and senseless mania of your origin in Matter consciousness, that possessive nature, the perversion of the Mother, which, failing to assess the fullness of cosmic possibilities, limits itself to the baubles and trinkets of temporal possession. Let heaven use your consciousness to expand its window into the infinite, and then behold at last the beautiful possibilities present in the most dire outer conditions. Give wealth to the poor in spirit, understanding to the rich, and compassion to everyone.

So often a lifestream may have in abundance the very qualities in which his neighbor is lacking. Exchange your virtues by exalting the valleys of another, and trust Life to remove the peaks of his pride as well as your own. Transmute the conditions in your own world that you do not want by determined and persistent effort. Every divine being who exalts the life of God within you knows that the power to do these things is in your hands this very day, within the reach of your intelligence and spirit.

Construct those spires of attainment which compose the Celestial City, and enfold the world of physical substance, the conscious mind, and the feelings of your heart with the radiance of immortal spheres. Gazing at the universe with renewed hope, behold the need to sustain the proper regard.

Vanity has held sway upon earth far too long. Wondrous opportunities, like spirits in the night, have vanished with the dawn, resisted by the cold shackles that imprison the soul in a mantle of disintegrating moments descending in the glass of the hours.

The son of Elizabeth inquired of the Christ, "Art thou he that should come, or look we for another?"[1] The reply of the Christ referred to his miraculous accomplishments: the deaf were made to hear, the blind to see, and the lame to walk. The lesson contained in his answer urges each life-stream to accept the greatness of his own Reality.

All should see that life has brought to them its great and wondrous graces through the "I AM He" consciousness which must emerge from the cave of materiality. The gross separation of the whole into weak and incomplete components— men's concept of themselves as particles remote from their Source—obliges their struggle through human misfortune instead of their acceptance of the grandiose concept of cooperative oneness charged with the power of love and freedom un-bounded.

Truth raises all and defeats no one save those enemies of righteousness whose shadowed misunderstanding makes them little more than savage animals in the jungle of human creation. Even these are given more compassion by Life than they deserve. This I know, because the record is laid before me. Beloved Kuan Yin has called for mercy and given it freely to all without limit and without price.

This is God's great gift: he always returns more love to life than life ever gives to him. Self-lessly, the magnitude of God sends forth a torrent of love when a few droplets would suffice and thereby sweeps mankind on the upward pilgrim way, regardless of men's erroneous notions.

Now, looking to another is not the solution to your problems; nor will it win the intended fulfillment God holds for thee, blessed son of man. As an alchemist enlightened by the torch of divine knowledge, aware of the magnificence of true Selfhood, you must summon the strength from the invisible realm and use the processes of transmutative alchemy within your own world and affairs to master daily all outer conditions by the spiritual means and physical appurtenances available to you.

To make bricks without straw[2] may not always be a requirement and may seem most difficult, but to the determined alchemist it is merely an obstacle to be overcome.

No one who occupies the earth at present should limit his recognition of the now-is-the-hour concept which mounts each wave of opposition and rides it forward into the crest of victory. Everyone should see his life—at any age or time—as amenable to change for the better and himself as possessing the capability to surmount any condition at will. Law and justice are natural factors of control, but the universe, guided by its own law, has the creative methods of transcending that law, approximating cosmic dimensions, and expanding geometrically into infinity.

Friends of freedom must disallow old ideas as quickly as they are able and discard outworn concepts as outmoded garments. It was difficult for men in Copernicus' day to accept his theory that the earth and the other planets revolved around the sun; they dogmatically subscribed to the belief that the earth, and not the sun, was the center of the universe. Chemical formulas of basic and complex matter are simple to the chemist but to the unlearned seem but a jumble of symbols.

Our purpose in this course is not merely to confer knowledge, but to effect your acceptance of that knowledge by an almost a priori methodology. This is needed because the categorical proof of alchemical laws is universally and necessarily seen through their action in man!

Let there be light within your personal orbit and within the sphere of your being. Life is not an experiment, but mankind have experimented with it. Humanity has ridden the tide of the peripheral world of effects while neglecting the inner causative realm. All unhappiness is rooted in basic factors of cause. Mend the flaws and you shall be self-healed and self-revealed.

I am interested in bringing about a complete reversal of deleterious human attitudes and replacing them by such right methods and concepts that each life can quickly rise out of the human force-field with its heavy, gravitational magnetism that hinders mankind's progressive ascension.

By transmutation let every would-be alchemist first act to transform himself here and now and gain thereby an inner peace and a sense of outer accomplishment—especially at the close of each life's term. Surely, unless both an interior and an exterior focus be maintained where Good is accented, one's concentration of positive control which has the power to alter substance within and without cannot manifest the blessing God intends all to have and exercise each day.

Beloved ones, a life lived for reward or punishment is not a raison d'être. The destiny inherent within life has escaped the intelligent comprehension of many on earth and is anchored in but a few. Thousands daily take pleasure in the sweepstakes, the races, or games of chance, hoping against fantastic odds to become a winner, whilst they ignore the most certain of all laws: the cosmic purpose.

Those who deny God or life itself do so out of a dearth of genuine experience. They have not witnessed the dawn of pure reason in themselves. They prefer to accept those popular ideas associated with "non-gullibility"!

Well, the losses of such as these are legion. And while I do not expect to change every such individual, I do repeat my admonishment here that all might be inspired to keep on keeping on. The search is worth all effort. I know the law; the alchemy of action is its own proof.

Those who desire to enter into debate to prove the nonexistence or the nonessentiality of a First Cause may not wish to lose the transient pleasure of so doing. But if they accede to the divine logic, the golden grain of truth will replace the husks of pride in the stifling, airtight systems of the human intellect which disdains the verification of any knowledge not experienced by the physical senses.

Frequently individuals like to think they are *en rapport* with hoary heads of wisdom. Now, I think that the centuries I lived before my ascension and those which have since transpired have entitled me to some distinction in this respect. Neither ego nor human motive would inspire me to write this series. I am aware only of the deep love I feel for the earth as a unit of cosmic progress, and I desire to impart herein something of the sweet simplicity of that love and the wisdom that is guided thereby.

Let us see now how reasonable it is to suppose that enough people serving in harmony can change the most calcified condition and create an influx of love that will sweep the hills and valleys with an inspired movement to heal the breach between the realities of eternal alchemy (the *all-chemistry* of God) and the artificialities which rise from the caves of base error. Then the emerging gold of personal integrity and personal integration will be a gift equally shared by all; individual man will reflect pure genius and the social order will reflect the kingdom of heaven.

The forces that would bind mankind to their past errors and thus prevent the flame of peace from being released in the present must themselves be bound as in heaven, so on earth.[3] And mankind must arise to sound the death knell of these forces here and now ere war shall cease. Freedom from confusion can be found only in the true understanding of life and the alchemy of being.

Step by step, I am leading you to the right understanding of alchemy. In the first lessons I reminded you of responsibility—your responsibility to prove the law of your being by the right use of alchemy. Now I am reminding you of the need to effect changes in yourself where change is desirable. Finally, I shall instruct you in the art and practice of precipitation.

A prerequisite to applying the methods of precipitation is knowing what you want to precipitate. It was this truth which Jesus taught in the Lord's Prayer and when he said, "Nevertheless not my will, but thine, be done."[4]

The will of God, the will of the Higher, is the will of your Real Self—the most important part of you. Because the lesser you, although it retains through the soul the capacity to contact this Higher Self, is but a bundle of impulses crowded with bits of human knowledge, I am advocating that you become acquainted with the Reality of yourself. For this Reality is the genie (genius) in you that can give the Aladdin (symbolizing the alchemist who rubs the lamp of pure knowledge) the right desires of his immortal being.

Ponder now the need to change (Thine is the kingdom), the power to change (Thine is the power), and the motive to change (Thine is the glory), and evolve out of the passing flame of earnestness the permanent sun of renewed hope.

Graciously, I AM

Saint Germain

✠

CHAPTER 6

Molding Factors

Ah, the mold—there's the rub! Aye, and the mowlde,[1] too, contaminates. But how beautiful is the original hope of heaven for each lifestream!

Following the descent into form and material substance come those formative years when the pressures, both clamorous and silent, make their impression upon the clean white consciousness of the individual. Beginning with the first fond gawking of parents and kin, there is a gradual buildup of environmental factors which serve to create patterns and concepts upon the tender screen of the embryonic mind.

These molding factors continue to exert their multifarious influence upon the plastic personality of man. That selfhood, then, which is first identified wholly with God-Good, is affected and shaped by myriad experience patterns. Thus does example, for woe or for weal, sculpt the mind and being of man.

Experience is not, however, the sole way to expand consciousness. For each moment spent with God or one of his cosmic band serves to exalt and broaden individual consciousness, conveying illumination on the instant—in the twinkling of an eye![2]

The empirical proof of human imperfection is epitomized in the past/present lives of mass humanity. Life in bondage and life in peril decries the meaning of existence. Religion and hope for salvation arise in the human heart and burgeon from the human tree! ("And he looked up, and said, I see men as trees, walking."[3]) The alchemy of change was needed in Jesus' day and is still needed, because all too frequently the mold is imperfect and the product cannot excel its matrix.

I have declared that the mowlde, too, contaminates; and thus I direct your attention to the untransmuted accumulation of human filth and misery which, like trash, litters the sidewalks of the human consciousness, reeking forth from the literary stalls of the world. The crusty mowlde masquerades as legitimate culture while undermining the decency of lusty souls.

Freedom of the press was not intended to give license to the corrupters of youthful minds; neither was it intended to be used to confuse and disorganize the populace, flooding their brains with jingoistic propaganda and prejudicial discriminations. Rather, the power of Light was intended to emanate from a free press and exalt everyone into a rightful sense of cosmic destiny.

America, my beloved country! How precious

are the footsteps of your heroes sung and unsung; but every mother's heart can take a just pride in offering with the "consent of the governed" the fruit of her life—sons and daughters of excellence who from the heart of this beloved nation serve the cause of freedom across the earth.

Because each dire effect of the mold and the mowlde must be counteracted, I am releasing these remarks pertaining to personal freedom through the correct use of alchemy. I do not say that more will not be spoken on the subject to parallel and conclude the course, but herein is my specific advice to those who would use alchemy to further their own personal advancement in the divine plan fulfilled and thus change their present circumstances for the better.

Those who are familiar with the process of refining precious metals are aware of the intense heat needed to liquify many metals. Heat is also necessary to release impurities and foreign material from the pure metal. Separation of the dross occurs in two ways: (1) a portion is vaporized and passes into the very atmosphere of the room wherein the refining furnace is operating, and (2) much of this unwanted substance is brought to the surface and skimmed off by the alert refiner.

Apropos of this, few parents exist who are equipped with the type of instruction which would enable their children to know from the beginning the tenets of their full freedom. I do not say that the world is not full of aspiration and good intentions, but the highways so paved do not seem to lead to the best places. Thus it happens that the children of the world become wiser in each succeeding generation in the arts and artifices of war and in the many customs of world society without ever becoming too stirred about the regenerate and peaceful society of saints!

In the main, few are born and come to years with a right understanding of the universal purpose. And of necessity, personal destinies, which often run crosscurrent to the universal flow, are periodically thwarted and broken.

The pages of history are full of the downfall of tyrants and the overthrow of monsters of misdirected purpose. Failures and successes in many fields draw recognition while the average man moves into the burial ground of mediocrity. Nothing is further from the plan of God and nature than these counterfeits of the golden mean.

How ill-equipped is the concept of a destiny which can be shaped by human misconceptions. How noble are they who acknowledge an Intellect, a Mind, a Spiritual Overseer, and a Creator whose forethought, greater even than that of his emissaries, is revealed as a mountain of universal purpose to be scaled by the brave who do not hesitate or fear to trust the wisdom of those early climbers of the rugged summit peaks.

Those linked to the lifeline of these spiritual pioneers are given greater guidance, for the elder brothers of the race lovingly extend to them the freedom of the ages as a gift of faith. This gift is extended to all who, by accepting that faith, can likewise summon the will to pursue it and the perseverance to let it fashion them in a mold made purer still and in an accumulation of that purity whose reality is the treasure of heaven!

Beloved friends of freedom, you stand now at the gateway to higher alchemical truths, which I am releasing in the seventh lesson; but it is needful for you to contemplate your life in a manner wholly in keeping with the Spirit of Universal Alchemy. No longer act from the vanity of desiring recognition, but from the valor of necessary achievement and because service is needed and worthy in itself. God needs a vehicle through which to manifest in the world of form, and you lend your hands and feet to him!

You must understand the mystery of oneness whereby a thread of contact between each life and its Source serves to connect all who live to one great central switchboard. Here the interaction of thought and feeling is guarded lest it hurt any part of life in the holy mountain of God.

Consider all the beauty of life which can be. Perceive this as pure gold. All causes of unhappiness, every vibration of discord, fear, doubt, suspicion, condemnation, criticism, judgment, self-righteousness, and all negative traits are part of either the human mold or the mowlde which must be purged as dross before purity can so regenerate a lifestream as to enable the individual to partake of the waters of Life freely.[4]

It is not enough that men come to drink when the invitation from higher sources has gone forth. They must make new skins to retain the new wine of infinite goodness and purpose.[5] This is spiritual alchemy; and wise are they who first master it in themselves before attempting to govern the elements in others or in nature, for thus is karma justified by wisdom and rendered benign. Sin does not come to the door of such a practitioner, for his motives, purpose, and methods are pure, and his acts are also just.

Gracious alchemists, the very fact that you are studying this course should denote your interest in improving. In the very word *improving* is a spiritual lesson to be mastered.

The words *impression* and *proving* combine here to denote that life brings its impressions to the heart of your consciousness to prove the worth of each impression. Every idle thought is thereby brought to judgment before the magnificence that is the higher glory of God, the upper light in the vaulted chamber of heaven.

The mind of Christ is synonymous with the mind of Light and characterizes one whose attunement is specifically directed to the Higher Intelligence. The inflow of impressions from the world at large should be directed by the student for comparison and proof to the pure patterns of the purposes of heaven.

When these are improved upon by the alchemical fire, they become part of each man's forte of useful objects and ideas—permanent matrices for good, drawing unto the consciousness of man more of their kind. Thus is the kingdom of Selfhood expanded on wings of heavenly wisdom proved day after day by the speech uttered from the hills of spiritual watchfulness.

The sincere alchemist knows that the vast Intelligence that created all that is, expands mighty wings of light over the all of the cosmos. As above in the Macrocosm, so below in the microcosm, in the miniaturized world of appearance, is this Intelligence individualized! The watchful care of God ever manifests to his wondrous purposes as a Guardian Presence who seeks not the defilement, but the glorious fulfillment of each person in whom dwells the flame of almighty, ever-present life.

So-called physical death does not represent the end of being. It merely divides eternal life into compartments of identity and experience whereby expansion and opportunity can be utilized to the fullest and each outworn mold discarded. Forgotten fragments can be pieced together by the seeker and woven strand by strand into a tapestry of such beauty as to thrill the beholder with a sense of gratitude for the perfection and glory present in each day of eternity!

I am aware of human discouragement caused by identifying with elements of disintegration in society. I know full well the deceits practiced in the name of religion. But my concern is not so much with these matters as it is with those lives that do emerge from the crucible of experience with a wonderful garment patined with pure gold.

Your life need never be vacant, for Life watches you and Life is intelligent and considerate. Life is tangible and real. Life is earnest and tender. Life is dramatic and moving toward glory.

The high road, as distinguished from the low road, is the way of the alchemist, whose heart is in the shining glory all the day and all the way that his pilgrim feet walk the dusty ways of man—transmuting, transmuting, and transmuting that dust into purest radiance!

I AM the life, I AM the truth, and I AM the way,

Saint Germain

✳

CHAPTER 7

Methods of Transfer

Light is the alchemical key! The words "Let there be light"[1] are the first fiat of the creation and the first step in proper precipitation. When man, who himself is a manifestation of God, desires to emulate the Supreme Father and precipitate, as a true son of Light should learn to do, he ought to follow those methods used by the Supreme Intelligence if consistent and worthy results are to be anticipated.

By examining the obvious methods of the Creator and by observing nature, you can deduce much of value if you will school yourself to think independently. For it is necessary to bypass mere human syllogisms and to penetrate the limitless consciousness of God, who is the great Master Alchemist, in order to "go and do likewise,"[2] ever beholding your services as good.

When you have determined within yourself to experiment with the art of precipitation, first create a mind blueprint of the object you wish to produce. This should incorporate definite size, proportion, substance, density, color, and quality in detailed picture form. When the visualization of the blueprint within your mind is complete, it ought to be immediately sealed. This is a vital step in its speedy and effective release into the world of Matter-form.

Do not misunderstand this step and think that by sealing your plan you are closing the door to the improvement of its design. Such is not the case, for improvements can be made in subsequent models; but unless you release the blueprint to the elementals and builders of form as a finished work, they cannot properly bring it into manifestation. The words "It is finished!" are therefore the second fiat of creation following "Let there be light!"

Now that you have created a thought matrix and sealed it against the intrusion of impinging mind radiation from others, set up either consciously (in some cases through jealousy or ego) or unconsciously by the mass mind's collective resistance to progress, you must observe the third rule to protect your creative intent and "tell no man." This, too, is a law of precipitation—one that allows you to circumvent concentrated beams of human thought and feeling patterns which can be most disturbing to a successful alchemical experiment unless certain safeguards are activated.

Avoid, then, the dissipation of energy by the intrusion of a multiplicity of minds, except where two or more individuals are specifically cooperating in joint precipitation. Those who are of a scientific nature and are familiar with Coulomb scattering and Rutherford's law will understand how thought-energy, as waves scattering other waves as if composed of minute particles, can set up a penetration of great enough intensity to break down the field of magnetic thought-energy focusing the specific pattern of the creative matrix.

Each student should recognize that geometric figures such as the square, the triangle, the circle, the ellipse, and the parallelogram are employed almost universally in creating within the macrocosmic as well as the microcosmic three-dimensional world. Although higher forms of creativity are found in the mathematical world of algebra, calculus, and trigonometry, the highest symbology of all known to us at inner spiritual levels is the science of engrammic rhythms.

This study deals with the control and release of energy, with engrams (which term we use to refer to the causative key behind the effects observed by worldly scientists and called by them engrams), with the use of mantras, with the storing of fohatic energy, and with safeguards activating principles of demarcation between the evolutions of the human consciousness in the planes of Matter and the world of perfect divine order that exists in the planes of Spirit.

When contemplating this science, one should bear in mind that even the infinite, omnipresent consciousness of God, as it extends itself into the realm of the material creation, moves through the gamut of creative expression from simple patterns to those of increasing complexity.

The student of alchemy should consider the memory, when employed as the instrument of the Higher Mind, as an invaluable adjunct to his experiment; for the processes of the human memory are remarkable indeed. And when these are coordinated with the mental body, superlative action is always forthcoming. Thus there are a number of individuals who can memorize and execute an entire symphony without noticeable flaw. Mathematicians, too, demonstrate marvelous faculties of mental control in their calculations which approximate infinite precision.

Let each student of alchemy, then, recognize that he has within himself a Higher Mind that is capable of holding patterns of infinite dimensions. This Mind functions independently of the outer mind without human restriction of any kind. Hence, as the vehicle of the Higher Mind, a purified memory body, feeding as it does the impressions of that Mind to the outer mind, is indispensable to the alchemist.

Let the sincere student who would ponder and practice methods of mind and memory control, which are the methods of God himself, acquire the habit of consciously giving to this blessed Higher Mind, or Christ Self, the responsibility for designing and perfecting the embryonic ideas and patterns of his creation. For many of these patterns which at first appeared to be consciously conceived by the alchemist frequently have their origin within this higher portion of the blessed Self.

Remember, twenty-four hours of each day your Higher Mind is active in expanded dimensions. This blessed Comforter, unknown and unexperienced by you outwardly, waits to be called into action and does function free of ordinary space/time limitations. Employ your Higher Mind, then, both as your apprentice and as your teacher; for the Holy Spirit of truth moving therein can lead you into all truth![3]

I would like to call to the attention of the students that if they so desire, they can immeasurably assist themselves in the alchemical arts through outside reading. Care must be exercised in this, however, so that the byways of technology and scientific theory do not serve to divert the mighty flow of alchemy as the greatest science into byways of materialism where the ends are said to justify the means.

I realize full well that many related subjects would not only be boring, but also beyond the comprehension of some of our students. Desiring not to limit the masses of mankind from having the blessings of alchemy, I have deliberately stated many of these points in such a way as to make them easily understood. Let no one feel, however, that all knowledge can be reached through a single approach or without effort and study.

I suggest for those wishing more technical information to augment the course that they study wave propagation, the mechanics of the quantum theory, elementary and advanced chemistry and physics, seismology, astronomy, geology, and related subjects. These studies, together with courses in the humanities, the world's religions, and the Shakespearean plays, will be of immense value as you are guided from within and also by your personal tastes.

Let none feel that the pursuit of such extracurricular subjects is absolutely necessary or the mandate of the Masters, for the teachings of greatest importance are included herein—albeit in some cases between the lines. Let God guide; and to those who do not recognize his reins, I say, fortune is as fortune does!

I am a bit hopeful that material science will not look too much askance on the control of Matter by the power of the mind and spirit. I doubt that religion could justly deny the so-called miracles which demonstrate (if they are to be believed) that individuals who have lived upon earth have been able to practice transmutation, which is simply changing one form into another, such as water into wine;[4] amplification and multiplication of the atomic and molecular substance, such as multiplying the loaves and fishes;[5] and precipitation of the elements, such as calling down fire from heaven.[6] Equally wondrous feats performed by masters unascended and ascended indicate a most exact science of control over Matter and energy.

I myself have never questioned the truth of these matters, simply because I have always retained in humility my faith in the power of Good to endure forever. Moreover, I am active in demonstrating the laws of alchemy which make of the entire process of the control of Matter and energy an everyday affair.

I realize that the uninitiated or those who have never seen these so-called miracles for themselves may easily question their authenticity. Alchemists of God, I do not now ask you to believe alone. I ask you to begin in some measure to demonstrate these truths for yourself!

A few students of higher law have been able to externalize successfully one or more visible objects directly from the Universal such as a rose, a precious stone, or a cup of liquid essence quickening both mind and body. Naturally, we are anxious to see people achieve the power of producing anything and everything directly from the Universal.

Yet such secrets can hardly be written down or spelled out in full, for we cannot upset the present economic system until greater justice is established by mankind on earth. But neither can these secrets be justifiably concealed from the worthy. Hence we have included marvelous keys in this total course which, to the eyes of the faithful or those who would strive to become so, will open many a door of progress.

Every Ascended Master has these powers to precipitate at will, and therefore he never lacks for any good thing. Let unascended mankind ask themselves this question: How long will you spend your energy struggling to eke out a bare existence from Nature's cupboard, which to some seems bare indeed, when all your needs can be met by mastering the cosmic laws which Christ Jesus and other great teachers have demonstrated by their own lives in the past?

The use of the term *light* in alchemy includes light in its known visible aspects as well as in its invisible characteristics, some of which are yet unknown to physical science. When I produced rare gems and precious stones by means of alchemy, the methods I used could not have been easily applied by the average person who had not by discipline, faith, and meditative quietude established the necessary mind control.

These methods are known to every initiate; and only an initiate could be so tempted of the dark forces as Jesus was, who, aware of his alchemical power, rebuked the temptation to use alchemy during the period of the testing of his faith. Rather than relieve physical discomfort by commanding "these stones be made bread,"[7] as he might have done, he rendered his allegiance to the supreme God Presence and the Word of God and acknowledged these as far more important than the demands of his physical body. This enabled him to pass his test and to prepare for the disciplines which gave him his victory on the cross and in the tomb and carried him upward from Bethany's hill into the arms of God.

However, the alchemy of spiritual progress seems less important to many who prefer the more spectacular modes of psychic phenomena to the attainment of those transmutative changes which will make them Godlike. Little do men dream that the assurance "All these things shall be added unto you"[8] includes the power of control over wind and wave, of substance and energy, once man has made the kingdom of God his first and most important objective.

Yet, balance is needed, and I am delighted once again to tell the students that the use of alchemy to work change in the physical octave is not inordinate in the least if it is properly used.

The methods of alchemy can be simply stated and easily absorbed, but its precepts require the practice of a master artist. Nevertheless, results can come forth in diverse ways if the student will at least begin and try. There are many methods of precipitation, but here I shall outline just one of them in part.

First design a mental matrix of the desired object, then determine where you wish it to manifest. If you know the material substance of which it is composed, memorize its atomic pattern;

if not, call to the Divine Intelligence within your
Higher Mind to register the pattern for you from
the Universal Intelligence and impress it upon
your memory body and your mind.

Recognize that light is an energy substance
universally manifesting on earth, thanks to the
sun center of being, the focal point of the Christ
in this solar system. Call for light to take on
the atomic pattern you are holding, to coalesce
around that pattern, and then to "densify" into
form. Call for the multiplication of this atomic
structure until molecules of substance begin to
fill the void occupying the space in which you
desire the object to appear.

When the total outline is filled with the
vibratory action of the fourth-dimensional substance representing the desired manifestation,
ask for the full lowering of the atomic density
into three-dimensional form and substance within the pattern established by the matrix of your
mind; and then await results.

Do not be tense if your manifestation is not
immediate or if after a reasonable length of time
it appears that results are not forthcoming. Remember, blessed ones, despair destroys the very
faith upon which your experiment is built. For
faith is the substance of things hoped for, the evidence of things not seen,[9] and you must hold your
faith as you hold the gossamer veil composing the
mental image.

If you have spent years in the grip of
human emotions absorbing the discord of the

mass consciousness and the doubts and fears by humankind, these records must be consumed by alchemical fires to make way for these nobler ideas and forms which you would image forth. To your new ideas you must give your time and your energy. Thus you begin to weave a web of fruition dedicated to spirituality, to the spiritualization of the material consciousness, and to the materialization of heavenly concepts right here on earth where the kingdom of God must come into manifestation.

I would like to point out that the scanning method used in the projection of television pictures, whereby an electronic stream effect fluoresces on a screen and the electronic particles sweep in a horizontal linear pattern to create within a microsecond an eye picture, cannot be successfully used in alchemical precipitation, but is most suitable for the projection of mental pictures at a distance. In precipitation, a rapid expansion of the light rays in three dimensions must occur; and in the screen method, the optical image is on a flat, single-plane dimension.

A study of cytology and embryology will provide the student with some understanding of how a single cell multiplies and reproduces. When you are dealing with instantaneous manifestation, the velocity and intensity of light must reach startling speed and power.

It must be realized that the exercise of such control over Matter by the mind is no ordinary process. While I do not say that ordinary people cannot master the technique of executing these laws and that the most humble individual cannot be invested with or invest himself with such authority within the inalienable rights that God gives to man, I do not wish a sense of frustration to arise within those who may attempt to precipitate and then feel discouraged because they apparently fail.

I say "apparently" because the law does not fail. In most cases where direct precipitation does not occur, if the effort and the technique be pursued in full faith that the call compels the answer, an indirect precipitation will sooner or later be brought about whereby through one hand or another the desired manifestation does take place.

Remember, this is divine artistry of the highest type. It is also co-creation with God and, as such, is best used by those whose purposes parallel the divine. Thus, when the will of man is aligned with the will of God, the light of God does not fail to precipitate that will in the fullness of time, space, and opportunity.

I have devoted six lessons to this subject, dealing with practical methods for assisting the spiritual scientist in obtaining greater personal happiness each day through the merger of the person with the patterns of Principle itself. Both inner and outer peace and a sense of personal well-being are required for the successful development of one's spiritual powers, albeit some individuals may thrive in the midst of conflict.

I admit that upon earth courageous leaders in many fields are needed to unfold and develop the type of society which could be considered to be designed by the gods.

In addition to the alchemy of instantaneous precipitation, the alchemy of preparation is needed, whereby the use of one's energies and opportunities is planned in an intelligent manner so that Life does not receive a hit-and-miss return on its investment of energy in an individual lifestream.

I am hopeful that my readers thus far have not been disappointed in the homey use I have made of their time and attention. I humbly submit that the rereading of this material may further enlighten you, each one, in the true depth of my perceptions, which are calculated to exalt those of various social and religious strata into areas of greater usefulness to themselves, to mankind, and to God. If, when the course is complete, I have in some measure accomplished that or augmented its possibility, I shall be content.

Some of you may desire my personal guidance as you attempt your first alchemical precipitation. I shall gladly assist all who will silently request my aid, providing the motive be right and the desired change beneficial to your life plan and providing you exercise care and prayer in seeking that God's will always be done.

Let me suggest, then, that you attempt as a first effort the precipitation of an amethyst in the form of a Maltese cross. You see, this would be most excellent, for I have personally used alchemy to make many experimental models. And I am most happy to add my momentum to your own!

From the simple to the complex, from the dawn of the beginning of the use of Light's ray to the noontide zenith of progress, let all move in the byways of life as in a caravan of faith. Let each would-be alchemist aim at the mark of achievement. You build in the eternal day right now.

I AM dedicated to your success,

Saint Germain

✠

CHAPTER 8

Commanding Consciousness

Now we approach with reverent hush, with the awe of sacred awareness, the great spiritual laws governing all outer manifestation. The purposes of God become more near to each one as they become more dear to him. Realize what folly it is to submit to the false tenets of any educational system. Yet it is equally foolish to deny the inherent truth and the tested precepts of academic knowledge.

To know nature, know thyself; but master the art of sacred synthesis. Thereby the justice of truth shall serve to integrate within the field of knowing that inner relativity and cosmic measurement between nature and the Self whose precise mathematical action indicates that as God geometrizes, so man is able systematically to perceive and demonstrate a correlated understanding of the wondrous works of God's hands—minus the fallacious wizardry of the carnal mind.

By stripping human thought and feeling vibrations from the creative grace enfolded within each atom of the creation, the whole substance of life gleams, purified by eternal hands. Now this is as it should be! The grossest error, the most intense suffering—all are caused by an erroneous approach to pure reason.

Do you realize, blessed children of mankind, that few there be upon earth who would knowingly persist in wrongdoing were they convinced with certainty that they were so engaged? It is up to the master alchemists of the race, then, to serve God and man to the ultimate by removing every trace of malice and ignorance from the screen of the human consciousness, commencing with each one's own personal concepts.

Knowing how tenderly the students of this course are hanging on my every word, I am also imbued with a sense of reverence for the service at hand. I cannot conceive of how we can do less than answer the calls made unto us in accordance with the Great Cosmic Law.

Even an ascended being in close contact with mankind can become almost possessed with a sense of urgency and a desire to cut the chains which hold any blessed soul in bondage! Yet it is only possible for us to point the way and give such specific guidance and service as the Karmic Board has prescribed.

The injunction "Man, know thyself" must be applied by you to the pure truth of being and not to human concepts of what that truth is. It is dangerous, however, to be critical of another or of his concepts; for only the individual can apprehend, through the screen of his own being, his world and the cosmos beyond.

When you realize the meaning of interpreting life for yourself, you will see how utterly impossible it is for you to perform this for another, inasmuch as the average person cannot successfully enter the consciousness of another lifestream nor accurately assess his complete thought and feeling processes.

This, by the grace of God, we are able to do; and the Karmic Board, in connection with the universally Christed Selves of all mankind, is able to mediate. We often hesitate, unless mightily appealed to, to interfere in individual karma. Yet foolish unascended mankind often rush in to decide how an individual ought to live or think. I trust the students of this activity will come more and more to realize how helpful they can be to one another by holding the immaculate concept for each one's life plan and then leaving the guidance to that one's Higher Self.

Well have I observed over the centuries how important is the service of ordered prayer. The daily offering of petitions has saved the lives of millions, expanded the lives of other millions, and blessed all life without limit.

Prayer opens the door of God's intervention in human affairs. It provides an avenue whereby the Ascended Masters and cosmic beings who desire to serve the planet earth and its evolutions can walk within the folds of universal justice and render special assistance because they have been called upon to do so. For the law decrees that the heavenly hosts must be petitioned by some among mankind, must be invited to intervene, before they are permitted to intercede on behalf of humanity.

After all, would men retain their free will if heaven thwarted the attainment of every inordinate desire? Yet can those guardians of the race who perceive the error of mankind's actions fail to invoke on behalf of their misguided brethren assistance from the higher intelligence of God to cut life free from the crystallized effects of their erroneous concepts?

To the alchemist the value of prayer is manifold. In addition to the aforesaid benefits, it provides an impetus to enhance his values and further the goal of divine truth while the mental mold is in the process of coming into physical manifestation.

The call of beloved Jesus at the hour of his greatest testing, "Nevertheless not my will, but thine, be done!"[1] teaches a more advanced law of alchemy. When spoken by the alchemist at the moment of the sealing of the matrix, this call ensures that the guiding forces of power, wisdom, and love will amend the precipitated pattern where necessary in order that the more perfect designs of the Creator may come forth in the world of form.

This places the whole process of precipitation within the forcefield of eternal perceptions and provides man, as a co-creator with God, with the added benefit of the assistance of the Almighty as he forms and develops his own idea-pattern of destiny in accordance with cosmic purpose.

In my most recent offering, I hinted at the possibility of other minds interfering with the process of precipitation. And while I wish no one to become fearful of this eventuality, I do want each one to be alert to protect himself by guarded silence.

Guarded action and guarded meditation are additional guarantees that the freedom to create which God intends all to have will be the lot of everyone. Your visualization of a blue light around yourself, your matrix, and its manifestation will serve to focalize the desired protection.

When Christ Jesus made the statement "Think not that I am come to send peace on earth: I came not to send peace, but a sword," it caused consternation to many who followed him as the Prince of Peace and it has continued to do so to the present hour. Beloved ones, that declaration, together with that which follows—"I am come to set a man at variance against his father, and the daughter against her mother, and the daughter-in-law against her mother-in-law. And a man's foes shall be they of his own household" [2]— have in common the purpose of conveying a message of protection to each lifestream.

The Saviour proclaimed to all mankind the need to protect the very God-design which belongs to them. Therefore, if some should presume to tell others how to live, they would be setting at variance family and friends. And if a man choose consciously to seek, find, and follow his own God-design, although that very pattern may not please father, mother, friends, or society, that man should accept it albeit it set him at variance with those who yet hold the world's concepts of fulfillment.

In following Bethlehem's Star—the inner lodestone of the Christ—one shares Gethsemane, Calvary, resurrection's morn, and ascension's hill. Thus no one can have true peace until the sword of divine discrimination enables him to discern Reality for himself and then to protect the inherent gifts and graces God has sealed within him in order to make of each lifestream a glorious facet in the master plan of the creation.

I do not allow that an excuse for human stubbornness should arise from my preceding statement. Surely it should be realized that many well-meaning parents and friends do give sound advice, that many religious and educational leaders do likewise, and that much can be learned from listening to the wisdom of the learned and the well informed.

I am, however, interested in each individual's mastering for himself the process of self-discrimination whereby he develops the qualities of leadership and the ability to weigh the advices of others, obediently looking to the God above to penetrate the density of human reason with the light of his benevolence—which, I repeat, is the dawn and the substance of pure reason itself. Greater logic hath no man than the incomparable wisdom of the Logos!

There is here, nonetheless, a point of danger, a thin-ice state of consciousness where foolish aloofness is sensitized within the student; and in this state he declares, "I need only God, and he alone must tell me all I would know." Well, dear ones, when the king bids the son to a feast, he employs servants to place the goods of his table before the son, who must then arise and partake of it for himself. So let all learn to recognize the true worth in others and in all things, but be not misled by the blindness of others.

Now I come to a place where I am anxious to convey to you a great mystery in a manner whereby the very correctness of your apprehension will enable you to reap permanent benefits in your mind and affairs. It is this: the alchemist's understanding of consciousness as the supreme ingredient.

Beloved ones, with God all things are possible![3] If you possess his consciousness, then it is now so for each of you—all things are, in fact, immediately possible to you in manifestation. If this is not your instantaneous experience, then you need more of his consciousness!

"So far, so good," you say. "But how do I go about acquiring that nebulous commodity called consciousness?"

Beloved ones, what and where is your consciousness? The minute specks of physical Matter or energy, atomic in nature, are composed of particles of light held within orbital paths, prescribed and imbued with intelligent action. This spiritual magnetism, infused with creative intelligence, power, and love, is a flux whose density permeates the entire sphere and realm of each atom, extending outward into molecular and cellular composition and thence through the elemental phases of nature, manifesting unto planetary scale. And when correctly understood, these particles shall be known to be whirling in infinitely fantastic orbital paths through solar, galactic, and universal densities.

Relative size has enabled mankind to feel that his consciousness is body-confined or cell-confined, as the case may be. This concept of the ghost chained within the human machine is a total mistake. Although the flow of interacting forces may become more complex, still the concept of an expanding consciousness, simultaneous with an expanding universe, must be reckoned with if man will correctly master his affairs.

Man is no more confined to his body than he is to an atom of substance within it or within his brain. Neither are the atoms of physical Matter composing that body confined to it and limited in expression by that body or Matter-mind density.

The power of reaching outward and becoming a part altogether conscious of a whole in a marvelously spiritual manner is the gift of God to all. No one loses any part of that which is already his own by so doing, and no one takes anything away from anyone else through this sharing of the glories of God.

The real meaning of the passage of scripture in which John the Revelator referred to the little book which would be sweet in the mouth and bitter in the belly[4] relates to his digestion of the idea of himself as containing the universe and the universe containing him. The Book of Life spoken of in Revelation[5] is the lexicon of God, and the lexicon of God embraces the entire cosmos.

Inasmuch as it spans all of the creation, let none take away another's portion or privilege to enjoy all of its cosmic truth; nor let anyone deprive himself of this, life's greatest privilege. To do so is to take away either one's own or another's portion, and surely then God, as Law, shall confine the one so doing to the same sphere of limitation to which he has confined another.

Let all in being their brother's keeper esteem the highest and best possibilities for everyone. Therefore, expand and contract the consciousness to sense not only the necessary internal realm of being, but also the externally expanding universe, and you shall find your consciousness leaping into the arms of the Eternal Alchemist himself.

Now, it is not my intention to leave the many subjects included in this course without a spiritual and physical synopsis and an appendage of daily usefulness. Therefore, the next lesson shall include the golden cord, which should perhaps be spelled *chord*, for it is intended to create a final harmonizing key in consciousness that will make this course of permanent and inestimable value to all.

I am hopefully including such instruction as shall serve to frame the whole in a setting rare and lovely. But the whole herein referred to is your whole life! Master your consciousness by properly directing its attention, and possess thereby the key to God's precious storehouse of eternal substance.

Fondly, I AM

Saint Germain

CHAPTER 9

The Crucible of Being

Breathes there the man, with soul so dead
Who never to himself hath said,
This is my own, my native universe!

Part I

If I could cite one area of application which the students need to work on more than any other, it is that of the expansion of the universal consciousness within the forcefield of the individual.

The greatest need of mankind today—and I say this unequivocally—is the development and the nurturing of the sense of the universal as belonging completely to the individual. From thence is drawn the foregone conclusion that the individual must also be sensed as belonging to that universal cosmos so conceived.

As the student of alchemy approaches the temple of being, of life, of oneness, he must, if he would correctly apprehend the meaning of existence and derive happiness therefrom, see himself as a diamond of Light's perfection set in a mounting of perpetual elegance. Acknowledging his origin in those permanent realities which the interpretative mind and heart of being are able to apprehend and hold in the proper focus of prospective progress, man shall once again renew his intelligently guided drift toward sublime Reality.

There is no greater deterrent to progress than the isolationism that evolves out of the sense of separation from Life wherein the smallness of the ego, pitted against indeterminate odds, lurks in the shadows of uncertainty. The unforeseeable events of the future, by reason of their opacity, project little comfort into the longing heart which awaits some word from the creative mind of God, some foreknowledge of the depth of that love which God feels for each part of the vast whole of the cosmos in all of its immensity and greatness.

From the least to the greatest minds of earth, all need the benefit of lasting attunement with the universal consciousness of God.

Mankind, through various religious concepts, have imagined God to be a "creature-creator" simply because they themselves are "creator-creatures." Using the tremendous outgoing energy of being, men have diligently imagined and imaged forth the nature of God, while only the few have apprehended the truth that God is consciousness, and as consciousness he is life, intelligence, will, and love manifest in a rich variety of dimensions and attributes.

Now I tell you, God is a benign Impersonal Personality, a Personal Impersonality, a Personal

Personality, and an Impersonal Impersonality comprising the manifold consciousness of being. He gives and gives of his creative Self to the creatures he has made in the hope that they will apprehend his purposes and emulate his consciousness to the fullness with which he has endowed them.

As they mature and grow throughout life, people imitate one another, consciously and unconsciously mimicking the personalities that touch their lives. They dwell in such a sense of unreality that they persist in identifying themselves as vile sinners. They accept not only the accusations of the "accuser of our brethren" whose machinations are exposed in the twelfth chapter of the Book of Revelation, but also the burden of mounting waves of mass condemnation which, like a raging sea, threaten to drown the Real Image of the Higher Self in an ocean of emotion.

The purpose of thought and feeling is to form the mold of fruitful and progressive experience which in turn endows mankind with the highest aspects of his Divine Self. You see, blessed alchemists, your thoughts and feelings are the collimation lines that adjust and align your energies, focusing them through the lens of consciousness according to your free will for either constructive or destructive designs in the world of form.

Mankind, in the mainstream of their influence, have misused the energies of their thoughts and feelings; and, unaware of the consequences of their mental and emotional inconsistencies, irregularities, and incongruities, they have molded Light's energies descending into their world into asymmetrical forms which, by reason of their nature, could never produce happiness for themselves or any other part of life.

The idea of a temperamental, vengeful, or unjust God is abhorrent from the outset. The concept of an arbitrary Deity who would show favoritism is likewise distressing. Hence, according to his awareness of the Deity, man himself becomes the arbiter of his destiny, and, according to his uses of energy, the harbinger of truth or error in his life.

The stratification of human consciousness from the aboriginal types unto the erudite twentieth-century man, skilled in philosophy, science, religion, and the higher mechanics of living, persists in its full range to the present day in various parts of the world. Honest individuals will even recognize in themselves these progressive steps of consciousness which, if progress is being made, are constantly in a state of flux.

Now, it is true that it may be more comfortable, at least temporarily, for mankind to vegetate neath the sun and the moon in an isolated reverie, remote from the challenges of life, without benefit of the sometimes violent but always disturbing alchemical heat which, as Christic fires, acts to purge mankind of his dross. But I am certain that the soul which desires to climb the hill of attainment to reach the summit peaks will neither find fault with nor reject the necessary chain of experiences that are intended to broaden the mind, sharpen the intellect, exalt the spirit, and test the mettle of a man.

While on the subject of the gradations of consciousness, remember that each level represents a phase of the alchemy of transition from the human to the divine. A just sense of the equal opportunity of all to apprentice themselves to the Master Alchemist is a prerequisite to personal freedom.

To recognize the potential of a mobile and malleable consciousness is to recognize the soaring of the spirit. To be willing to accept personal responsibility for changing unwanted conditions within the domain of the self is to accept the responsibility of being a son of God. Those who cater to their egos and allow the energy patterns (i.e., vibrations) of personal jealousy to block the doorway to self-mastery as they court the attainment of another lifestream will be hindered in their progress on the Path until they have transmuted this propensity.

Jealousy is in fact rooted in the doubt and the fear that Almighty God himself is unable to bestow upon each one every good and necessary talent contributing to the fulfillment of his divine plan. Inasmuch as jealousy and competition between individual expressions of God are among the basic causes of all unhappiness upon earth,

I would definitely underscore the students' need to put them to the flame.

The threats to the alchemist's self-mastery posed by jealousy manifest in many subtle modes —so much so that many honest-hearted people are unaware of the fact that such tainted vibrations do from time to time play upon their feelings. Application made in prayer and supplication or as invocations and affirmations (called decrees) made in the name of God for the freeing of oneself from all conditions of struggle and strife will bear the fruit of an active yet peaceful progress.

You see, false identification with family and friends, the acceptance of limitations through heredity and environment, attachment to persons and places, to one's race, religion, nationality, or ethnic group must also be submitted to the flames of the Refiner's fire for transmutation. Personal attitudes must be adjusted to impersonal laws, and thought and feeling patterns must be molded after more noble designs if the individual is to make true spiritual progress.

I do not say that individuals should not be loyal to those whom they love and in whom they believe. But I do declare that man's first loyalty should be to his True Self, his own God-identity, and to his Christed being, and then to those of like mind. Above all, the purposes and uses of life must be rightly understood and practiced.

To awaken each day to another round of pursuing vain pleasures and the questionable hope of mortal expectation—herein lies a state of flaccid misery in which the soul is scarcely exercised. When the purposes of heaven are truly understood, man will welcome the dawn and receive each new day with joy.

In the fullness of life man can hardly fear death. As I wrote in my essay "Of Death" (under the name of Francis Bacon): "It is as natural to die as to be born; and to a little infant, perhaps, the one is as painful as the other!"[1] Thus we now stand at a point in our alchemical studies where we must understand the meaning of the mortification of the body of untransmuted substance.

Through the centuries men have taken great pride in the body: they have glorified it and deified it. Artists have painted it, sculptors have created beautiful statues exhibiting it, and in the end it has fallen into dust and decay.

All the while this process of decay has been going on, the spirit of man has supposedly been creating houses of perfection eternal in the heavens.[2] And this is true in part, for every good deed which man does while in the body is recorded to his credit in the great concentric rings of light and electronic substance which comprise his causal body—the body of First Cause which is the dwelling place of the Presence of the Most High God.

As each individual man who is a manifestation of God has a causal body, so each individual has an I AM Presence pulsating as the sacred fire in the center of that body. And in the auric forcefield surrounding that Presence are the markings of his achievements for good upon his planetary home.

One law, then, would I instill in the hearts of the students of alchemy: God is absolutely just— the universe is absolutely just. All injustice arises either in man's misinterpretation and misunderstanding of the flow of events or in man's mishandling of justice. Those who have not apprehended life correctly, those who remain ignorant of the laws of divine as well as human justice, cannot be relied upon to preserve the flame of justice.

As I have stated before, every student must be willing to throw off the shackles of the false teachers and their false teachings. Every student must determine to break the chains of error even while he rejects the image of the world as a place where integrity is lacking and the suggestion that individuals are here to take advantage of one another.

The well-known and often-quoted entrepreneur P. T. Barnum said, "There's a sucker born every minute." Of course, people do not like to think that they are being taken advantage of. Therefore, they often try to outdo the other fellow before he outdoes them. This attitude is responsible for a most unhealthy climate in both commerce and society.

While it is true that the responsibility rests with the world's leaders in every field to set an example of integrity, nothing should prevent the world's followers from manifesting that integrity which their leaders ought to manifest or from exalting virtue as an example before them. There is much in the world's thought about itself that is accurate, but its inaccuracies have come to be accepted by individuals without question. Such tacit acceptance makes for both a weak civilization and a weak individuality.

Therefore, in strengthening the bonds of freedom throughout the world, a new man must emerge from the social milieu: a New Atlantean must step forth clothed with the righteousness of the Sun! A golden man for the golden age! This is the Master Alchemist!

If this spiritual man—clothed with the power of the Sun, clothed with the power of spiritual alchemy, clothed with the virtue that he already possesses but of which he is far too often unaware—is to stand forth today, it must be because he has offered the "body" of his corrupt substances to be thrown into the crucible of the alchemical furnace!

The early Christian mystics and writers referred to this experience when they said that a man ought to die with Christ if he expected to live with him. [3] This death of the old man with his deeds [4] is confined to the crucible of the spiritual-alchemical experience; thus it is possible for all unwanted conditions in a man's life to be changed, that he may pass through a glorious transmutative epic culminating in the putting on of the new man. Free at last of the dross of the human experience, man stands forth in all of the shining glory of the divine experience that is the wholeness of the resurrection.

The agonies of Gethsemane may be compared to the spiritual preparation that the individual alchemist must make before knowingly and consciously committing himself to the crucible of life in order that he may emerge in the true glory of his being. This is dying with Christ in the certain hope that he will live again.

Beloved ones, bear in mind that those who do not do so willingly and knowingly will still pass through the change called death, even if they persist in following the ways that lead to destruction. But this change, without the prior putting off of the old man, will not lead to the indestructible Christhood that God intends every son to manifest. It is a supreme demonstration of faith when a living soul, forsaking even self-love, offers himself as a living sacrifice in order that Christ-victory be glorified through him. Such is a career son of God!

In closing Part I, I advocate that the seeker make any sacrifice necessary to the seeking out of the golden possibilities that gleam through the mists of time and space as spiritual reality—the hope of every man upon earth!

Part II

Beloved ones, just as heaven is not lost by a single thought or deed of a lifestream, so heaven is not gained by a single thought or deed. Nevertheless, your life can become a daily round of victories whereby each step taken aright propels you into an expanding awareness of the beauty and glory of the newness of life. This is the resurrection from dead works of carnality into the living exaltation of the Christ consciousness of spirituality, vesting each one so dedicated with the mission of Jesus the Christ—one of the greatest alchemists of all time.

Speaking of resurrection, I am reminded of the words "In the beauty of the lilies Christ was born across the sea, / With a glory in His bosom that transfigures you and me: / As He died to make men holy, let us live to make men free, / While God is marching on."[5]

The newly resurrected man—in whom Christ is born, in whom there is a transfiguring glory—is resurrected by the power of change, by the science of divine alchemy. In him the dawn of each new day takes on a spiritual significance never before experienced. He holds each day as a chalice of opportunity to live free and to make all men free.

Then all of nature, in sweet communion with the yearning of his lifestream to fan the fires of freedom, extends immortal hands of felicity. The trees, the flowers, the rocks, the earth—all of the variegated expressions of nature—bow to that man who has made himself the instrument of freedom and extend to him the care and consideration of the Master Gardener himself.

The Father who created the paradise of God referred to in Genesis is now perceived to be in fact the Creator of all loveliness. The sylphs of the air, the undines of the sea, the fiery salamanders of the flame, and the gnomes of the earth are recognized as elemental spirits created to assist that one Father in bringing forth a kingdom of supreme loveliness and beauty.

It is recognized by the perceptive alchemist that the carnal nature of man has been outpictured in part by the nature kingdom; for the elementals, from the smallest to the greatest, are great mimics of the human scene. As they have taken on human concepts of duality, thorns and thistles, pain and parting have been brought forth upon the screen of life. Yet with all of the despoiling of the virgin beauty of the earth by mankind's discord and inharmony, much that is lovely has remained, showing that the power of God is greater than the power of the deification of evil.

Through friendship with the servants of God and man in nature, the compassionate alchemist learns to utilize the great spiritual flow of elemental life and finds in the presence of the Holy Spirit a cooperation with nature which formerly he did not even dream existed. Looking upon the blessed earth with the grandeur of its rolling plains, its fertile valleys, and its mountain ranges, gazing upon the crystalline mirrors of its lakes and flowing streams interlacing the terrain and conveying the water element in channels of varying depth, mankind become filled with reverent wonder.

The planetary veins and arteries conveying the tireless energy of the Eternal One from place to place upon the spinning globe of the world, the blue dome of the sky with the golden sun disk to warm and revivify mankind, the silent night with the crystal moon and diadems of stars like unto the Pleiades—all of these are flooded with a sense of unity which pervades all things. Nowhere is unity felt with greater meaning than in the depths of the heart of the individual who is in complete attunement with God and his own I AM Presence, the individualized identity of the perfection of the Creator himself.

That body of historical error composed of myriad carnal events and human misqualifications is changed now by the alchemical fires of spiritual regeneration, and in its place the wholeness of the Real Being of man stands forth. He is no longer a part: he is the all of creation!

These valleys and hills, these diadems of stars and far reaches of space are a part of himself. He is all of them and in them all! With this supernal sense of ever-present wonder, man is able, as an integral manifestation of God, to perform the miracles of the Great Alchemist and make his world the wondrous glory of the resurrection! Old senses are passed away; all things are become new.[6]

With that I wish to give the students a coup d'oeil into advancements which shall be forthcoming in the world of science. I am interested in offering a preview of man's greater control of the elements in this *Studies in Alchemy*, because some of our would-be alchemists can be instrumental in the production of these new techniques or in calling them forth from the Universal.

Let us consider for a moment the development of the mind-switch. At present, lights, elevators, doors, and many devices are activated by switches or electronically; and engineers are at work upon a typewriter which will type phonetically sentences spoken directly into it. The mind-switch is even more revolutionary, for it will enable men to direct mechanical apparatus and electrical functions through brain waves by the mastery of the energy currents flowing through the mind.

Of course, many amusing situations could be construed in which two individuals might transmit divergent impulses simultaneously. This should pose no problem, for they would but cancel each other out or the stronger would overcome the weaker of the transmitted thought waves.

Another development of the coming age will be a camera so sensitized that it will make possible the photographing of the human aura. This will enable physicians to discover the fundamental causes of many physical diseases as well as the solution to psychiatric problems related to the emotions and subconscious records of past experiences, even in previous lives unknown to the patients themselves.

The wave patterns caused by criminal tendencies and crimes recorded in the etheric body will also be "photographed," or recorded by sensitive instruments in graphic form similar to the process now used to record brain waves and impulses of the nervous system. Evidence of guilt or innocence will thereby be afforded those administrators of justice who formerly relied on incomplete knowledge of events in the penalizing of delinquent individuals.

With the advent of greater understanding of magnetism, it will be possible to so amplify the power of magnetism as to suspend furniture in midair without any form of visible support. A new optical development is forthcoming which will increase mankind's exploration of the submicroscopic and atomic worlds.

In this field the magnification of images with great clarity will become possible by methods not previously encountered. With this advancement certain methods of transmutation will be made known to the chemists of the world whereby the synthesis of new elements will be achieved as simply as a child plays with blocks.

A new form of aeronavigation and transportation will be made possible by utilizing an electronic ray played upon the metal of which the airship itself is composed, negating the gravitational influences upon it and giving it a quality of lightness similar to helium. This will enable it to rise in complete resistance to the power of gravity. The ship can then be directed by atomic jets in such a manner that a safer form of locomotion will be made available to all. A breakthrough in color television enabling increased clarity in the ranges of color tones and values should come forth before too long.

Through the means of orbiting satellites such as those that are currently circling the earth, a new method of studying the weather and of mapping it will cause mankind to realize the need for a central control station for the weather in order to direct its conditions over most of the landed areas of the world. I feel, however, that this could be the subject of much controversy and may eventually be dropped until the time when greater unity and amicability exist between various interest groups and among the family of nations.

The work begun many years ago by Luther Burbank—who acted under the direction of the hierarchy in his experiments with nature and the grafting of plants—will be brought to a new degree of perfection as certain influences within the hearts of the seeds themselves are revealed through advanced studies in cytology. Within the heart of the desert cactus is locked a secret whereby the arid areas of the world can indeed be made to blossom as the rose[7] and produce all manner of fruits and vegetables with far less moisture than is presently required. Water shortages may thus be alleviated.

The present surge in world population, which seems to have caused many demographers to review and revise the doctrines of Malthus with the aim of extinguishing or limiting human life in complete contradiction to God's laws, will prove of less concern to future societies as they become aware of marvelous methods of increasing agricultural production, of harvesting the wealth of the sea, and of the unlimited use of atomic energy in advanced city planning as well as in interplanetary colonization.

There is a purpose in the plans of God which far transcends the understanding of the human intellect and the memory of history upon earth. The wonders that are to come will soon be dwarfed by still greater wonders, and therefore all life should live in a state of constant expectancy.

It is the joy of the mind of God to give richly of his blessing. But above all, may I counsel you now, students of the Light and all mankind: Obtain first from God the Father the wisdom to live peaceably, to deal gently and courteously with one another, to promote the education of mankind the world around, and especially by honest efforts to prevent the increase in number of those indigent individuals who are prone to commit crimes against society.

The value of training the young in a proper manner and encouraging them to live lives of useful service and good character cannot be overestimated. Political scandals within the nations of the world and the harshness of police-state methods (as enforced in Communist-dominated countries) must be overridden by the sword of the Prince of Peace.

The Prince of Peace is imaged in the compassionate Christ going forth to teach all nations that the way of God is good, that his wonders are intended to be used and possessed by all and exclusively by none. A higher way of life than vain competition must be pursued. Men must become God-spurred and less motivated by status seeking.

Teach this truth! The sharing of the grace of heaven is a message of eternal watchfulness from the Great White Brotherhood to all upon earth.

Abundance and peace go hand in hand, and this state of felicity is the will of God. Let this planet, by the power of spiritual and natural alchemy, arise to build new homes, new churches, new schools, a new civilization, new concepts, new virtue, new greatness—all in the bonds of eternal confidence which blazes forth from the very heart of God and is anchored within your own physical heart as the expanding flame spark of the Immortal Alchemist himself!

Part III

The feeling of aloneness should be transmuted and superseded by the certainty of all-oneness. Man came forth from God as good, and he shall return to that goodness by becoming like it through the dignity of freedom and choice.

The power, love, and wisdom of God are never tyrannical but gently bestow upon each individual creature of the creation the blessedness of opportunity to know God without limit. Forgiveness, mercy, justice, peace, achievement, and progress toward ultimate supremacy are the gifts which Life holds for all.

Through the process of descent into Matter and form, man, as a part of God destined to become ultimately victorious, is made the conscious master of all he surveys, so long as he is not forgetful of his Source. By identifying with the gross, man becomes almost at once entangled in a web of human creation whose snarls, like the thread of Ariadne weaving through the labyrinthian cave of subterranean Matter, bring him face to face with the Minotaur who dwells in the lower octaves of consciousness waiting to devour the Christ.

Escape is freedom. That which descends and is committed to form and density must, in obtaining its freedom, ascend back to that Source from whence it came.

To do this prematurely is in error; and therefore the Father, or I AM Presence, knows of each

lifestream the day and hour when he is truly
ready! Until the fullness of outer circumstance is
transcended and transmuted in a manner whereby the lifestream has fulfilled his original purposes for entering the orbit of Earth, he should
continue his training and preparation in accordance with the universal plan.

Surely thoughtful individuals will quickly recognize that marrying and the giving in marriage,
procreation and the perpetuation of present modes
of civilization are not of themselves the ultimate
purposes of life. All the world as a stage is not the
cosmic coliseum; and ere the curtain is drawn on
the final act, the drama of man's existence shall
be played out in many corners of the universe
undreamed of by either early or modern man.

Men's dreams of heaven are but fond
glimpses into the imagery of Elysium graciously
afforded mankind as encouragement until the
time when they are able to expand their own spiritual vision and behold reality in the wonders of
the Father in his many cosmic mansions.[8]

The supreme purpose of God for every lifestream upon earth is the selfsame victory which
beloved Jesus manifested from the hill of Bethany. The accent of Christendom upon the agony
of Gethsemane, the crucifixion, and the vigil
in the tomb of Joseph of Arimathea has often
eclipsed the great significance for every man,
woman, and child of the glories of the resurrection
and mysteries of the ascension.

Misunderstanding of the law of cause and effect and failure to apprehend the at-one-ment of the Universal Christ originated in the human concepts that were introduced in the parable of Eden and continue to the present day, perpetuated by the hoary mists of time and dogma. Unfortunately, the vicarious atonement has been ignorantly accepted and is widely used as an excuse for wrongdoings and their continuation. Thus, surrounded by an aura of godly but needless fear, men have persisted in passing on fallacies from generation to generation in the name of God and Holy Writ.

The registering of discord and wrongdoing upon man's four lower bodies (i.e., the physical, mental, memory, and emotional bodies) is effected by scientific law, cosmically ordained and itself the very instrument of creation. As creators, men have sown the wind and reaped a karmic whirlwind. [9]

The victory of the Universal Christ, which beloved Jesus demonstrated, was intended to show to man the way that would conduct him safely back to God's image. That way was revealed as the Christ, or Divine Light within every man that cometh into the world. [10] It is this wondrous light, then, which is the light and life of the world [11]—of every man's individual world. Only by walking in the light as he, the Universal Christ, is in the light [12] can men return to the Father's house.

The forgiveness of sins is a merciful instrument of the Great Law whereby retribution, or the penalty for wrongdoing, is held in abeyance in order that a lifestream may have the freedom to "go and sin no more"[13] and then be given the opportunity for greater spiritual progress. However, forgiveness does not absolve the soul of the requirement to balance the energies misused by the alchemical fires of transmutation. The balancing of wrongs done to every part of life, including the self, must be accomplished in full with cosmic precision; hence every jot and tittle of the law must be fulfilled[14] either here or hereafter.

This process need not be a fearful looking for of judgment,[15] but it should preferably be a happy expectation of opportunity for service to life and the freeing of Life's imprisoned splendor. For by ministering unto life individually and universally and by calling forth the alchemical fires on the altar of being, the individual can undo all of the inharmonies which he has thoughtlessly cast upon its beauteous presence. Truly, those who have been forgiven much can love much;[16] for they perceive the need to be everlastingly grateful for the goodness and mercy of God which endure forever![17]

One of the major causes of recalcitrance, arrogance, willful wrongdoing, disobedience, rebellion, and stubbornness is the vain hope of individual attainment without individual effort or of personal salvation without personal sacrifice. Mankind do not relish the idea of painstakingly withdrawing every thread and snarl they have placed in the garment of life or of attaining heaven by honest application.

Yet they must one day face this truth of themselves. Therefore, the present, when truth and justice of opportunity are at hand, is the right and accepted time. "Behold, now is the accepted time; behold, now is the day of salvation." [18]

The desire to find a scapegoat for one's sins in a world teacher or saviour is not in keeping with the cosmic principles undergirding the law of the atonement. A master of great light such as Jesus the Christ or Gautama Buddha may hold the balance for millions of souls who are not able to carry the weight of their own sinful sense. This holding action is a staying of the law whereby, through mercy and through the personal sacrifice of one who keeps the flame for all, mankind might find their way back to God and then, in the power of the rebirth and in the presence of the Holy Spirit, return to take up the unfinished business of balancing their debts to life.

Christ is the saviour of the world because by his immaculate heart he postpones the day of judgment, affording humanity additional opportunity in time and space to fulfill the requirements of immortality.

I cannot, in the holy name of freedom, resist speaking out on these matters. For many have suffered in the astral world after the change called death, and when they came before the Lords of Karma to give an accounting for their lives, they were found wanting. Unfortunately, this may have been only because while on earth they accepted false religious doctrine and, in their misguided state, failed to do well in the time allotted to them. Then came to pass the words God spake to Adam's son, "Sin lieth at the door"[19]—that is to say, the record of the misuse of God's energy is at hand: render an accounting.

In God's scheme of world order, the propitiation for sin is permanent and effective; for the violet fire will transmute every unwanted condition and balance all by Light. This Light is the Universal Christ.

The precious violet flame, an aspect of the Comforter's[20] consciousness, is the friend of every alchemist. It is both the cup and the elixir of Life that cannot fail to produce perfection everywhere when it is called into action. After the violet flame has performed its perfect work, then let all rest in their labors that God may move upon the waters (waves of light) of the creation to produce and sustain the righteousness of his eternal law.

The climax or initiation of the ascension can and will come to all, even to little children, when they are ready for it—when at least 51 percent of their karma has been balanced (this means that 51 percent of all the energy ever given to their use has been transmuted and put to constructive purpose) and their hearts are just toward God and man, aspiring to rise into the never-failing light of God's eternally ascending Presence.

When this gift is given to anyone by his own I AM Presence and the Karmic Board, the appearance of age drops from him as swiftly as a smile can raise the lips, and the magnetism and energy of that one becomes the unlimited power of God surging through his being. The dross of the physical, the weariness of the emotional body, tired of hatred and its monstrous creations, the ceaseless rote of the mental body—all drop away and are replaced in perfect ease by their divine counterparts.

The feelings become charged by the love of God and the angels. The mind is the diamond-shining mind of God—omnipresent, omniscient, omnipotent. The total being is inspired and aspiring!

Thus that which once hopefully descended now ascends back into the Light from whence it came. One with the company of angels and the nature and friendship of the Ascended Masters and in fellowship with the august fraternity of the Great White Brotherhood, each such one, by the divine merit within, attains the fullness of all that God would ever bestow upon each son without respect of any man's person, but in joyful acknowledgment of man's victory: Thou art my beloved Son; this day have I begotten thee![21]

Epilogue

Religion and spirituality are no shame. These are the implements of the eternally creative arts. These are the friends of the alchemist who would change every base element of human nature and all life into the gold of Christed accomplishment.

In this teaching are keys to the highest portal. They must be fitted in the lock to gain entrance to the highest initiation. I AM the door to the progressive unfoldment of ever-ascending planes of consciousness—all within your lovely God Presence, I AM.

Blessed ones, you are not limited in alchemy merely to the drawing forth from the universal light of three-dimensional objects. Alchemy can be mastered in order to illumine the mind, to heal any unwanted condition, and to spiritually exalt man's total nature from its base state to the golden standard where the golden rule is law.

With you—as with God—all things are possible. There is no other or higher way. For example, the brilliance of present Soviet science cannot win the universe for the blessed children of Mother Russia. Only God can bring eternal satisfaction to the whole earth. Let the ungodly tremble, for they shall be cut down as grass;[22] but the righteous shall shine as the sons of the Great Alchemist, Almighty God!

Further studies in alchemy are available to all who would progressively advance in this science of self-dominion. Some of this material I am releasing in the lessons of the Keepers of the Flame Fraternity, some in the weekly Pearls of Wisdom written by the Masters of our Brotherhood, and some I shall bring to you individually in answer to your heart's calls. But call you must if this cause which is just shall be fulfilled in you!

"Call unto me, and I will answer thee," [23] declares the Most High God. The Father shall reward you openly for each prayerful call you make in secret. [24] Within the inner recesses of your heart, unknown by any man, you may ever silently call. There in your heart is the crucible of the eternal essence, the white stone, the elixir and full potency of Life.

Alchemists of the sacred fire, here is the sacred cosmic formula: Theos = God; Rule = Law; You = Being; *Theos + Rule + You = God's law active as Principle within your being* (TRY).

I AM in constant attunement with your true being,

Pax vobiscum

Sanctus Germanus

✠

The
Mystical
Origins
of the
United States
of America

No people can be bound to
acknowledge and adore
the Invisible Hand which conducts
the affairs of men more than those
of the United States.

– GEORGE WASHINGTON
First Inaugural Address

An Invisible Hand in the affairs of men? In an age of power politics, scientific miracles, and ultimate threats, it may come as a surprise that one of the most widely accepted and ancient of ideas was that a divine hand established and ruled the nations. Early Americans believed that an unseen intelligence directed the course of the American Revolution and guided the destiny

"America was designed by Providence," wrote John Adams, who helped draft and also signed the Declaration of Independence and the peace treaty with England.

of this nation. John Adams wrote, "America was designed by Providence for the theatre on which man was to make his true figure." And Patrick Henry said, "There is a just God who presides over the destinies of nations."

Evidence of the invisible hand of God is nowhere more apparent than in the affairs of our nation. For the swift ascent of the American Republic was nothing less than miraculous.

From a loose coalition of seaboard states united as much by their dislike of the British king as by brotherly affection, the United States grew from a tiny preindustrial community to the world's preeminent economic, technological, and military power in less than two centuries. America became a land of political and religious freedom, a beacon of hope to the nations, and a stage for the playing out of a great historical epic.

By the twentieth century, America had become a proud land—the American with history as his witness, self-assured. So it was doubly surprising after World War II when the Republic was at the apparent zenith of her power, that Americans found themselves reeling under the hammerblows of events. Emerging out of the 1950s, the Republic plowed into heavy seas.

Campuses, college towns, and inner cities erupted in flames and violence. A gulf opened up between youth and aged, hip and square, black and white, conservative and liberal and radical. Various and sundry revolutions tore through the nation like a series of earthquakes—drugs, rock, and rebellion against the establishment among them—shaking the Republic to its foundations.

With the suddenness of lightning, President John F. Kennedy, the image of our youth, was struck down. The nation mourned and was never the same. Then the Martin Luther King and another Kennedy assassination followed.

And darkness covered the land. Or was it a brooding spirit? Who could see the outworking of an inner design, the gleam of hope, or the turning of the tide?

By the mid-seventies, the storm had largely subsided. But the nation was rudderless and in the doldrums. Vietnam and Watergate troubled the national psyche and left most Americans unsure of their purpose.

The Ford years were aimless and lackluster. During the Carter term, U.S. prestige so declined that our allies no longer considered us leader of the free world, but let us know we were now an "equal partner." Soviet imperialism was unchallenged because it was presumed to be unimportant or not to exist.

Patrick Henry declared, "There is a just God who presides over the destinies of nations," and, "Is life so dear, or peace so sweet, as to be purchased at the price of chains and slavery? Forbid it, Almighty God! I know not what course others may take; but as for me, give me liberty, or give me death!"

America, it seemed, had become a helpless, hapless giant. The capture of sixty-six Americans in Iran was the height of ignominy. Or was it? It turned out, in fact, to be the turning point. First there were tremors of shock and indignation. Then the seizure galvanized a growing but largely unnoticed wave of patriotism. Yankee ingenuity, humor, and determination returned.

The Soviet invasion of Afghanistan mobilized American resolve to resist Communism. And suddenly the apparently dormant American spirit awakened to the dawn of a resurrection.

President Carter was out of step with the new mood. The electorate swept him from office and installed a man who promised to lead America to a restoration. Ronald Reagan, fortieth American president, rode the resurgent American spirit to a resounding victory.

Although one of Ronald Reagan's campaign themes was the return to American greatness, his election was more of an effect than a cause—he was riding the wave, not causing the tide. Something subtle, yet more powerful than any man, is and always has been propelling the nation forward towards some unnamed goal.

Even though the pomp and circumstance of American heritage is back in style, the new patriotism is still more of a feeling than a conscious articulation of values. There is still confusion about what course of action *We the People* should take. The problem is not one of indecision, but one of identity—when you know who you are, you know what to do.

America, who are we?

Most of our founding fathers knew. Many early Americans knew also: they were Israelites.

Since only a few were Jews and none were citizens of a then nonexistent Israeli state, in what way did they deem themselves Israelites? They were Israelites because of their mystical identification with that ancient people and their God.

Historians have recognized that the early Americans saw a striking similarity between their own hardships, history, and condition, and those of the children of Israel under Moses and Joshua. It was as if they were reliving history: they baptized their children with the names of the Hebrew prophets and patriarchs and likened their present condition to "Egyptian bondage," King James to "Pharaoh," the ocean whose dangers their ancestors had encountered to the "Red Sea," and their new home in the American wilds to "the wilderness." Washington and Adams were often referred to as "Moses" and "Joshua." All that was missing were the desert sands of Sinai.

The Bible was more than a religious guide to the early New England settlers. It was their political textbook as well. The early criminal codes of the Plymouth and Massachusetts Bay colonies were modeled on rules found in Exodus, Leviticus, and Deuteronomy.

By 1776, it was widely accepted that God had established a new American Israel. The idea was preached to approving congregations in sermons with titles such as "The Republic of the Israelites: An Example to the American States" and "Traits of Resemblance in the People of the United States of America to Ancient Israel."

The idea was so deeply rooted that the first design proposed for the seal of the United States depicted Pharaoh sitting in an open chariot, passing through the divided waters of the Red Sea in hot pursuit of the children of Israel. Rays from a pillar of fire shone on Moses as he raised his hand over the sea causing it to overwhelm Pharaoh and the Egyptians.

Yet America was nearly four millennia removed and 6,000 miles away from the ancient lands where the Israelites had appeared.

The story of the Israelites is a historic epic in which the God of Israel revealed himself, established his covenant with Abraham, Isaac, and Jacob, renamed Jacob "Israel," and promised "a nation and a company of nations shall be of thee."

God's plan to liberate his people spiritually and temporally required great foresight and planning. Talk about invisible hands! God revealed the Egyptian captivity to Abraham before there were any Israelites to speak of. Jacob's son Joseph, sold into slavery by his brothers, now risen to governorship under Pharaoh, told them that God had brought him to Egypt. Jacob and his other sons followed suit, surviving in Egypt during the seven-year famine. But after Joseph and his generation passed, the children of Israel multiplied greatly and what Abraham had once seen in a dream came to pass—four hundred years of bondage.

Throughout their historical trek—even to the present—it has been axiomatic that when the Israelites are obedient to God all goes well. When they fail to keep his commandments, God often uses neighboring peoples to illustrate to them the inexorable nature of the law of karmic recompense. The purpose of the Egyptian captivity was to allow the people to experience firsthand their own recalcitrance heaped upon them through their Egyptian taskmasters.

When it came time for their liberation, God sent Moses to lead them out of Egypt to the edge of the promised land, and Joshua to push them over the hill of their remaining waywardness. Under the brilliant leadership of Joshua, the Israelites took the land of promise in a lightning military campaign.

One striking feature of the Israelites was their organization into a tribal federation that gave each tribe considerable autonomy. This was the venerated republic that the early Americans admired and sought to re-create.

The fortune of the Israelites was anything but constant. Again, the people became rebellious, were carried off into captivity by neighboring nations and later entirely dispersed.

But all was not lost. Around 732 B.C., Isaiah prophesied that one day the LORD would "assemble the outcasts of Israel, and gather together the dispersed of Judah from the four corners of the earth."

There is considerable difference of opinion among scholars and theologians about the meaning of this prophecy. Some believe it refers to the Israelites' return from the sixth century B.C. Babylonian captivity, some the return from Assyria, some to the formation of the modern state of Israel, and some believe it refers to the regathering of the twelve tribes of Israel on American soil.

It seems that in the great odyssey of the Israelites, nearly twenty-two centuries passed before there were visible signs of how this prophecy would be fulfilled. The stage was being set for a regathering of the Israelites, but the land to which they were destined to return had to be prepared. In fact, it had to be discovered.

This assignment was given by the Invisible Hand to Christopher Columbus, who discovered America by prophecy. In carrying out his mission, he wrote, "Neither reason nor mathematics nor maps were any use to me: *fully accomplished were the words of Isaiah.*"

Columbus' life is clothed in mystery. The exact date or place of his birth is not known. Some claim he was Greek, others Genoese, and

Man of destiny. Christopher Columbus discovered the New World by prophecy: "Neither reason nor mathematics nor maps were of any use to me: fully accomplished were the words of Isaiah."

still others a Spanish Jew. He was steeped in astrology, the writings of Marco Polo, the Old and New Testaments, and the Apocrypha. And the two words of his name, Cristóbal Colón, mean "Christ-bearer" and "colonizer."

This mysterious figure was adept in the poetical language of the secret societies of the fifteenth century and, quite possibly, a member of the Great Guild of Weavers. Secret societies, such as the guilds, Knights Templars, the Rosicrucians, and the Masons were repositories for the ancient, sacred mystery teachings that were handed down to initiates throughout history.

The idea that there is *a* mystery teaching may seem to some to have a ring of exclusivity out of step with their enlightened notions of freedom of choice. Yet behind the world of effects is an inner world of cause whose light has illumined men and women throughout the ages, shining in virtually all beneficial social, scientific, and spiritual movements. Indeed, most religions have an inner teaching that is so similar and so ancient that Aldous Huxley called it "the perennial philosophy."

Secret societies were sponsored by a Brotherhood of highly evolved spiritual beings—known as the Great White Brotherhood—who magnetized the sacred fire to their heart's altar. The white light emanating from their auras gives them the appearance of being white-robed, and they are referred to by John the Revelator as the saints robed in white.

This Brotherhood of adepts has always sought to elevate and enlighten the children of God. Working from beyond the veil (or secretly, right in the very midst of the people), they have sponsored the great movements for religious liberty, scientific advancement, and political freedom.

The tradition of the secret societies is ancient. They existed at various times in Chaldea, Egypt, Greece, Italy, among the Hebrews, Christians, Muhammadans, and others. Virtually all the great teachers of mankind—Homer, Moses, Pythagoras, Gautama, Jesus, Paul, and others of like stature—were initiates of the sacred mysteries.

It was Columbus' sponsorship by this mystical Brotherhood that made his voyage to the New World something quite out of the ordinary. America had been "discovered" again and again by Basques, Phoenicians, Druids, Libyans, Egyptians, Chinese, Arabians, Norsemen, and Danes for nearly 2,500 years before Columbus. But Columbus bore in his heart an idea—even the archetypal image of a new race destined to be born out of the old. It was an idea whose time had come. The mantle of destiny descended on Columbus. And the next scene in the great epic of the Israelites was about to begin.

As a result of the Brotherhood's sponsorship, the "Christ-bearer colonizer" captured the Old World's imagination and began the enormous colonization movement.

A new nation
was thus conceived
and dedicated to what
Roger Williams, founder of
Rhode Island, called "soul liberty."

But there was much to be done. For
there was no Declaration of Independence
and no Constitution. And few understood the
karma of an ancient people who had lived even
before the Great Flood on a lost continent called
Atlantis—much less why or how that past civilization would affect the New World.

According to Plato, Atlantis was a land of
gleaming white cities and golden temples that
sank beneath the sea as a result of violent earthquakes. Sixty million were reported to have
perished in a single night. Plato received his
knowledge of Atlantis from reports brought back
from the mystery schools of Egypt by one Solon,
an Athenian lawgiver.

Early Atlantis was the scene of golden-age
civilizations whose inhabitants lived together in

great spiritual harmony.

Later, discord, warfare, and the misuse of advanced technologies created the karmic conditions which caused the continent to sink.

Although Atlantis is a legend to many, legends have a way of moving from the realm of myth into reality with a few timely discoveries. In 1933, Edgar Cayce predicted that "a portion of the temple [of Atlantis] may be discovered . . . off the coast of Florida." Two pilots intrigued by this prediction kept watch as they flew over the area.

In 1968, they discovered submerged ruins off Andros island near Pine Key.

The timing of their discovery is linked, at least by coincidence, to another Cayce prediction. In 1940, he said that the western part of Atlantis "will be among the first portions of Atlantis to rise again. *Expect it in '68 or '69.*" Since then, the submerged ruins of step-pyramids, raised stone platforms, and great construction projects have been discovered on the ocean floor throughout the Caribbean and western Atlantic.

Although Atlantis may rise again physically, in one respect it had *already* returned through the reincarnation of its people.

Reincarnation is widely accepted as a fact of life in the East. While still not universally embraced in the West, it is gaining wider acceptance even in the scientific community—more often through individual experiences and recall of former lives.

General George Patton, the spectacularly successful World War II strategist, believed in reincarnation. Benjamin Franklin predicted his return "in a new and more elegant edition, revised and corrected by the Author."

An individual may reincarnate many times seeking to perfect the soul and balance karma. Likewise, entire civilizations reincarnate together to balance karma and work out their group destiny.

Among those who had kept a standard of integrity on Atlantis during its period of iniquity were children of God who reincarnated as the early Israelites. Since then, the seed of Abraham has reincarnated again and again in all nationalities, races, and religions. Thus Israelites are distinguished solely by their devotion to the person and the principle of the one God. Indeed they are the issue of the Christic seed imparted to Abraham—yet, through reincarnation, they have been scattered across all boundaries of race and religion.

The eastern seaboard of North America, a portion of the New World where the Israelites were destined to reincarnate, was a part of Atlantis that did not sink. But even years after Columbus' voyage, the New World was far from habitable.

One initiate of the Brotherhood worked tirelessly to reestablish the golden-age civilization of Atlantis and to provide the proper environment for the Israelites to fulfill their fiery destiny—the incomparable Francis Bacon.

Where has there arisen a genius of equal stature? Lord Chancellor of England, philosopher, author, statesman, scientist, orator, and humorist, Bacon was one of the prophets of the scientific revolution. He instigated the formation and influenced the course of the Royal Society and was a driving force in the Elizabethan Renaissance. Editor of the King James Version of the Bible and the first English essayist, Bacon is thought by many to be the true but concealed author of the works of Shakespeare and other Elizabethan literature.

Francis Bacon secretly founded the first Lodge of the Free and Accepted or Speculative Masons.

Freemasons laid the foundation for national unity in America and helped direct the course of the revolution. George Washington, Benjamin Franklin, Paul Revere, Alexander Hamilton and nearly all the signers of the Declaration of Independence and the Constitution were Masons. George Washington (right), wore Masonic collar, sash and apron while laying the cornerstone of the Capitol. The apron (below) was a gift to Washington from a fellow Mason, the Marquis de Lafayette.

In his most celebrated work, *Novum Organum*, Bacon presented a method of inductive logic. In *Instauratio Magna*, Bacon offered a plan for the "total Reconstruction of Sciences, Arts, and all Human Knowledge" to restore man to mastery over nature. According to Alfred Dodd and other authorities, in 1580, at the age of twenty, Bacon secretly founded the first Rosicrucian Brotherhood, the Rosicrosse Literary Society, and the first Lodge of the Free and Accepted or Speculative Masons.

But what Bacon did for England is dwarfed by the unseen work he performed on behalf of his great dream, the establishment of a New Atlantis. In addition to everything else, Bacon secretly laid the groundwork for the establishment of the United States of America.

Bacon entitled an allegorical literary work about a utopian commonwealth the *New Atlantis*. Perhaps it was inspired by his recollection of the Atlantean golden ages. Thought to be an allegorical reference to America, the book is said to contain the keys to the rituals of Freemasonry.

Bacon, the Master Mason, built for the future. In building for the future, one must instill in others the vital essence of one's own purpose. Bacon's dreams were realizable because the early Masons embraced his purpose.

Although few Masons today understand the inner meaning of their own traditions, W. L. Wilmshurst, author of *The Meaning of Masonry*, points out that Masonry offers "a philosophy of the spiritual life of man and a diagram of the process of regeneration."

This philosophy is symbolically embodied in its three degrees, or steps of initiation. According to Wilmshurst, "From grade to grade the candidate is being led from an old to an entirely new quality of life. He begins his Masonic career as the natural man; he ends it by becoming through its discipline, a regenerated, perfected man.... He rises from the dead a Master, a just man made perfect, with larger consciousness and faculties, an efficient instrument for use by the Great Architect in His plan of rebuilding the Temple of fallen humanity, and capable of initiating and advancing other men to a participation in the same great work.

"... The real purpose of modern Masonry is, not the social and charitable purposes to which so much attention is paid, but the expediting of the spiritual evolution of those who aspire to perfect their own nature and transform it into a more god-like quality."

The challenge of Masonry is to be reborn "incorruptible" which must be preceded by the death of the lower nature. The Masonic third degree is the allegorical crucifixion, death, and resurrection of Hiram Abiff, the teacher, or guru, who is analogous to Christ. Thus the intention of Masonry is not the building of a temple, but the greater science of soul building. On a macrocosmic scale, as applied to America, this meant the resurrection of the golden-age civilization of Atlantis by the resurrection of the divine identity of her citizens in the New Atlantis.

Bacon was an unheralded partner in the Virginia Company that established a settlement in Virginia. He was a confidant of the English explorer, soldier, courtier, writer, and colonizer Sir Walter Raleigh and received correspondence from John Smith, who became president of the Jamestown Colony after being saved from death at the hand of Powhatan by the chief's daughter, Pocahontas.

Because Bacon worked behind the scenes, there are only a few identifiable traces of his work in the New World. In 1910, he was honored by Newfoundland on their tricentennial commemorative stamp as "THE GUIDING SPIRIT IN COLONIZATION SCHEMES."

With the flowering of Masonry in America, the prophecy of the restoration was nearly fulfilled, but not quite. America was still a British possession.

In the mid-1700s, the spirit of the Revolution swept the American colonies. It grew out of the reaction to British tyranny and the Great Awakening, a religious revival that gave rise to the belief that God had founded a New Israel in America. The Great Awakening gave impetus to the millenarian movement which took things one step farther—a belief that God would establish in

The Great Seal

The Great Seal of the United States is an emblematic representation of the mission and identity of the American people portrayed by the great eagle, the pyramid, the mottoes, and the numerological symbols.

The eagle is the ancient symbol of spiritual vision without which the people perish. The olive branch in the right talon indicates the rule of the Prince of Peace by the authority of Jehovah. Jehovah, the Hebrew name of God, is taken from the verb "to be," more literally "that which was, is, and will be." Thus, Jehovah signifies that which transcends time and space—I AM THAT I AM, as the LORD revealed himself to Moses.

The gift of that name—the Lost Word of Masonry—was the dispensation for the twelve tribes, who were destined to establish peace in America through their realization of the inner Christ consciousness, or the Masonic Hiram Abiff as the archetype of each one's Real Self—the mediator between the soul and the universal Spirit.

The number thirteen is used so frequently in the Great Seal that even those who love "coincidences" would be compelled to admit that its designer had a purpose in mind.

The Spirit of '76 is composed of digits which add up to thirteen. The eagle holds thirteen arrows in the left talon. There are thirteen pieces for the escutcheon, or coat of arms. The mottoes, *annuit coeptis*—"He has smiled on our undertakings"—and *e pluribus unum*—"one out of many"—both have thirteen letters. There are thirteen rows of masonry on the pyramid.

The frequent repetition of thirteen reflects the determination of the founding fathers to remind us that we are the twelve tribes and the thirteenth—the Levites—of Israel.

The incomplete pyramid is symbolic of the great work of perfecting the soul unto the image of the living Christ and the nation into a golden age.

America a millennial kingdom as promised in Revelation 20; Christ would then reign a thousand years.

The religious millenarian language adapted the framework of apocalyptic history to commonly held political ideas. American liberty was God's cause; British tyranny was Antichrist's. Sin was failure to fight the British.

It takes more than a fiery sentiment to make a revolution—it takes organization. The Masons and only the Masons were sufficiently organized. It is doubtful that the American Revolution could have ever happened without them.

According to historian Bernard Faÿ, "Masonry alone undertook to lay the foundation for national unity in America." It fostered a feeling of American unity in a small but prominent class of people. There could have been no United States without it because the states were too deeply divided among themselves. By 1760, there was hardly a town, big or small, where Masonry was not preaching fraternity and unity.

By 1773, Boston was the center of American discontent. Feelings ran high. When colonial tempers rose, there was a revolutionary movement ready to direct the spirit of resistance—the Masons.

What made tempers rise? The tax on tea. Who hosted the first act of revolution in America? The Masons. And the affair? The Boston Tea Party!

On December 16, 1773, Masons from the St. Andrew Lodge in Boston and some local radicals dressed as Indians, sailed to the British ships, and dumped the tea. The victorious "Indians" sailed to shore, and with songs and hurrahs, marched to a local tavern, disappeared inside, and were never seen again. Later, however, a lot of excited Masons were seen leaving the place!

America owes an unending debt of gratitude to George Washington for the success of the Revolution and the establishment of the Republic. The fact that the colonies fielded an army at all from 1776–83 was due alone to Washington.

Always with his soldiers, he was the general in the field. His example buoyed up their morale. He wrestled with Congress to procure food and ammunition, and when Congress became entirely helpless, he kept his men alive out of his own pocketbook.

The clergy proclaimed that he was an instrument of God—"one of thine own sons"—who saved this country. They called him the "great preserver," "so great a deliverer," and compared him to Moses, Joshua, and Gideon. When even Benjamin Franklin could not persuade the French king to give the American revolutionaries further material assistance, Washington prevailed by sending his own aide-de-camp to Versailles—and by prayer.

Like no other, Washington put his life, fortune, and sacred honor on the line for the cause. Washington was a Master Mason—in fact, he was the Master of masters.

Masons seemed to be the moving force at every key step in the building of a new nation. Paul Revere was a Mason. Estimates vary, but as many as fifty-three of the fifty-six signers of the Declaration of Independence were Masons. All but five of the fifty-five members of the Constitutional Convention were Masons.

All the leading generals in the Continental Army were Masons. The leading lights of the Revolution were Masons—among them Alexander Hamilton, John Marshall, James Madison, Gen. Nathanael Greene, Gen. Charles Lee, and Gen. John Sullivan. They united around their rising sun, George Washington.

George Washington's role in creating the new government was at least as important as his military role. Serving as president of the Constitutional Convention, he was the sun in the midst of the solar system that held the states together. It is doubtful that the states would have so patiently forged a union had he not been there.

Not only was he universally recognized as the only acceptable candidate for the first president, but he was the office incarnate. No one at the Constitutional Convention had *any* idea what the president would be like except that he would be like Washington. They created the office and established its requirements by their perception of his virtues.

The great efforts of Bacon and Washington came to fruition with the adoption of the

Constitution, a document that embodied the principles of the Brotherhood. It provided that each individual would prosper based on his own efforts—the civil application of the initiatic path of the Masons. And it protected by law freedoms such as no land had ever enjoyed—speech, religion, press, and assembly. Each person might then be free to work out his individual destiny as he saw fit.

Thus, with the great gathering of the elect in the promised land, there was reestablished the community of those who were free not only to keep the LORD's covenants but to elect to do so by the gift of free will. It was a community based on true individuality.

Individuality proceeds from the Hiram Abiff of the Masonic tradition, the inner Christ, the Immanuel of Isaiah of whom it is prophesied, "The government shall be upon his shoulder." This idea was embodied in American notions of individual sovereignty.

And God has smiled on our undertakings—*annuit coeptis.* Thus reads the motto on the Great Seal of the United States—once disparagingly

Commemoration of Washington, *depicts two angels, Time and Immortality, lifting Washington into heaven. This and other works executed both before and after his passing show that many Americans believed in a heavenly hierarchy and revered Washington as the patriarch of our nation.*

COMMEMORATION OF WASHINGTON.

called "a dull emblem of a Masonic Fraternity."
Masonic, yes. But it is anything but dull. The
seal's symbolism proclaims the true identity of
the American Israelites in the tradition of the
ancient mysteries. (See p. 127.)

The motto *novus ordo seclorum* represents
the great work that the Masons had made their
own—the establishment of the *new order of the
ages!*

A considerable number of early Americans
apparently accepted the presence and divine intervention of heavenly intercessors as a natural
part of life. The art and literature of the period
frequently depicted angelic beings, gods and god-
desses, and clouds of glory.

The Goddess of Liberty, patroness of their
"sacred cause," was perhaps the most revered of
all the heavenly hosts. In 1775, Thomas Paine
honored her in a ballad called "Liberty Tree."

*In a chariot of light, from the regions
    of day,
The Goddess of Liberty came,
Ten thousand celestials directed her way,
And hither conducted the dame.
A fair budding branch from the
    gardens above,
Where millions with millions agree,
She brought in her hand as a pledge
    of her love,
And the plant she named Liberty Tree.*

It was the Goddess of Liberty who appeared to George Washington and gave him a vision of three trials that America would face: the first trial was the Revolutionary War; the second, the Civil War; and the third is held at bay by the Invisible Hand while We the People yet resolve by law and by love the fate of our destiny. (See p. 142.)

This period of crisis was foreseen not only by George Washington, but also by the prophet Daniel who wrote, "And there shall be a time of trouble, such as never was since there was a nation even to that same time." Historian Arnold Toynbee used the phrase "time of troubles" to describe the chaos that accompanies the disintegration of civilizations. From a historian's point of view, many agree that we are now living in that "time of troubles."

Despite our nation's new buoyant mood, feelings alone won't see us through this crisis. We are vulnerable to any number of potential disasters—economic collapse, nuclear war, crime, pollution, toxic wastes, and dangerous new technologies, not to mention the genetic engineering of the coming race.

It will take more than enlightened leadership to meet this challenge. No mere mortal can solve our problems. Whenever the Israelites charted a course independent of God, the results were calamitous. If the ancient Israelites could not solve their problems without God, should we be so foolish as to try?

Toynbee said that a civilization in the time of troubles would collapse if its people did not go through the process of spiritualization from within or, as he called it, "etherialization." He was looking toward a veritable *revolution in higher consciousness.* That is the key to salvation and the moral regeneration for which America was established.

Now that we know who we are and the nature of our legacy, what should we do to survive the chaos theorized by Toynbee, foreseen by Washington, prophesied by Daniel, and predicted by our Lord as the Great Tribulation?

We the People ought to be comforted and strengthened by the message of history—that God and his heavenly hierarchy, the Great White Brotherhood, conceived, bore, watches over, and is involved in the affairs of our nation. We ought to get personally involved in finding solutions to our problems. But, most of all, American Israelites should do what their fathers did—Call upon the LORD! After all, would the God of history, the God of Israel, lead his people so many millennia and then abandon them at the last moment? Not if he remains true to himself and to us. And the I AM THAT I AM of the exodus is The Faithful and True, the same, The WORD of Revelation.

As all the adepts in the tradition of Christ have taught, prayer is a spiritual technique which combines the esoteric sciences of sound and invocation to create thoughtforms on the inner planes. These have the power to change the course of events in the world of form because their fulcrum is the Word itself.

In these final days, we are reminded by the holy angels to address our calls not only to Archangel Michael, whom the LORD named to Daniel as "the Great Prince which standeth for the children of thy people," but also to the great adept of the Brotherhood who is the sponsor of the United States of America and presiding Master of the Aquarian Age—Saint Germain.

It is an irony of history that the name Saint Germain isn't on every schoolchild's tongue and that every American president has not earnestly sought his counsel. For it was Saint Germain who embodied as the "Christ-bearer colonizer," Christopher Columbus, and as the founder of Freemasonry, Francis Bacon. And who but Saint Germain held the vision of a New Atlantis based on the principles of spiritual freedom and civil liberty for millennia?

Indeed, Saint Germain worked tirelessly for the reassembly of the tribes of Israel and Judah in the New World, and labored to infuse the land of his dreams with the one virtue for which he gave his life again and again—*Freedom!*

Saint Germain invites us to rise to higher levels of consciousness, to find immortality in

God—to be free. And if that isn't what the mystical tradition of America is all about, what is?

So, every Fourth of July remember that behind the effect of the joy felt by millions from those brass bands, the fireworks, the watermelons, the All-Star Game, and the carefree atmosphere of summer, there is a cause: the cause of freedom, the cause of Saint Germain, and the cause of the saints who move among us robed in white.

And when you hear those old patriotic songs, listen to the lyrics. They express a true love and recognition for the Great White Brotherhood and Saint Germain, the Master Alchemist who translated Our Father's gift of free will into the greatest system of political, economic, and spiritual freedom the world has ever seen.

> *Our Father's God! to thee,*
> *Author of Liberty!*
> *To thee we sing;*
> *Long may our land be bright,*
> *With Freedom's holy light,*
> *Protect us by thy might,*
> *Great God, our King.*

OVERLEAF: *This nineteenth-century work, entitled "Family Monument," is a memorial to America. In the lower right-hand corner, we see the symbolic depiction of the discovery of "Vinland" (so-named because of the abundant grapevines) by the Norse mariner Leif Ericson in the year 1000. His Vinland has been variously identified as the coast of Labrador or Newfoundland, but also of New England, which is suggested here. Moving left in the picture, we see the historic discovery of America by Christopher Columbus in 1492, and the first permanent settlement in Jamestown, Virginia, in 1607 (center). To the right are scenes from the Revolutionary period, culminating in the center, where America (the eagle) is victorious over Britain (the lion and unicorn). Ascending the pyramid, we see the first president, George Washington, with the Constitution, flanked by the celestial beings Liberty and Justice. The feminine figure seated before him displays the Declaration of Independence, and behind him stand the succeeding fourteen presidents, backed by the U.S. Capitol. Beyond, to the left, lies Saint Germain's vision for the future—America as the land of promise, the "new Atlantis," where golden-age culture and science will rise again.*

Washington's Vision of America's Trials

Originally published by Wesley Bradshaw
Copied from a reprint in the National Tribune
Vol. 4, No. 12, December 1880

The last time I ever saw Anthony Sherman was on the fourth of July, 1859, in Independence Square. He was then ninety-nine years old, and becoming very feeble. But though so old, his dimming eyes rekindled as he gazed upon Independence Hall, which he came to visit once more.

"Let us go into the hall," he said. "I want to tell you of an incident of Washington's life—one which no one alive knows of except myself; and, if you live you will before long, see it verified.

"From the opening of the Revolution we experienced all phases of fortune, now

The stained glass window in the Prayer Room of the U.S. Capitol shows the Great Seal and Washington with verse from Psalms 16:1, "Preserve me, O God, for in Thee do I put my trust."

THIS NATION UNDER GOD

GOD FOR IN THEE DO I PLACE TRUST

good and now ill, one time victorious and another conquered. The darkest period we had, I think, was when Washington after several reverses, retreated to Valley Forge, where he resolved to pass the winter of 1777.

"Ah! I have often seen the tears coursing down our dear commander's care-worn cheeks, as he would be conversing with a confidential officer about the condition of his poor soldiers. You have doubtless heard the story of Washington's going into the thicket to pray. Well, it was not only true, but he used often to pray in secret for aid and comfort from God, the interposition of whose Divine Providence brought us safely through the darkest days of tribulation.

"One day, I remember it well, the chilly winds whistled through the leafless trees, though the sky was cloudless and the sun shone brightly, he remained in his quarters nearly all the afternoon alone. When he came out I noticed that his face was a shade paler than usual, and there seemed to be something on his mind of more than ordinary importance.

"Returning just after dusk, he dispatched an orderly to the quarters of the officer I mention who was presently in attendance. After a preliminary conversation of about half an hour, Washington, gazing upon his companion with that strange look of dignity which he alone could command, said to the latter:

"'I do not know whether it is owing to the anxiety of my mind, or what, but this afternoon as I was sitting at this table engaged in preparing a dispatch, something seemed to disturb me. Looking up, I beheld standing opposite me a singularly beautiful female. So astonished was I, for I had given strict orders not to be disturbed that it was some moments before I found language to inquire into the cause of her presence.

"'A second, a third, and even a fourth time did I repeat my question, but received no answer from my mysterious visitor except a slight raising of her eyes. By this time I felt strange sensations spreading through me. I would have risen but the riveted gaze of the being before me rendered volition impossible. I assayed once more to address her, but my tongue had become useless. Even thought itself had become paralyzed. A new influence, mysterious, potent, irresistible, took possession of me. All I could do was to gaze steadily, vacantly at my unknown visitant.

"'Gradually the surrounding atmosphere seemed as though becoming filled with sensations, and luminous. Everything about me seemed to rarify—the mysterious visitor herself becoming more airy and yet more distinct to my sight than before. I now began to feel as one dying, or rather to experience the sensations which I have sometimes imagined accompany dissolution. I did not think, I did not reason, I did not move; all were alike impossible. I was only conscious of gazing fixedly, vacantly at my companion.

"'Presently I heard a voice saying, "Son of the Republic, look and learn," while at the same time my visitor extended her arm eastwardly. I now beheld a heavy white vapor at some distance rising fold upon fold. This gradually dissipated, and I looked upon a strange scene. Before me lay spread out in one vast plain all the countries of the world—Europe, Asia, Africa and America. I saw rolling and tossing between Europe and America the billows of the Atlantic, and between Asia and America lay the Pacific.

"'"Son of the Republic," said the same mysterious voice as before, "look and learn." At that moment I beheld a dark, shadowy being, like an angel, standing, or rather floating in mid-air, between Europe and America. Dipping water out of the ocean in the hollow of each hand, he sprinkled some upon America with his right hand, while with his left hand he cast some on Europe.

"'Immediately a cloud raised from these countries, and joined in mid-ocean. For a while it remained stationary, and then moved slowly westward, until it enveloped

America in its murky folds. Sharp flashes of lightning gleamed through it at intervals, and I heard the smothered groans and cries of the American people. A second time the angel dipped water from the ocean, and sprinkled it out as before. The dark cloud was then drawn back to the ocean, in whose heaving billows it sank from view.

"'A third time I heard the mysterious voice saying, "Son of the Republic, look and learn," I cast my eyes upon America and beheld villages and towns and cities springing up one after another until the whole land from the Atlantic to the Pacific was dotted with them. Again, I heard the mysterious voice say, "Son of the Republic, the end of the century cometh, look and learn."

"'At this the dark shadowy angel turned his face southward, and from Africa I saw an ill-omened spectre approach our land. It flitted slowly over every town and city of the latter. The inhabitants presently set themselves in battle array against each other.

"'As I continued looking I saw a bright angel, on whose brow rested a crown of light, on which was traced the word "Union," bearing the American flag which he placed between the divided nation, and said, *Remember ye are brethren.*"

"'Instantly, the inhabitants, casting from them their weapons became friends once more, and united around the National Standard.

"'And again I heard the mysterious voice saying, "Son of the Republic, look and learn." At this the dark, shadowy angel placed a trumpet to his mouth, and blew three distinct blasts; and taking water from the ocean, he sprinkled it upon Europe, Asia and Africa.

"'Then my eyes beheld a fearful scene: from each of these countries arose thick, black clouds that were soon joined into one. And throughout this mass there gleamed a dark red light by which I saw hordes of armed men, who, moving with the cloud, marched by land and sailed by sea to America, which country was enveloped in the volume of cloud.

"'And I dimly saw these vast armies devastate the whole country and burn the villages, towns and cities that I beheld springing up. As my ears listened to the thundering of the cannon, clashing of swords, and the shouts and cries of millions in mortal combat, I heard again the mysterious voice saying, "Son of the Republic, look and learn." When the voice had ceased, the dark shadowy angel placed his trumpet once more to his mouth, and blew a long and fearful blast.

"'Instantly a light as of a thousand suns shone down from above me, and pierced and broke into fragments the dark cloud which enveloped America. At the same moment the angel upon whose head still shone the word Union, and who bore our national flag in one hand and a sword in the other, descended from the heavens attended by legions of white spirits. These joined the inhabitants of America, who I perceived were well-nigh overcome, but who immediately taking courage again, closed up their broken ranks and renewed the battle.

"'Again, amid the fearful noise of the conflict, I heard the mysterious voice saying, "Son of the Republic, look and learn." As the voice ceased, the shadowy angel for the last time dipped water from the ocean and sprinkled it upon America. Instantly the dark cloud rolled back, together with the armies it had brought, leaving the inhabitants of the land victorious.

"'Then once more I beheld the villages, towns and cities springing up where I had seen them before, while the bright angel, planting the azure standard he had brought in the midst of them, cried with a loud voice: *"While the stars remain, and the heavens send down dew upon the earth, so long shall the Union last."* And taking from his brow the crown on which blazoned the word "Union," he placed it upon the Standard while the people, kneeling down, said, "Amen."

"'The scene instantly began to fade and dissolve, and I at last saw nothing but the rising, curling vapor I at first beheld. This also disappearing, I found myself once more gazing upon the mysterious visitor, who, in the same voice I had heard before, said, "Son of the Republic, what you have seen is thus interpreted:

"'"Three great perils will come upon the Republic. The most fearful is the third (The comment on his word 'third' is: "The help against the THIRD peril comes in the shape of Divine Assistance. Apparently the Second Advent) . . . . passing which the whole world united shall not prevail against her. *Let every child of the Republic learn to live for his God, his land and Union.*"

"'With these words the vision vanished, and I started from my seat and felt that I had seen a vision wherein had been shown to me the birth, progress, and destiny of the United States.'

"Such, my friends," concluded the venerable narrator, "were the words I heard from Washington's own lips, and America will do well to profit by them."

Those who understand the real purpose of prophecy realize that events of the future are foreseen not because they are predestined, but because they offer enlightened men and women the opportunity to unite and determine that the impending peril which could come to pass does not because we take action and because we pray. It is up to our generation to decide whether or not the third vision will occur—and the key to our victory is in our love, our unity, and our wise and judicious use of our spiritual and material resources. But to call upon the intercession of the LORD and his hosts is to insure the continuing blessing of the Invisible Hand— all too visible in time of trouble.

Book Two

Intermediate
Studies in
Alchemy

Alchemical Formulas for
Self-Mastery

Saint Germain

Wherein lies happiness? In that which becks
Our ready minds to fellowship divine,
A fellowship with essence; till we shine,
Full alchemiz'd, and free of space. Behold
The clear religion of heaven!

KEATS, *Endymion*

CHAPTER I

"Create!"

When the Great Alchemist's Spirit breathed into man's nostrils the breath of life, the fire of creative Spirit filled the clay tabernacle. An embryonic god was born.

The practical aspects of alchemy are to be found in manifestation only in the one who has developed the power to execute the design of freedom. Whatsoever bindeth is not the friend of the alchemist; yet it is the goal of the alchemist to bind the soul to its immortal tryst in order that the pact of life might be sanctified even as the precious gift of individual identity is accepted.

Now, the identity of the alchemist is to be found in the mandate "Create!" And in order that he might obey, the fiery energies of creation are dispensed to him each moment. Like crystal beads descending upon a crystal thread, the energies of the creative essence of life descend into the chalice of consciousness. Neither halting nor delaying in their appointed course, they continue to fall into the repository of man's being. Here they create a buildup for good or for ill as each iota of universal energy passes through the recording nexus and is imprinted with the fiat of creation.

The fiat reflects the intent of the will of the individual monad. When the fiat is withheld, there is an idling of the great cosmic furnace as the talent of the descending chaliced moment is rejected by the consciousness and becomes an opportunity lost. Where there is no qualification, no fiat of intent, the energy retains only the God-identification of the talent without the stamp of individualization; and thus it falls into the coffers of the lifestream's record without having received so much as an erg of qualification.

The creative process, then, is of little significance to the individual who does not recognize the mandate to create, for by his nonrecognition he forfeits his God-given prerogative. As a result of man's neglect of his responsibility, the fiat of God was given that is recorded in the Book of Revelation: "Thou art neither cold nor hot: I would thou wert cold or hot. So then because thou art lukewarm, and neither cold nor hot, I will spue thee out of my mouth."[1]

The fiat to create must be heeded, but let us pray God that men heed well the sovereign responsibility that Life has given them to create after the pattern of the divine seed. Well might they emulate the elder gods of the race and the royal priesthood of the order of Melchizedek in their creative endeavors, that they might convey upon the energy chain of life that peculiar and fascinating aspect of cosmic genius that is the nature of the eternal God.

So long as individuals allow themselves to be kept in a state of constant fear, so long as they deny themselves the great benefits of universal hope, so long as they fail to take into account the meaning of the promise "His mercy endureth for ever,"[2] so long shall they continue in ignorance to deny themselves the bliss that exudes from the rightful exercise of spiritual privilege.

To belittle the soul of man, to cast it down into a sense of sin, frustration, and self-condemnation is the work of the princes of darkness. But it is ever the forte of the sons of heaven, of the Ascended Masters, and of the cosmic beings to elevate that supreme nobility which is both the fabric and the content of the soul into such prominence in the life of man that he might hear the dominant word of the eternal God in ringing tones, "Thou art my Son; this day have I begotten thee."[3]

Man must enter into a pact of universal trust based on his own inner commitment to the grace of God that will not prohibit him from exercising the power of the living Word to emulate the Masters, to emulate the Only Begotten of the Father, to emulate the Spirit of comfort and truth. And when he does, he will find opening to his consciousness a new method of cleansing his soul by the power of the LORD's Spirit. Then he will come to understand the meaning of the statement made concerning Abraham of old that Abraham's faith "was imputed unto him for righteousness: and he was called the Friend of God."[4]

And so it is "not by might, nor by power, but by my Spirit, saith the LORD of hosts,"[5] that man accomplishes the alchemical feat of transmuting the base metals of human consciousness into the gold of Christed illumination. Human might and human power can never change man's darkness into light, nor can they deliver humanity from the sense of struggle that bans from their lives the acknowledgment of the God-given potential that lies within the domain of the self.

The victorious accomplishments of the Master Jesus, together with the "greater works" which he promised that the disciples of Christ would do "because I go unto my Father,"[6] remain in this age, as in ages past, a fiat of universal freedom. Thus the works of the alchemists of the Spirit beckon the souls of men to forsake their attitudes of self-condemnation, self-pity, self-denegation, self-indulgence, and overreaction to the errors of the past. For when men learn to forgive and forget their own mistakes, their hearts will rejoice in the acceptance of the word from on high "What God hath cleansed, that call not thou common."[7]

Recognizing, then, that the potential of every man rests in his immersion in the great soundless-sound stream of living light-energy from the heart of the Universal Christ, we say: Let the power of the Holy Spirit, worlds without end, exert its mighty cosmic pressures upon the soul of the would-be alchemist until he emerges from the fiery furnace pliable, whited, and pure in the willingness to obey the fiat of the LORD to create first a clean heart and then to renew in self a right spirit.

God is a Spirit; and as the Supreme Alchemist who has the power to work change in the universe, he is able to convey his passion for freedom to the soul of any man who will accept it. His is the passion which produces in man the miracle of unfoldment through a sense of the real. His is the passion that will drive from the temple those money changers and bargainers who would literally sell the souls of men in the marketplaces of the world.

We are concerned with creating in the student of alchemy a conscious awareness of the power of the Spirit to convey the transmutative effect of the Universal Alchemist into the lives and beings of embodied humanity. It is through this awareness that they shall be exalted in a manner which they have never before experienced, for at last they shall have recognized that within themselves the cosmic key-seed of universal potential lies literally entombed.

To resurrect, then, the Spirit of the Cosmic Alchemist means that we must seek before we shall find, that we must knock before the door shall be opened. We must, in the ritual of true faith, be content to commit ourselves to him who is able to keep and to save to the uttermost those who believe in his manifold purposes. These are centralized in the one purpose of unfolding the consciousness of the stone which the builders have rejected, of the Christ that is the head of every man. [8]

In the concept of the abundant life is to be found the radioactive principle of the expanding God consciousness into which any man may drink without depriving his brother of one iota of his inheritance. There is no need, then, for jealousy or a sense of struggle to function in the lives of the true alchemists; and wise are they who will submit themselves to the pressures of the divine law, who will seek to purge themselves of all unclean habits stemming from mortal density and of doubt and fear, which are the root cause of man's nonfulfillment of his destiny.

Those who dare to submit to the will of God will come to the place where their souls can at last welcome, face to face, the overcoming Spirit that makes possible the transfer of the consciousness of the Great Alchemist to the consciousness of the lesser alchemist. Through this transfer, hope is amplified in the microcosm of self and the miracle of emerging chrysalis is beheld. Then the soul, feeding upon the living Word which throbs within, finally understands its raison d'être in the fiat of the light "Create!"

It is incumbent upon each life, then, to create according to the patterns made in the heavens. [9]

He who can produce the miracle of these patterns in his life is also able to have all things added unto him; for by his seeking first the kingdom of heaven, the earth herself yields to his dominion.[10]

In this series on intermediate alchemy, I am, in the name of Almighty God, creating in the consciousness of the disciples who apply themselves to this study a spirit of inner communion. Through this spirit—a focus of my own flame—the Most High God and the hierarchy of Light shall focus, by the power of universal Love, a climate within the consciousness of the student that shall enable him to obtain his rightful place in the divine scheme. Then the kingdom will flower and men will perceive that they need not engage in struggle or seek by violent means to obtain that which God is ever ready to give unto them.

The lingering fear in the worlds of men is of the dark, whereas faith, hope, and charity are the great triune bearers of light who exalt Reality and lead men toward the light.

Ready for action,

I remain the Knight Commander,

Saint Germain

✠

CHAPTER 2

Practical Alchemy

The history of man's devotion to the cause of freedom may never be written either for the planet or for the individual. Therefore, man will never know by outward study the true story of freedom. Nevertheless, through the outreach of the Spirit of God in man and its wondrous attunement with the central clearinghouse for every part of life, he may enter into the akashic records of those solemn moments in the lives of other men and thereby perceive how they obtained their victory.

Even as the alchemist builds on the discoveries of his predecessors, so there is an inner teacher within every heart who tutors the outer self, subduing it when necessary and guiding the fires of the mind in their search for the oftentimes invisible strands of reality.

When the subject of creation is given more than ordinary consideration, man begins to realize that his own destiny lies as a gift in his hands. He has always looked to God for assistance, and God has always looked to man that he might convey to him every good gift and all the support which man could reasonably receive and acknowledge. Unfortunately, even in those periods of their most advanced meditations, mankind have seldom glimpsed the necessary cosmic pattern of what they are and what they shall be.

The secrets of alchemy are always to be found in the domain of creation. If man has not the power to create, he is not truly free. Therefore, the stream of energy that God is giving to him in ceaseless descent must needs be channeled into matrices of creative desire patterned after the divine will; but when misqualified, these energies form the links of the chain that binds him.

Our first step, then, is to abort and to transmute the negatively qualified substance in the world of every would-be alchemist. The power of the violet transmuting flame, as an agent of the Holy Spirit, can be called forth from God for the purification of man's world.

It should be noted, however, that this power is seldom recognized until the alchemist has invoked the flame for a considerable period of time. But, practice as he will, his use of the flame will not be enough to transform his world unless the correct scientific attitude is maintained. The alchemist who insists on exalting his own human will and ego in contradistinction to the Divine Will and Ego cannot possibly receive the great gifts which the Spirit seeks to convey.

I know that many people are reluctant to

release themselves completely into the hands of God. They are willing to go part of the way, and they gingerly step forward when the higher will seems to flatter their own; but because they have not let go of the human will, they find in the end that their efforts are unrewarded.

Man cannot bargain with God. Nevertheless, Cosmos is far more ready to give every good and perfect gift to man than man is ready to receive it. The problem, then, lies not in the ocean that is filled with pearls, but in the diver himself, who must be willing to acknowledge the presence of the treasures of heaven in the cosmic depths— treasures that heaven intends man not only to discover but also to possess.

By incorrect attitudes, men have kept themselves from the kingdom of heaven. They have sought through magic and, unfortunately, even through witchcraft to win for themselves that which could be obtained on a permanent basis only by willing submission to the will of God, to his intents and his purposes.

How long will men deceive themselves? How long will they prevent themselves, by their fears, from surrendering to the living purposes of God? It is as though they would not relinquish their money to the merchants in the shops until they held in hand the intended purchase.

There is no bargaining with God or with Cosmos. Cosmos is ever willing to convey the highest and best gifts to man, but in order to receive them, man must change his attitude.

Those who are schooled in the knowledge of the world may believe in their hearts that they have found through academic pursuits the key to the governing of the senses and to gaining entrée into the realms of the Spirit. We say, not so! For neither by intellect nor by self-righteousness shall men obtain the highest gifts.

These gifts will come as the natural unfoldment of the soul who submits to the grace of God and understands that having done so, he can rightfully expect the divine revelation to manifest within himself. And when that revelation comes forth, it is received within the hallowed circle of righteousness and reason—a righteousness that does not do despite to his neighbor, that seeks no harm to any, and a reason that understands that the best gifts of the Spirit relate to the realm of the practical.

The practicality of God must not be employed as a weapon to destroy the mystical beauties of the Spirit. On the contrary, it must be used to draw the divine mystery to the focal point of individual manifestation. As the flesh came forth and was animated by the Spirit, so practicality must come forth and be animated by the creative purposes of God.

Then God will take man by the hand and lead him through the realm of perfect order to a place where man will perceive that the world and all things in it were originally created according to a perfect cosmic pattern. Here he will be shown that each individual was intended to manifest a specific facet of the divine intent and that each facet of the grand design was created to complement the other and to produce thereby the miracle beauty of an everlasting kingdom, worlds without end.

How can men imagine that the Mind that created man in all of his wondrous parts—the universe, the stars, the suns, the spiritual realms—would be so lacking in foresight as to fail to provide a way of escape for those who might wander from the cosmic blueprint? Did not his practicality bestow upon man the fullness of the divine conveyance expressed in the command "Take dominion over the earth"?[1] Man, then, was and is intended to be a practical manifestation of God, learning how to master his environment by cosmic wisdom united with his own natural intelligence.

We have seen, however, that man becomes discouraged when he realizes that although he has exercised his mental faculties to the point where his mind is literally crammed with an encyclopedic knowledge of the world, he is nevertheless mentally muscle-bound and powerless to take dominion over his personal affairs—much less the earth—because he is spiritually anemic.

Now, such discouragement is the result of the individual's failure to recognize the fact that he is actually a monadic part of God. He does not know—for he has not been told—that in his silent eternal union with the mind of God, he is tied to a giant computer. Through this computer all knowledge is immediately available by spiritual transmission to those who will use it to do the will of God.

But the bounds of man's habitation—including the bounds of his mental probings—which are prescribed by cosmic law, cause this wisdom to be withheld from that part of the universe which is not yet ready to assume its role in taking dominion over the earth and in making itself functional with the powers of the Universal Christ.

The key, then, to the practice of advanced spiritual alchemy lies in the alchemist's understanding of the purposes of the Brotherhood and in his consciously yoking himself together with those who are pledged by word and deed to the fulfillment of those purposes.

Little do men realize when they begin to pursue the study of alchemy how deeply involved it will become and how deeply they will become involved in it. For unless there is an immersion of the self in the sea of universal wisdom and purpose, the soul cannot be saturated, the sponge cannot be wetted, and the energy so needed for transmutation cannot be evoked.

If I seem to be releasing the secrets of the ages slowly into the minds of the hurried and harried students who would like to overcome all things in a moment, let me say that you today are receiving from the retreats of the Brotherhood more information than we ourselves received in the past when we were undertaking our own novitiate.

In your patience, then, possess ye your souls;[2] but be diligent in studying the various aspects of being which from time to time will be pointed out to you—sometimes from the most unexpected sources. Be ready to find in the smallest gift an intricate treasure that, like a piece in a great puzzle, may not at first seem relevant.

Again I say, be patient. For time, in marching on, reveals eternal patterns. Therefore, to decline the search or to reject the means of cosmic study which makes possible the search is an error of the first magnitude.

Let all who are receiving this form of instruction rejoice and be glad, seeing in the very opportunity for self-study the need to render the service to the brothers of acquainting others with the teaching. Thus, by making available the gift of life to receptive souls, Heaven shall respond and give a greater gift to the souls of you who have proven that you are willing to labor and to wait.

Perfection is forthcoming, and it is the perfection of a master mason—a builder who, in idealizing perfection in the universe, has no alternative but to idealize it in himself. This is the builder who sees the need to cleanse the very foundation of residue in his world, to submit to the washing of the water by the Word[3] and to the cleansing of the sacred fire. This is the builder who sees the need to know what the tools of the aspirant are and how these tools may be employed in the service of self, in the service of humanity, and thus ultimately in the service of his God.

Let us, then, reiterate for all
That life is not so simple as men have dreamed.
But it is a scheme so vast and tall
As to literally enfold us all—
Men and gods and Masters, too,
Parts of life you do not view
Right now, but one day will
If you will only learn to listen and be still,
Knowing I AM God within.

To his glory I live,

Saint Germain

✠

CHAPTER 3

Spiritual Alliance

Little does the beginning alchemist realize the need for a spiritual alliance. If men are critical of the appearance of oppositional aspects in religious endeavor such as struggles among the brethren, their ungodly attitudes, their criticism, condemnation, and judgment of one another, let them realize that that which is below is not the product of that which is Above, but remains a part of human creation which is no real part of God.

It is to genuine spiritual brotherhood, then, that we would direct your attention, for the alchemist who seeks but his own unfoldment can never manifest aught but a relatively weak potential. Those who ally themselves with the Brotherhood of Light are utilizing the functional power of the Great Alchemist not as a mighty ocean pouring through a narrow inlet, but as the great ocean roaring to the perfection of itself. Thus in all true striving, the hand, aware of the head, blesses the feet that march in progress toward an appointed goal.

Freedom, then, is a name and a game, but the stakes are very high. The Great Alchemist demands absolute obedience from every adherent and from all who would practice the game of victorious becoming.

Man is a limited creature. He is limited by the mésalliances he has formed, often in the bane of ignorance. Therefore, we must commence by literally turning the being of man upside down and inside out. We must ferret out the little tricks that have been employed by the finite self in maintaining its own sovereignty over the lives of others, for it is the sense of struggle that has actually created a struggle in the lives of countless millions.

But when they shed that sense, when they perceive that the universe is a harmonious working-together of light serving light, they will hasten to be about the Father's business of transmuting the shroud that covers the earth, the shroud that is composed of the elements of mankind's own insanity and destructive emotional patterns.

The sacred fire has been distorted through the misuse of sex, and sacred music has been aborted through the introduction of astral and voodoo rhythms. The new moralities of the people must be seen for what they are—simply the old and sordid outworkings of Sodom and Gomorrah come again. Children are taught to pay homage to personalities, and thus they follow after rock 'n' roll idols who themselves are the victims of the demons of darkness. The brutal noises of these pied pipers jar the fine sensibilities of the soul and destroy the inner electronic machinery that would enable the youth to attune with the Spirit of God and to decipher the tongues of angels.

The game now is to draw the youth into a spirit of rebellion before they have the opportunity of developing a correct understanding of life and of their destiny[1] as heirs of God. But I cannot honestly say that their elders have excelled in virtue, nor do I find that the power of example has been spread abroad in the world as it should.

The ancient proverb "Train up a child in the way he should go: and when he is old, he will not depart from it"[2] has failed of expression in many generations. Nevertheless, we must not destroy the foundation of hope in the world; for although there have been failures, there have also been numerous successes, many of them unchronicled in the annals of the race.

And so whereas we do indeed, and rightly so, condemn mankind's increasing lack of morality, their licentious spirit and struggle for ego-expression, and whereas we do condemn the violent and indiscriminate overthrow of institutions and standards long upheld by the Brotherhood as guidelines for the working out of karmic imbalances, we also accede that an enormous amount of God's energy has been misqualified in this and past ages. Therefore, the trends toward misqualification must be challenged at the same time that they are being reckoned with as karmic factors by those who are determined to override man's density and to bring into manifestation the long-awaited kingdom.

Have men failed in the past? Then the record of that failure is a magnet to draw them down, and strong counteracting forces must be kindled. The power of heaven must be reharnessed and men must turn from darkness toward the light.

There is, then, a purpose for spiritual alchemy. But before I go into it enough to enable you to draw forth greater measures of cosmic energy and to learn how to qualify this energy correctly, I must show the relevance of this study to the present age.

The destructive energies which poured through the Beatles and entered the subconscious minds of the youth, popular though they were in the world of form, are gradually working their way to the surface, revealing their true colors and Satanic origins. These unholy emanations have drawn many young souls into the mistaken belief that the taking of drugs, the practice of witchcraft, and illicit sex can give them freedom from all imposed limitations. Instead, these indulgences have held them in bondage to the legions of darkness.

Would it not be, then, of greater value and virtue if the resurgent power of regeneration were allowed to come forth through many hearts as a great cosmic flow? The forward movement of this flow is able to engender in men a spirit of willing acceptance of cosmic beauty, which in turn brings about the flowering of hope in the youth—hope for a greater measure of inward satisfaction, hope for a greater measure of attunement with the realities of the universe. For the tides of reality continually pour through the cosmos whether man is aware of them or not.

The certitudes of life are often unknown by the young in heart who, while they are borne upon the tide of human events, are seldom able to compass those events with a relevancy that would give greater meaning to their lives.

I am therefore advising all to eschew the evil and darkness that enter the forcefield of the four lower bodies when the attention is placed on the jangle of modern jazz. I advise all who would truly be alchemists of the Spirit to seek out the classical music of the world's greatest composers—of Beethoven, Bach, Chopin, Haydn, Handel, Wagner, Liszt, Mozart, Mendelssohn, Mahler, and many others who have been commissioned by the Brotherhood to bring forth the music of the spheres.

I advise all to learn to seek in meditation those peaks of cosmic elevation that will enable them to understand and interpret the language of the angels. I advise all to take the time to learn what is real and to develop passions of genuine love toward humanity. But let not these passions take the form of mere devotion to communal efforts or to the raising of one segment of life into a more advanced state of economic development; rather let them take the form of raising men to new levels of spiritual appreciation of their own divine potential as sons of God.

Only by this form of devotion shall their hearts, touched by the hands of the Infinite Creator, be imbued with such reality and love that they will move with precision to execute the divine will. Thus shall men behold the outworkings of a Providence that has for so long yearned to find greater expression in mortal affairs, that those affairs might become truly guided by the power of Life from on high.

Then shall liberty live in human lives. Then shall freedom in honor raise men to a state where they can invoke, by the creative power of the Spirit, a golden age that will transcend the age of Pericles and every other golden age that the earth has ever known. This shall come about through the establishment of a fountain of living flame-power, -wisdom, and -love.[3]

That fountain shall inundate the souls of men and drench their garments with so much of the essence of freedom that they will perceive spiritual alchemy as the means to every cosmic end. And the glory of the threefold flame, now saturating their consciousness with a fiery brilliance, will evoke an equal response in the very heart of God.

The bond thus established between earth and heaven shall raise this star to a position of greater brilliance than the Star of the East that heralded the approach of the Master Jesus two thousand years ago, for this light will signify the victory of the Christ consciousness not only in one Son of God, but also in all mankind.

I am the exponent of freedom for this age, and in revealing these facts about the science of alchemy, I cannot restrain myself from voicing these sentiments as apropos of the struggles of the times. Are men filled with idealism? Let them turn that idealism toward the Light where divine ideas flow out from a central fountain of living flame. There let all kindle and rekindle the torches of being, and let the fires of their minds be saturated with new hope for a new age born of the Spirit.

Life was never meant to be a cesspool of defeat, but a pillar of victory whose crowning laurel speaks of a living abundance. Blooming within the soul, that abundance extends itself out of the lonely room of self into the larger domain of the universe.

The Ascended Masters' consciousness is a vital power which will assist the devotee in performing a more than ordinary activity of genuine service and renewal. For we are about the Father's business of renewing the consciousness of men— not by applying old patches over old patches, but by renovating the entire garment of consciousness.

As we prepare, then, to make the would-be spiritual alchemist more effective in performing the Father's will and in enhancing the value of freedom, let us say unto every man:

The LORD is your shepherd. You shall not want[4]—if you will only understand that he longs to guide you correctly, if you will only understand that whereas evil has no real existence, its shadowed veil has been the means through the centuries of binding man to the earth. And you shall see that by cutting the bonds of evil and by acknowledging the power of Good, you will no longer strain at a gnat and swallow a camel,[5] but you will enter straightway into the City of God, into the consciousness that transcends the world and its options by recognizing the spiritual options that lie as a gift in your hand.

Man is the Divine Alchemist in physical form. In his right hand the gift of life lies beating. It is the pulsation of cosmic effort. Without acknowledging the gift, man fades away as a vapor upon the glass. By acknowledging it, the cosmic breath strengthens the manifestation of self until death is swallowed up in victory[6] and Life stands forth transcendent and splendid to every eye.

Onward we move progressively toward freedom in action.

I AM

Saint Germain

✠

CHAPTER 4

To Penetrate Matter

Ere we begin to school the alchemist in more advanced methods of producing the seeming miracles of love manifest right before his eye, we are duty-bound to make further exhortations calculated to prevent the spread of danger through the misuse of higher powers. What do you think the story of the Garden of Eden reveals to man if it does not reveal his disobedience to the divine mandates and his misuse of sacred power?

We will consider, then, the solidity of substance. Matter that presents so hard an appearance to the eye is actually composed of the whirling energies of Spirit. When the Higher Mind examines the nature of Spirit and makes known its findings to the mind of man, he becomes imbued with what we shall call his first awareness of the potential of the self to penetrate Matter.

Matter is no longer solid, but yields to the probing fingers of his mind and spirit. Its density can be calculated and comprehended by the self; and with the speed of light, the consciousness can reach out and pass through dense substance as easily as the swimmer cuts through the water with his arms in motion.

The more the individual becomes aware of the inner power of the self to sense the various shades of reality, the more his powers magnify. At this juncture, the astute and godly man is aware of the need to guard the way of the Tree of Life.[1] Gazing around him upon the world scene, he sees a mixture of good and evil and he knows within himself that in reality you can never blend the two; for whereas black and white may be mixed, their combination will always bring forth a gray tone.

In dealing with the human self, man has been convinced over the years that this blending of black and white is the true nature of man. It is almost as though mankind were stigmatized and hypnotized by the concept that the die of sin, like a die that is cast, is itself immutable.

It is to the shattering of this erroneous concept that I dedicate this rendering. Whereas the scriptures of the world are filled with admonishments against sin—and certainly the jangle and discord of the world bears witness to the diabolical inferno that can ignite in the consciousness of man—yet grace and mercy also appear, and beauty, together with the myriad and magnificent qualities of nature.

How, then, shall we distinguish between the darkness and the light as these take shape in mortal consciousness and combine in manifestation?

There are those who argue that the brilliance of the Absolute would lack definition without the tonal values that dilute the pure light into various shades of gray and even black. They say that the darkness is needed as a medium of contrast on which the light can appear.

Let me hasten to say that these individuals do not yet have the knowledge that the cosmic law would vouchsafe to them; therefore, let them hold their peace until they know whereof they speak. For they have not considered the introduction of the color spectrum and the emergence of the beautiful pastel hues radiantly functioning in the spiritual world without ever requiring a single shade of gray or black to delineate the many facets of the consciousness of God. Black is the absence of light and of the color-qualities of life, whereas white contains all of the rainbow rays as the prism clearly shows.

Let me say, then, that within the realm of the Absolute, within the goodness of God, within his power to create, lies a chromatic scheme so dazzling and so splendid as to literally propel the consciousness of man out of the socket of mortal vicissitudes. Why, then, do men and women tarry in the Troys of the denizens of darkness? I say it is through a common ignorance and the unfortunate spread of suspicion and doubt.

This distrust of the invisible yet all-powerful spiritual world by men and women is a strange phenomenon, for they are so easily persuaded to give their all in the cause of faithlessness. Contending that God is not and expounding and expanding upon their doubts, they never seem to realize that the energies that they use, if properly directed toward a higher faith, would produce the miracles of alchemy. And these tangible manifestations of the divine power would utterly convince them as to the rightness of the divine plan and ideal.

It has always been inconceivable to the many sincere and religious people that any man would succumb, as Faust did to Mephistopheles, and sell his soul to the forces of nihilism. But this is not so hard to understand if men will recognize that it is possible for faith and doubt to live side by side in the consciousness of the individual.

The presence of two opposing forces creates vacillation. Therefore in moments of faith, individuals are able to believe in the miraculous powers of nature and of alchemy; but when they allow projections of doubt concerning their own reality to be anchored within their consciousness, they are able to rationalize their selfish conduct.

Through habit, men use the energies of God to draw forth the elements of the good life which they desire. At the same time they take pleasure in preventing the manifestation of good in the lives of the innocent and those who may be far more virtuous than themselves.

Hence we warn of the degradations of witch-craft and black magic. Remember that the goal of spiritual alchemy is to create nobility in the soul and virtue everywhere, particularly in the realm of the self. For how can men extend to the boundaries of other lives that which they cannot manifest in their own?

Here lies the great error of the impatient black magician or the advocate of witchcraft. He is not willing to wait for the externalization of his own spiritual dedication and the release of the divine afflatus into the capsule of identity be-fore exerting his energies on behalf of controlling the universe.

Now, this chapter is the last that I shall write in this vein. In succeeding ones it is my intent to release some very interesting keys to the students of the light. But cosmic law demands that I ex-plain that the light must always be used to pro-duce the fervent beauty of dedication to God, love for humanity, and those divine qualities that enable the soul to adhere to the tenets of the Great White Brotherhood.

When this is accomplished, we are certain that we will have not just a few students in our class on the science of alchemy—or the science of wondrous change, as our students have come to call it—but we will have many. And these many will also be forewarned and forearmed against the misuse of energy so that all of their earnest efforts will cooperate successfully in achieving the divine plan for the golden age oncoming.

Only the few are aware of the enormous effort being made in the higher reaches of cosmos to assist humanity in awakening from the lethargy of their long sleep in the realm of the human ego—that fantastic and complex forcefield of individuality out of which a god can be born and out of which can emerge monstrous forms of discord and confusion—to the domain of the Real Self that has locked within it, waiting to be released, the greatest secrets of all time.

Today is the LORD's day. Today is the day of the God Self. The ages have not marred the power of him who has said, "I AM the same yesterday and today and forever."[2] Therefore, be assured of a kindly response to those efforts which are made in hope, in faith, and in charity, for the greatest Masters function in this domain.

To be a mortal adept, to move mountains for the sake of greed and the aggrandizement of the human person, is as nothing. For he who has said, "Seek ye first the kingdom of God and his righteousness, and all these things shall be added unto you"[3] meant every word of it.

Right now, today, you stand upon the threshold of fulfillment in your lives as you realize the beauty of nobility so ably stated by Sir Galahad of old: "My strength is as the strength of ten, because my heart is pure."[4]

Let us ready ourselves now for that purity which precedes the greatest alchemical manifestation.

For your advancement and achievement, I remain

Saint Germain

✠

CHAPTER 5

Formulas for Precipitation

Not what might be, but what will be because man envisions, invokes, and equates with universal law. Alchemy! The wondrous science of change that fulfills the heart's deepest desires, orders man's affairs, and renews the sweet purity of his original communion with the Great Progenitor.

The concept of the multiplication of cells points to the law of nature that provides for a continual addendum. This law which governs the reproduction of life after its kind does not involve the physical body alone, but the mind, the feelings, and the memory as well as the pure Spirit of man. Coordination between the four lower bodies and the higher vehicles enables man first to control his environment and then to create—on condition that he can understand and not be hindered by the obvious illusions of the appearance world whose point of reference is time and space.

Now, the presence or absence of certain factors may either lengthen or shorten the time of precipitation even though all other components be in order. Therefore, when these factors are known, they can be systematically eliminated in order to shorten the time of manifestation. The primary deterrents to precipitation should be recognized as (1) inharmony in the feeling world, (2) a sense of loneliness or abandonment, and (3) a sense of smallness or insecurity and doubt.

Sometimes the presence of these factors can be minimized by a simple act of faith. At other times it may require more earnest application to the Deity and a strengthening of the positive counteractions which are designed to eliminate completely the negative influences manifesting within and without one's world.

It may seem strange to some of you that I call to your attention these simple facts. But may I honestly say they are not so simple, for the effects of these mood energies upon the creative intent are of far greater consequence than humanity are willing to admit.

By pointing out the need to correct these conditions and making the would-be alchemist aware of the influence they exert upon his desired manifestation, I feel that we are taking a big step in the right direction. For this knowledge applied will avoid the introduction of discouraging factors at a later time when for some the anticipated results will not be immediately forthcoming for the very reasons I have stated.

This brings me to the place where I want to amplify, at the beginning of my instruction, the need for perseverance. Frequently, failure to persevere in the correct course has nullified all fruitage just before the harvest from the invisible world was ready to release itself into the hands and use of the seeker.

We would mention now some of the great and vital alchemical factors whose positive power should also be considered. Chief amongst this list is faith. This includes a belief in the whirling power that keeps the electrons in vital motion revolving around their nucleonic centers.

This power resembles a tightly compressed, almost omnipotent spring. It is central to every solar system and atom whose magnetic flux and emanation, while centered in its own nucleus, is able under cosmic law to tie into limitless energy fields to produce whatsoever miraculous manifestation is the requirement of the moment—when the individual is able to convince himself and the universe that his course is right.

Now, we have all seen men who were remarkably successful in producing wrong action simply because they were convinced that their course was right, even though they were actually wrong. This does not mean that Cosmos itself is proverbially blind; it is simply indicative of the cosmic need to protect the secrets of creation from the eyes of the curious and to guard the treasures of heaven through the systems of initiation evolved by the Brotherhood.

For this very reason the fiat of God went forth "Behold, the man is become as one of us, to know good and evil: and now, lest he put forth his hand and take also of the Tree of Life and eat and live for ever: therefore the LORD God sent him forth from the garden [guard-in] of Eden, to till the ground from whence he was taken."[1]

The inner necessity of the universe to protect its secrets from the profane can be seen in the activities of the Luciferian hordes who, from time to time during the long history of the planet, have involved the sons of God in a misuse of the creative and sacred power of life. This they have done through psychedelic perversions, dangerous drugs, their infectious spirit of rebellion against order—which is heaven's first law—and the spread of chaos, often in the name of idealism.

But this brand of idealism has always been based on intellectual pride; it is put forth as the counterplan of the carnal mind that competes with the Divine Mind, considering itself superior thereto. Therefore, if I have seemed overly protective in this intermediate course in alchemy, heaven knows there is a reason for it.

And now I say to each one, taking into account the semantics of alchemy, let us recognize that the word *altar* signifies a sacred place of change. Here all change is wrought by God's law.

God is law. His law does not exist without love. But unfortunately, owing to the very generosity inherent within the Divine Nature which allows various functions of the law to be used by evolving humanity, it has been possible for man to separate the law from love.

Thus, the more mechanical aspects of alchemy, called magic, have been employed down through the centuries by those who have used their knowledge of God's laws for selfish ends. This was demonstrated at the Court of Pharaoh when Aaron, a true alchemist of the Spirit, was challenged by the magicians who cast down their rods that also became serpents. [2]

The mechanical aspects of the law are often combined with trickery to produce phenomena which in the eyes of God are meaningless. Once a man has attained the position of a true spiritual adept, he has developed the powers of love and wisdom within the framework of universal law. He is innocent of harm to any, and his alchemical feats reflect his selflessness. Then the miracles he produces are of far less importance in his own eyes than the miracle of his oneness with his Creator.

So now as we face the altar, the place consecrated to the science of wondrous change, we must recognize the two courses before us. The first is to choose a course of action based on the highest knowledge made known to us. We decide what we wish to change. We decide why it needs to be changed. This gives motive power to our alchemical experiment.

At the same time, we recognize the limitations of man's knowledge and the superiority of the God Self and of the elder brothers of Light to assist him in working out his individual destiny. Therefore, the second course of action is to be aware that right change can be produced without conscious knowledge of what that change ought to be. We simply invoke from God the purity of his divine plan for right change.

In other words, we command in the name of the LORD—which man as a co-creator with God has the right to do—an alchemical precipitation of the gifts and graces of the Spirit that will endow the blessed son with the qualities of the Christ, thereby making him more capable as a spiritual alchemist and more integrated with the universal plan. I have found that wherever the second alchemical technique is employed, it strengthens the first course of invocation (invoked action) and fills the gaps in man's forte of knowledge, covering his ignorance by the cloak of true spirituality.

As we face the altar, aware of the realities of God and of the potential for their realization in man, let us also take into account those masterful beings who have already secured for themselves the ability to produce change at will. Surely the assistance of those who have been successful in the alchemical arts will be invaluable in producing the fruit of our desires. Invocations and prayers of one's choice are then in perfect order.

With an awareness of the law, faith in its impersonal operation, and a determined intent that once the formula has been developed the desired manifestation must be released into form, we shall proceed with the business of creating change.

Now, one of the most effective means by which change can be produced—and this which I here make known to you is a deep and wondrous secret held by many of the Eastern and Western adepts—is through what I will call "the creation of the cloud." Saint Paul referred to a "cloud of witnesses." [3] I am referring to a cloud of infinite energy which, somewhat like the ether so popularized by the scientists of a century ago, is everywhere present but nowhere manifest until it is called into action.

At first reading, to those who are empirically minded—skilled only in the material aspects of science and in what the senses can perceive—my foregoing remarks may seem to be just so much foolishness. If any think that, I can only have compassion for them.

I cannot help them, nor does the law require me to apologize; for I have proved this principle many times with the greatest of success. And I think that where the great adepts do not consciously use it, then it is automated for them through their contact with the Higher Mind. But for most of our beginning and intermediate students, it will be essential that they learn the process carefully in order that they can first consciously create the cloud and then wait until its appearance becomes an automated process in their beings.

I shall continue next week with this very important activity—"Create!" and the cloud.

Onward,

Saint Germain

✠

CHAPTER 6

"Create!"
and the Cloud

How deeply, how deeply many have yearned to know how to produce constructive change both in themselves and in the world. Let them realize, then, that to bring about change is a creative act. Alchemy is the creative science whereby man is enabled to obey the original fiat of God "Take dominion over the earth!"

This command was indicative of the Father's plan for his son, and the means to implement it are discovered as one learns the ancient secrets of this sacred science. Practicing the principles of alchemy, the individual is able to rise from being a puppet to the will of other egos, to the will of disobedient spirits, to the passing fancies of the times, or to the dictates of the brothers of the shadow who induce the young adept to practice black magic and witchcraft, flattering his ego and often quoting scriptures, saying, "If thou be the Son of God, command that these stones be made bread."[1]

Now we are on the verge of taking our initial steps in producing change—not a change that gears man to the contemporary scene where his every effort is molded by environmental factors, but a change that will bring him closer to his Real Image. We will create the means whereby change can be produced by our sovereign will, whereby we can take dominion over the earth. For it is here on earth that we are obliged[2] to create the desires of our hearts. It is right here and now that we are indeed obligated to become co-creators with God, thus to fulfill the purity of his intent.

Whereas I recognize that there may seem to be mechanistic factors in the scientific direction that I am about to give you, I am sure you have noticed the many safeguards which I have inserted into this course to make certain that you are never of the wrong opinion; for none should ever assume that by a mere scientific or mechanical ritual he will be able to perform the highest types of alchemical manifestation.

Not so! For the highest alchemy, the greatest change, is that which changes man into a god, wherein the son becomes one with the Father; and this can never be accomplished by mechanical means.[3]

Stand now before your altar, honoring the living God and his fiat. For he who is God has commanded it: "Take dominion!" You are rightfully functioning, then, as you do just that. You are about to create, and you will first create the cloud from the enormous power of God stored at every point in space, waiting to be invoked.

The power of vision is central to our invocation. Therefore, we shall create in our minds first a milky white radiance, and we shall see this milky white radiance as an electronic vibratory action of vital, moving, ineffable light. The concentration of the light, which we call the density of the light, is that which makes the milky white color. If the cloud were attenuated, we would be able to see through it as though the scenes around us were enveloped in a fog.

Now, having created in our minds this form of a bright translucent cloud, we allow it to enfold our physical bodies and to occupy our forcefield. For a moment we become lost in the midst of the cloud, and then it seems as though it has always been there. Its atmosphere is familiar, comfortable.

We recognize that the mind has the power to expand its circle of influence, but we must not try to move far from the parent tree of self. Let this bright and shining cloud at first be nine feet in diameter around oneself. Later, perhaps, we shall expand it to a diameter of ninety feet, then nine hundred feet and further.

In our early meditations we shall concentrate on intensifying the action of the white light in our minds. From thence we shall transfer that action to the nine-foot area around the physical form. Once we have developed the sense of this cloud being around our physical forms, we shall understand that whereas the cloud can be made

visible to the physical sight, our primary concern is
to keep its high vibratory action purely spiritual.

Those of you who are familiar with electronics and the workings of a rheostat will understand
that by a simple twist of the dial of consciousness,
we can intensify the vibratory action of the cloud.
In this case, we coalesce more light around each
central point of light; for our cloud is composed
of many light points whose auras diffuse and
blend with one another, making the total effect
one of a lacy yet highly concentrated white radiance, a pure swirling cloud of cosmic energy.

What is this mighty cloud that we have created, this forcefield of vibrating energy, and why
did we create it in the first place?

Actually, whereas I have used the word *create*,
it would be more appropriate if perhaps I used
the word *magnetize*; for we are actually magnetizing that which is already everywhere present in
space. We are amplifying an intense action of the
light from within its own forcefield—more than
would normally manifest in a given area. We are
thereby drawing upon universal God-power to
produce this cloud that first penetrates and then
hallows our immediate forcefield in order that
we may have a spiritual altar upon which we may
project the pictures of reality that we desire to
create.

Bear in mind that this cloud can be used ther-
apeutically for the healing of the nations and the
soul of a planet, or you can use it as a platform to

invoke, as Christ did upon the Mount of Transfiguration, the presence of the Ascended Masters—of beloved Jesus, Mother Mary, the Master Serapis Bey from Luxor, the Maha Chohan, Lord Maitreya, Archangel Michael—to assist you not only in your alchemical experiments, but also in your ministrations to life.

Where you are yet ignorant of just what you ought to produce for yourself and others, you can, in a gentle, childlike manner, ask God to produce out of the great pool of his light-energy the miracle of his healing love not only in your life and in the lives of your loved ones, but also in the lives of the multitudes in the world at large.

You can ask the power of God and of the kingdom of heaven to come into manifestation upon earth. You can ask for the golden age to be born, for an end to strife and struggle and all negative and hateful manifestations. You can ask for Love to take dominion over the world. If you will open your heart to the needs of the world and to the love of the Divine Mother that seeks expression through your uplifted consciousness, limitless ideas for universal service will flow into your mind.

But here again, let me hasten to sound a note of warning, especially for the benefit of those who have been psychically inclined or who have a tendency, as humanity would say, to "go off the deep end." Beware! You are dealing with sacred creative power. Beware! It is better for you

to ask the Masters to interject their ideas for you—
without necessarily defining or releasing them to
your conscious mind—than for you to be carried
away from the tether of the alchemical norm.

The Ascended Masters are not only sane
and well organized, but they are also godly and
profound to the nth degree. It is essential, then,
that you become likewise. Above all, be not carried away by pride or by the exaltation of the self
over others.

As you gain spiritual power through these
periods of meditation upon the cloud—which at
first should not exceed fifteen minutes a day—try
to understand that the creative cloud, once it is
dispersed by your fiat at the conclusion of your
creative ceremony, will continue to expand and
expand and expand throughout the universe as a
globe of translucent white fire, eddying in ever-
widening spheres to contact all that is real and
that is really yours.

The cloud, as the manifestation of the power
of your creative energy, the fire of your Spirit,
will draw into your world the very consciousness
of God himself. Evoked from the central pores
of being and beautifully expanding as an altar of
God, the cloud will hallow space wherever it
expands.

Christ was able to produce the miracles recorded in the Gospels, and many more, because
he had first mastered the correct use of energy.

He called the holy energy of Spirit "Father"; and of a truth, father the Spirit is to all manifestation.

The Father is all-loving, all-knowing, and all-powerful, and he will make you all that he is. But we have only begun to touch upon the correct use of his energy. Therefore, I seek to develop in your consciousness, through your reading of this material, a proper attitude that will enable you to function, under the guidance of your own God Presence and Christ Self, as an efficient co-creator with God and the Brotherhood of Light.

We need alchemists of the Spirit—men and women who will produce physical, mental, emotional, and etheric alchemical manifestations. Welding them all into one creative act of abundant living, these shall at last understand the meaning of the Master's words "I AM come that they might have life and that they might have it more abundantly."[4]

Alchemy is not a devilish means of bringing forth riches and honor. It is a spiritual, all-loving science of changing the base metals that make up the synthetic image of man into the pure gold of the Real Image that he may implement his wise dominion over the earth.

Eventually the Great Alchemist will teach the apprentice the seraphic science whereby man shall produce that wondrous final change of which Paul spoke: "Behold, I shew you a mystery; we shall not all sleep, but we shall all be changed, in a moment, in the twinkling of an eye, at the last trump: for the trumpet shall sound, and the dead shall be raised incorruptible, and we shall be changed."[5]

Bear in mind that I have only lightly touched upon this great creative energy that is within you even now.

In the name of the Master of Masters, in the name of the Lord Christ, I remain his servant and your advocate forever,

Saint Germain

✠

CHAPTER 7

The Science
of Picturization

Remember that once you have held the vision of the cloud and turned it over to your Higher Self to sustain, to the latent God-faculties within you, your God Presence will sustain it for the required period. In time you will find that the glow of the cloud will softly suffuse itself through your physical body, and as this takes place there will come a sharpening of the mind and a new sense of awareness of all life everywhere.

As you perform this ritual-exercise of creating the cloud through attunement with the creative power of the universe, becoming thereby a co-creator with God, you will gain a feeling of detachment from the world as though you were merely an observer to what is taking place around you. This will occur as you allow yourself to flow automatically into the great creative power of the Macrocosm.

This experience in flow, whereby the lesser consciousness of man flows into the greater consciousness of God, is what is known as "going up into the mountain."[1] It is called a mountaintop experience because through it man discovers the Summit of his being, the place where the lower self is wed to the Higher, and Matter and Spirit merge.

Therefore, throughout this ritual your consciousness must be kept pure, charged with love, aware of the infinite potential of the cosmic mind of God, and completely identified with all constructive momentums. If there is an introduction of hatred or even mild dislike of anyone or an attempt to interfere with the cosmic flow of the infinite plan through any part of life, such activity will, of course, create a karmic situation that will prove most unfortunate to the individual who allows his energies to become so engaged.

Those who have irresponsibly used alchemical techniques, whether in ignorance or with the intent of bringing harm to other lifestreams, have in fact brought about great harm to themselves. Others who harbor feelings of criticism, jealousy, and irritation concerning the actions and accomplishments of friend or foe may create just as much harm as those whose malice is intended. Gossip itself is one of the most deadly forms of black magic and can bring about the physical death of its victims.

Seeing that all harm eventually returns to the one sending it forth, would it not be well for all true alchemists to take the vow of harmlessness, at the same time recognizing that the defense of truth and freedom sometimes necessitates making a choice between the lesser of evils?

I urge, then, that all understand the need to magnetize the grand design of God for all parts of life. Naturally, everyone cannot be expected to be in sympathy with your aims. After all, on the great ladder of souls ascending progressively (hopefully toward the light of purpose), there are many levels of attainment.

None should condemn those of lesser understanding or do aught except to emulate those of greater understanding. Above all, do not be jealous of those who may be more successful than you in their application of the science of intermediate alchemy. Remember that it is practice that makes perfect, that it is motive that transfigures design, that it is beauty that transfixes the soul.

Thus the loving purposes of God come to fruition in man as he originally intended them to do, for the Garden of Eden was a place where the beauty of communion with the LORD and the understanding of his laws could be imparted to man. It was intended to be the most beautiful school in all the world, where the dreams of God could flow through the branches of the tall trees, where the billowing clouds of morning, of noon, of even would be highlighted by the sacred glow of the luminous sun, "a light to light the day."

Lament not, for the Edenic school shall be reestablished in this day and age to fulfill the plan of paradise ere the golden age shall manifest. And it shall appear when enough alchemists of the Spirit unite in the common goal of bearing witness to the truth.

Now let us place our attention upon the science of picturization, for without it nothing shall appear. You will find this science illustrated in the story of Jacob, who used alchemy to increase the numbers of his cattle.[2] Visualization is important to the alchemist, because it is the overlay of his visualization upon the creative cloud that actually produces the miracle of alchemical manifestation.

If you wish a more youthful appearance, you must visualize yourself as having just that. If you wish more vitality, you must visualize yourself already having that vitality—your muscles rippling with God's energy, your mind brimming over with vital ideas, tingling with life and light and love. You must feel and know that the energies of God are flowing through your fingertips and toes, emanating into space the glow of abundant health and a transfiguring countenance.

As you proceed with this exercise, there will be produced, without additional effort on your part, a beneficial effect upon those whom you contact. But you must be very careful not to seek recognition for this service; otherwise, as it is written in the Book of Life, "ye have no reward of your Father which is in heaven."[3]

I know that you will smile when I say that we are aware of some students who, when they are given this material, may become so enthused with it that they will say to those who are uninformed of their efforts to become more godly, "Do you feel something when I am near?" And of course this will spoil the whole effect of any virtue they may have developed during their study.

Calling attention to one's accomplishments produces a concentration of energy upon the personality and away from the soul whence the radiance of the source is derived. Whereas the inherent God-qualities of the soul are like radioactive substance imbedded in and composing the soul, the radiant cloud is the soul's own alchemical altar which makes possible the soul's expansion—like unto the expanding universe—from the fires of its own central sun out into space.

Some may ask, How can we produce miracles that affect others without taking that energy which belongs to them or without depriving them of the opportunity of producing their own wondrous changes? These seem to be of the opinion that the fires of God have a decay rate and that sometime, somewhere these fires will come to an end or burn themselves out.

Let me hasten to assure you that though all of the suns in the physical universe were to fall as burning cinders into the central sun and the central sun by God's law were to be dissolved in its physical manifestation, the fires of the soul of God would never burn out. They are immutable, infinite, and eternal. Have no fear, then, that you are using up God's energies or that you are taking that energy which might be used more profitably by another.

When the fiat "Create!" went forth, it was the signal of God's gift of freedom to man. Therefore, man should be free to create. Moreover, he should be free to create without condemnation. To insure his freedom from the impinging thoughts of others, the matrices of his mind must become receptive to and fortified by the thoughts of God and there must be spaces in the time of the day when, apart from the creating of the cloud, the alchemist attunes with the mind of God and drinks in the fragrance of his being.

True alchemy draws man close to God and to his Christ, and it enables him to fulfill the ancient fiats "Man, know thyself!" "Create!" and "Take dominion!" The benefits of man's communion with all life through the sacred science can and will spread abroad throughout the earth. These benefits can and will exert the pressure of the higher techniques of heaven upon the world below.

Have you not read "Be not forgetful to entertain strangers: for thereby some have entertained angels unawares"?[4] Let men entertain you as angels unawares. Do not sully your alchemical results by imposing the dregs of the human personality upon any man; rather continue in the joyous faith that God will expand and expand and expand the domain of yourself in limitless light and love.

One of the most important points for you to understand in the science of intermediate alchemy is that whereas you are only beginning your training, this is not the only opportunity you will have to use these laws. For you will be able to use them not only all the days of this life, but should you not win your ascension at the close of this embodiment, you will find that so long as you live upon this earth, the science of God's alchemy will help you to be changed "from glory to glory, even as by the Spirit of the Lord."[5] You must understand that there is nothing counter to his law in the correct use of alchemy, for true alchemy *is* the change from glory unto glory by his Spirit.

I know that some who are reading this course may not have considered themselves religious at the beginning. Perhaps the intended functions of the spoilers, the brothers of the shadow, to ruin the purposes of religion by ruining the lives of those who profess to follow religion may have corroded your acceptance of the laws of cosmos.

But I think that some of you have already begun to experience profound results in your lives through the practice of the rituals I have given you. And I am certain that those of you who have not will begin to do so as your faith mounts and as you counteract all your negatives by the exhilarating sense that you can change your world and that you can make your life what God wants it to be and what you, deep inside, want it to be. For you can find success in all that you are doing. And that success need not be confined to the spiritual side of life, but it can also include the material.

The Lord has said, "Seek ye first the kingdom of God and his righteousness; and all these things shall be added unto you." Therefore, fear not to ask that ye may receive of the earthly things that you need even as you have first sought the heavenly.

Remember the story of our Lord who, when he would ride into Jerusalem, told two of his disciples to go to a certain village where they would find "a colt tied, whereon never man sat." They were instructed to fetch "the colt, the foal of an ass,"[6] and to tell those who might question them, "The Lord hath need of him."[7]

Will you develop this sense of knowing that what you have need of, God will supply? Oh, build and build, brothers of Light! Build, sisters of Light! For God needs you. The kingdom needs you.

Lovingly, I AM

Saint Germain

✠

CHAPTER 8

What Alchemy Can Mean to a Decaying World

The moon rules the night side of life and is the lesser light, the reflective light of the solar energy of God. In its reflective state it exerts enormous control over the tides and over the water element.

Luna, the moon, the great whirling satellite that rules the night, governs in part, then, the emotional body of man and can easily become either his greatest enemy or his best friend. For when properly harnessed, the energies of the moon (being put under his feet[1]) can help him to achieve alchemical control over his emotions (over his energy-in-motion). Let us see how this is so.

The moon reflects the astral body of earth. When dealing with the moon, then, we deal with the reflected light of the sun When the astral body is under the dominion of the Christ, its power becomes limitless. When its purified energies are magnified in turn by the moon, which is nothing more than a giant reflector, their power is multiplied in almost infinite proportion.

But until such time as the mass consciousness is ruled by the light of the sun instead of being ruled by the night, the moon will reflect the astral effluvia of the planet. Thus men will continue to be the victims of their own horrendous miscreations, and that to an even greater degree during the cycle of the full moon.

Now, the alchemist uses his purified consciousness as a reflector of solar energies much like the moon reflects the light of the sun. The waters of his mind reflect the light of the day and the night even as the waters of the sea reflect the golden pathway of both the sun and the moon. But the Christ consciousness, the prism of purity like the "sea of glass,"[2] filters out the impurities of the moon even as it refracts the light of the sun.

All energy being God's energy, the humanly misqualified energies reflected by the moon (sent back to the earth from whence they came, according to karmic law) may be freed from the impositions of the carnal mind through the process of transmutation. They may then be used to create, in the tradition of the Great Alchemist, more perfect works of art until the patterns in the heavens transform the patterns in the earth and the moon becomes a golden orb of rarified power.

Most of you know only too well that when your emotions become disturbed over outer conditions, feelings, or concepts, there is a moment when you are yet able to wrest control of your energies from your own emotional body. Subsequently, if these energies are permitted to continue to rage unabated, that moment of control is lost; and then it is easy for people to do, to think, or to say that which they will one day regret.

Conversely, most of you are aware of the great joy and peace that has come to your souls when you have been able to accomplish something for someone else. This happens because deep within yourself there is a loving desire to serve your fellowman.

This desire is what prompted the descent of the Christ, the sun of David, in his role as the Messias of old. The shepherd king, a man after God's own heart, communed with God and prepared himself for greater service as he tended his sheep. Nowhere was the luster of his soul more apparent than in the beauty of his meditations upon the Spirit of the LORD recorded in the Book of Psalms.

One of the most skillful ways in which the tired businessman or executive, the frustrated mother or wife, the confused young man or woman can find integration and wholeness for themselves is to develop the discipline of being able to direct their emotions to do for them exactly what they want. Such discipline will completely change their outlook, for they will then face life with joyous expectancy, not with dissatisfaction.

For example, if it is love for another that you would express, then you must always guard against that love which is selfish, which would exact from the beloved the expectancies of your own mind and heart without ever understanding the givingness of love. In order to love as God loves, you must first give freedom to all parts of life, including yourself; and then you must place your trust, as does a nestling bird, in the heart of God, in the heart of goodness and mercy.

Having given all, you will then receive the most joyful, eternal gifts from God that you could ever imagine—and some even beyond that which you could imagine. These will come not only through the chalice of your own heart, but also through the hearts of your compeers. If, then, you would truly love, you must learn to discipline the base emotions of selfishness, envy, jealousy, resentment, stubbornness, and ingratitude.

We urge, therefore, at this juncture in our alchemical studies that the control of the emotions be considered, for the emotions will play a very important role in the creative cloud action which we are considering and out of which we are functioning.

The only way to be truly happy is to give oneself totally to the universe and to God, at the same time being aware of and expecting from God the return gift of one's Real Self. One of the greatest dangers in the religious quest has been brought about as men have given themselves to God, thinking that that was all they had to do. Not understanding the responsibilities of free will, they then acted the part of the nebulous ninny. Having no will of their own, they would flip and flop back and forth, blown by every wind, obsessed with what we will call the law of uncertainty. "For if the trumpet give an uncertain sound, who shall prepare himself to the battle?"[3]

Men should understand that although their surrender to God be complete, following surrender they must wait for the fiat of bestowal that is pronounced by the God Presence as a restatement of the blessing given by God at the birth of his offspring: "Thou art my beloved Son: this day have I begotten thee." This takes place when one has relinquished the control of his four lower bodies to his Christ Self, thus enabling his True Self, the Christ, to obey the fiat "Take dominion over the earth!"—the earth being one's own footstool kingdom, the four lower bodies.

Remember that even Jesus the Christ came to the moment of his anointing. The Holy Spirit descended and the voice of God renewed the ancient covenant "This is my beloved Son, in whom I AM well pleased."[4] This is the timeless fiat of creation uttered from the foundation of the world, reconsecrating the soul who has pledged to renew in service his vow taken at inner levels to do the will of God.

Therefore, when man's right to function as a son of God is restored, the moment of creativity is born because he has once again recognized the power of God's love to forgive his sins (to set aside his karma until such time as he has gained enough self-mastery to stand, face, and conquer his human creation). Now the bond of life within itself weds him to the highest purposes of alchemy and that, mind you, without ever robbing him of his true identity.

What shall it profit a man if he shall gain the whole world through the use of alchemy and lose his soul?[5]

We ask the students to understand that gaining control of the soul (of the energies composing one's identity pattern) is one of the most essential functions of alchemy and that this control is gained through surrender and through humility. When the Christ entered the Holy City riding upon "a colt, the foal of an ass," as we mentioned in our last lesson, his mien was one of utter humility; yet he was crowned by God and man with the highest honors.

And so it is essential that we develop in the students those same Christlike qualities that will make them pillars in the temple of God that cannot be moved by human emotions, no matter what their guise: criticism, condemnation, judgment, self-pity, gossip, treachery, tyranny, or human deceit. The alchemist must be oblivious to all human conduct yet not unaware of worldly thought to the point where he plays the fop. To him the fulfillment of the fiat "Be wise as serpents and harmless as doves!"[6] is the order of every day.

But we are concerned with the sinews of mission, and the mission is freedom for all. If we would have freedom be the joy of all, then we must give freedom to all, for then none can exclude freedom from us. It is therefore to the passions of freedom that our experiments in alchemy must be dedicated. We must rise to emotional control; for when God said, "Take dominion over the earth!" He meant individual dominion over one's energies, one's consciousness, and one's four lower bodies.

Collective dominion comes about when the contributing spirit of the group, the nation, the planet—recognizing all that it has received from life—joyously offers itself and all that it has received to the Great Spirit of life. At that point, man the individual and man the collective unit ponder the enrichment of the Real Self and the true mystical identity of the group through the increase of individual talents. These gifts of God, when multiplied, are like stars in the firmament of being that glow in the grand design of universal destiny.

When man becomes one with God, he realizes that he truly is God. This is not blasphemy, but the fruit of total surrender. The return gift of Life's own identity, as God gives himself to his son, is far greater than the token sacrifice of mortality left on the altar by the beloved son. Nevertheless, it is typical of the Deity to be the Great Giver and thus to precipitate the highest alchemical manifestation—the prism of the Christ consciousness. This must be and always is the reward for the relinquishment of human error and the full realization of the divine life in every man.

All nature then trembles within the cup of the Christ mind. The heart of the Christ is brimming with the creative essence which pours out the unifying experience that identifies him with life, him with the alchemist, and the alchemist with him. Who can hurt or destroy in all my holy mountain?[7] Who can aid in all the holy mountain of God? Why, every atom, every electron, is a rushing unto God!

"And a cloud received him out of their sight. . . . Ye men of Galilee, why stand ye gazing up into heaven? This same Jesus, which is taken up from you into heaven, shall so come in like manner as ye have seen him go into heaven."[8]

The Second Coming of Christ is antedated by the fulfillment of the prophecy "One shall be taken, and the other left."[9] For when one is taken and another is left, it denotes that the world lieth yet in wickedness and that only the few have accepted the kingdom. But when the Second Coming of Christ comes to the quickened world, it will be because the nature of the Divine has become understood as a priceless gift of freedom to every man.

When this miracle of Christ-love is produced in the world, it will be because the students of alchemy—whether known by that name or any other, whether in the churches or out of the churches, in fact whether in the body or out of the body[10]—are expressing universally the radiance of the Christ-design. Imbued with the fires of the Holy Spirit, their minds will then become a cosmic reactor, a central furnace of universal ideas for freedom and for the breaking of the chains of bondage that a recalcitrant humanity have forged.

Now we reveal in this eighth lesson what alchemy can mean to a decaying world, what it can mean to slaves in bondage to the senses, what it can mean to the self surrounded by confusion and chaos as it becomes an ordered, purposeful exhibit of universal grace expressing through the forcefield of the individual identity of man.

Do you see now why El Morya and Mother Mary and all of the Ascended Masters are offering their energies freely for the good of humanity? Do you see why the creative cloud invoked by us, literally an individualized cloud of witness by day and a pillar of fire by night,[11] enables man to understand that the crucible of identity, while it may at first be nothing but an experimental test tube, can become a radiant altar of Reality?

Faithfully, I AM

Saint Germain

✠

CHAPTER 9

Anxiety and the Anxiety Syndrome

For this lesson we will permit the students to experiment with and develop proficiency in the creation of the cloud while we go afield for a moment to discuss one of the major deterrents to successful alchemy. I refer to anxiety and the anxiety syndrome.

Strange as it may seem, most negative manifestations stem from anxiety, including the awful sin of masochism.[1] Since it is generally acknowledged that humanity have a desire to be happy and that they have the right to pursue happiness, we ask this question: Would it not be wise for people in all walks of life to work toward the healing of those conditions which they bring upon themselves through their unfruitful anxieties?

We avow that there are lawful concerns and that men and women should make reasonable provision for their future and for eventualities which they know from personal experience may arise. But it is so unnecessary for them to become apprehensive about life in general, or even life specifically, to the point where their apprehensions unbalance their thinking, their emotions, and their entire psyche.

Anxiety is the great warp of life. It warps perspective without producing any perceptible benefit whatsoever. Anxiety is the cause of people's tendency to hoard the goods of this world. Like frantic squirrels they pile up their winter's supply of nuts. They accumulate an oversupply of every imaginable item, and they deprive themselves of happiness by their unwarranted concerns and their unnecessary and time-consuming preparations for every eventuality.

Just as we do not expect that the students will cease to be providential, so we do not expect that they will become unduly involved in anticipating a doomsday that never arrives. Anxiety is a symptom of insecurity; it stems from man's incorrect concept of himself and from his lack of perspective. Many people feel unfulfilled, unloved, unwanted, and they are not sure of just what they should be doing with their lives. Their uncertainties under adverse conditions are easily turned into mental and emotional states of depression bordering on extreme self-deprecation.

Considering these facts and bearing fully in mind the power of creative energy, we have decided that before going more deeply into our study of alchemy, we shall advocate for all of our students an utter mental, emotional, and even physical catharsis. We shall achieve thereby a purification of the consciousness and being of man—an emptying, if you will, of unstable conditions so that our alchemical creation may take place under the most sterile and clinical conditions possible.

You see, it is so easy for a negative ingredient to creep into our formulae that we must take every possible precaution before we begin our experiments. Without first purging ourselves of all undesirable qualities, we would find ourselves, with the best of motives, amplifying our negatives instead of our positives as we proceeded to employ the wondrous power of alchemy.

This is one of the problems that arise among those who follow some of the so-called mystery schools where the ego is catered to at the personal level instead of being disciplined at the impersonal level. As these students develop "soul power," it is inevitable that they amplify their negative momentums along with the great positive qualities which they seek to manifest. For whatever is in their worlds when they are brought into direct contact with the sacred fire must expand even as their total consciousness expands.

In some cases the negatives completely cancel out the positives; and many times, because of earthly affinities, the additional boost of power that comes about as the result of experimentation will make a magnet out of their negatives even when they are completely involved in the divine search. Thus will their own negative momentums, hidden in the recesses of their subconscious minds, draw to themselves more of their kind from the thoughts and feelings of others. This phenomenon is often the underlying cause of disharmony in religious groups.

Now we earnestly desire to have the body of God upon earth forewarned about these conditions, for unless the deterrent forces which are imbedded in the psyche of man are brought under the power of divine grace and emptied of their content (i.e., of the misqualified energies which sustain their forms), they will peer as haunting specters waiting to devour the offspring of all benign activities and to literally turn man's light into darkness.

We would do the opposite. We would create in the lives of the would-be alchemists the transmutative effects that will enable them, through awareness and through dedication to the Christ Spirit of living harmony, to manifest all good things under divine control. Thus shall divine grace fill the temple of the mind and heart of the alchemist and make him truly a wonder-worker for God.

How many times have we seen concern for his fellowman take shape in the consciousness of the student. As he gazes upon world conditions or upon the problems of his own family, he is often almost obsessed with the desire to produce the miracle of saving grace for his loved ones as well as for those who are in need in the world around him. So strong does this desire become that his

brotherly love is many times the central motivation behind his search for greater spirituality and
self-realization.

Ours is not to discourage those who would
serve, but to help them realize their objectives in
peace and in honor. Therefore, "consider the lilies
of the field, . . . they toil not, neither do they
spin: and yet I say unto you that even Solomon in
all his glory was not arrayed like one of these."[2]
The care of God for the birds of the air, the great
abundance manifest in nature and in the "lilies
of the field" shows the supreme value that God
places upon each of his children. Let us look to
him, then, to teach us how to meet the needs of
our brethren here below.

Anxiety stems from a lack of faith in the ultimate purposes of life. The hard experiences that
have come to many in childhood and in later
years, creating stresses and strains and producing
the fruit of bitterness, have prevented their development of that refined spirit which would enable
them to shed their anxieties.

In reality, the lessons Jesus taught on the
Father's watchful care for man and nature should
give all the understanding that will heal their insecurity, their anxiety, and their personal pain involving the mind and self. This healing is brought
about through the overpowering radiance of God's
loving concern for every man.

I urge, therefore, that all students take into
account the tender care and consideration of the

universe manifest in the wondrous working of the physical body when it is not interfered with by human pollutants. And I urge that they then make an attempt throughout the coming days to heal the breach caused by their sense of separation—the separation of the individual from his true identity and hence from the Eternal One.

In him you live and move and have your being. Without him you have neither life nor identity.

Ask yourself this question: Is it wise for you to pollute the Divine Identity by the intrusions of self-will and self-indulgence? Ask yourself this question: Have you really given the Father a chance or has yours been an on-again, off-again, vacillating attempt to realize God?

There is nothing complex about the origin of the soul and its everlasting communion with him. To become as a little child, then, as we shall see in our next lesson, is to prepare the way for the greatest manifestations of alchemy.

Now, alchemy is not witchcraft; it is not variance. It is the exercise of a stable God-intended control over nature, and it involves far more than men imagine. Through alchemy the shedding of your anxieties can be accomplished, but first you must build a mountain of faith to counteract the negative thoughts of the world which are primarily responsible for man's failures.

How is this so? Each time individuals have a failure and lament it, each time they have a

problem and sorrow over it rather than commit
it unto the Father, each time individuals resent
their problems and see them not as the return of
karma or as a test but as an act of Deity whom
they defy, they are building up in their own
worlds frustration, resentment, anxiety, and confusion. And these momentums draw to their
own doorsteps the negative conditions of the
outside world.

If ever there was a secondary enemy to anxiety, it is confusion. This, too, can and should be
healed by the fires of the Christ mind. For we
know that the Christ mind is calm yet capable of
focusing the fiery energies of the Creator to overthrow evil both in the self and in society.

But let us make clear that this is a fire whose
burning is controlled by the mind. It can be slow
or fast. It can leap like a young deer and take its
freedom, its dominion, its God-control, or it can
stand in midair like hieroglyphs of living flame
and say to all that would hinder the alchemical
manifestation, Pass no further!

I urge you to consider, then, the negative
thought pools of the world with a view to disen-
gaging your energies and your activities from
involvement with the misqualified energies contained therein. And I urge you to make your God-
determination that you are going to clean your
consciousness inside and out of all residual substance which is there as the result of your contact
with the cesspools of human consciousness.

Anxiety must go. It must be replaced by faith and solemn confidence in the outworking of the divine plan. This certain knowing, I say, is a happy state! When you begin to understand fully what I mean, you will see that the developing of this confidence in the real is one of the greatest ways in which all deterrents to successful alchemy can be vanquished. In fact, all deterrents to abundant living can be knocked down as you cease to fight "as one that beateth the air," [3] as Saint Paul once said.

You were born to win, and I say this to counter the lie that man was "born to lose." And if you will make this statement, "I AM born to win!" as an act of supreme faith, it will overcome the world's consciousness of failure—a deadly weight of sin if there ever was one.

It does not matter what problems you have faced, for even the most dire situations will yield to the mighty forcefield of God-potency that will be built up through your practice of spiritual alchemy. But why should man draw God's energies for alchemical experimentation and creation when his own world is still full of the miscreations of the mass mind and the weeds in his garden that will choke out his efforts and destroy the good fruit as well?

I do not mean that you should not continue your experiments with the cloud. I do mean that you should understand the duality of life and realize that anxieties must go. But in order for this to take place, you must make the conscious determination that it shall be done. And if you do, I promise you that your experiments will not only be purer and more successful, but also that they will produce happiness and the fruits thereof for yourself and the whole human race.

Oh, we have so much more, for each Master loves each servant-son!

For freedom to all, I remain

Saint Germain

✠

CHAPTER 10

Nature Yields to the Childlike Mind

The most important key we can release to the alchemist at this stage of his development is found in these words of Jesus: "Whosoever shall not receive the kingdom of God as a little child shall in no wise enter therein."[1] All of the pristine beauties of nature—the ethereal highlights whose gentle glow can be sensed by the budding spiritual faculties of the children of God—hold as their essential content the sweet creative longing of a child.

I do not wish to disabuse the minds of the children of men who have held such high and mighty opinions of the Masters of cosmos of any false glamour with which they have clothed our office under the Godhead, almost as a gilding of the cosmic lily. However, I do feel the need to point out, not only from my own experience but also from the experiences of those who are above me in the hierarchy, that the higher we have gone in our contact with the Deity, the more childlike, the more simple, the more beautiful has been his representation.

Therefore we conclude that the innocence of Nature herself is perhaps the greatest key to her potential for wondrous alchemical creations. We amplify, then, the need of the children of God to empty their minds of the dregs of turbulent emotions that have engaged their energies through the centuries and kept them bound to a senseless round of confusion and struggle.

The great barrier to spiritual progress has been that men confuse holy innocence and becoming like a little child with playing the fool. The highest Masters are childlike, sweet, and innocent. Nevertheless, when functioning in the world domain, they sharpen their "worldly senses" in order to execute judgment in human affairs.

The reason I introduce the subject of becoming "as a little child" into our study of intermediate alchemy is that every factor of thought and feeling impresses itself upon the sensitive matrices of alchemical manifestation. No thought or feeling, then, can be termed unimportant or irrelevant. Without hesitation, I declare that the most important of all alchemical factors in drawing forth the highest aspects of creation is the childlike mind—pure and guileless.

The child mind is the greatest mind because its innocence is its best and sure defense, because it is not surrounded by crowding concepts, and because it is free to develop symmetry, color, sound, light, and new ideas. In short, it is free to create; and its supreme goal is to spread happiness in all of its forms and manifestations, all the while maintaining the purity and harmlessness of the child.

Let me say, however, that the idea of harmlessness is applicable only to the world of human beings, for how can there be a need for harmlessness unless there first exist harm? When you destroy harm, you no longer have need to create harmlessness. In the absence of harm or harmlessness, the innocence of childhood prevails, enabling the souls of men to commune gently with nature and nature's God.

The vast drama that keeps the way of the Tree of Life, that guards the alchemical secrets, has also been born of necessity. Man's disobedience to cosmic law, his hesitancy in matters of the Spirit, his gathering momentums of destructivity upon earth—these have necessitated the curbing of his activities in heaven.

In a very real sense, then, man has been confined to the earth to work out his destiny. Eden, the Garden of God, and the secrets of life contained therein have been denied him because he would not heed the divine injunction "In the day that thou eatest thereof thou shalt surely die!"[2]

Now and always man must understand that when he partakes of the consciousness of evil, he becomes subject unto the laws of mortality. Yet God has always been ready to receive him again as a little child.

The compassion of the Christ toward those who had lost their innocence was apparent in his lamentation "O Jerusalem, Jerusalem, thou that killest the prophets, and stonest them which are sent unto thee, how often would I have gathered thy children together, even as a hen gathereth her chickens under her wings, and ye would not!"[3] We come, therefore, before the court of innocence, and we plead for a communication to humanity of the flames of purity, truth, and cosmic innocence.

Among the greatest misconceptions that have ever been formed in the minds of men is that which concerns the nature of spiritual realms. Men either think that heaven is remote, unfulfilling, and lacking in the joys of this world, or they imagine that it is the ultimate goal—the reward of the faithful and their relief from the oppressions of a world of sin, a place where they will have nothing further to do and all progress will cease.

In both cases the fallacy is in thinking that the future will bring man something that is not available to him today. Life is abundant—here, now, and forever. Wherever you are, it needs only to be tapped.

May I say, then, that I have walked and talked with the elder gods of the race. I have met with the greatest interplanetary Masters, cosmic and angelic beings. I have attended ceremonies in the grand halls of the retreats and strolled the cosmic highways. In short, I have had the most wondrous experiences since my ascension, and with me still is the memory of all of my earthly experiences prior to my ascension.

But none of these are worthy—even the highest of them—to be compared with the experiences I have had in the mind of the Divine Manchild. Thus should the alchemist realize that neither heaven nor earth can give him that which he has not already found within himself.

Truly, "eye hath not seen, nor ear heard, neither have entered into the heart of man, the things which God hath prepared for them that love him."[4] What a pity that more cannot shed this false sense of a far-off and future good! The secrets of life are to be found here below as above. The changing of base metals into gold would produce only earthly beauty and earthly wealth. But the changing of the base nature of man into the refined gold of the Spirit enables him not only to master the world of the Spirit, but also to take dominion over the material world.

If all power in heaven and earth is given unto me,[5] then I can give it to whomsoever I will. Yet would I will to give it to those who would abuse and misuse it to the hurt and harm of their brothers?

Why was the flaming sword placed at the east of Eden?[6] Why was the continuity of existence interrupted by death? Why did illness, warfare, and brutality flash forth and take hold in human consciousness? Why was anger sustained? Was it not because people have been afraid of loss—loss of self-respect, loss of individuality, loss of relativity? Actually, what have they to lose? Nothing but their fears, nothing but their negatives. For that which is tethered to reality can never be lost.

Let men learn to empty themselves completely of their attachments to the earth; so shall they begin to enter into the childlike mind and spirit of creative innocence. The greatest angels who keep the way of the Tree of Life cannot deny those who have reunited with the wholly innocent mind of God access to Eden. How can they, then, deny it to the Divine Alchemist in man, who in honor reaches forth to take the fruit of the Tree of Life that he may indeed live forever?

The meaning of the allegory is quite simple. So long as man lives according to the "earth, earthy," according to the concepts of "flesh and blood," he cannot inherit the kingdom of heaven,[7] he cannot sustain the heavenly consciousness. But when in childlike innocence he enters into the divine domain, he finds that all of the universe is his—for now he belongs to all of the universe.

This sweet surrender to the mighty currents of cosmic law and purity shows him the need to transfer from the higher octaves of light into the lower ramifications of self the power and the glory, the victory and the overcoming, the transmittal and the transmutation.

He must shed the glitter and the glamour; he must replace it by light and purity and do all things well. He must seek for the spirit of excellence; he must forget limitations and all things that are behind. He must have faith in that which he cannot yet see and know that Nature herself holds a cornucopia of loveliness and light waiting to be showered upon him when the magic word is spoken.

How beautiful then is the cloud—the cloud of witness. But how important are harmlessness and simplicity. How towering is faith! How gentle! Sweet yet mighty is the faith that moves mountains.

Because we are approaching a time of greater discovery, I have carefully prepared the mind and consciousness of the students for the most beautiful experiences in the world, but I have not kept them confined to the domain of temporal life. I am creating in you states of inner awareness that will assist you in evolving spiritually, whereby, even if the body were shed, the mind of the Holy Spirit would flow through you and teach you the way of the Christ, the way of the Helper, the way of innocence, and the way of happiness.

Humanity are bored, they are frustrated, they are ungentle. Through what you would call the "hoopla" of life, they have taken on the phoniness that the dark powers have created, spread abroad, and popularized as worldly sophistication— the antithesis of the childlike consciousness. "Ye are the salt of the earth: but if the salt have lost his savour, wherewith shall it be salted?"[8] We reiterate the Master's statement because it reminds us that the essential flavor of living is in the cultivation of the inner sense of beauty and reality.

That which you receive from God is never denied to anyone; they only deny it to themselves in their ignorance. We all have a responsibility to encourage the light to expand in all people, but each one must open the door for himself. Each one must enter into the realization that the Divine Redeemer is the Divine Creator and that since man's descent into the lower octaves of human consciousness, the Lord of Light has continued to emanate his radiance everywhere.

He is available yet hidden.
He is real, yet cloaked with unrealities
By the minds of men and their life experiences.
He is light sometimes covered over
With the darkness of men's misqualifications.
He is the Great Supplier
Of every good and perfect thing.
He combines the green shoot and the crystal
    snow.
He combines the ethereal in the sky that glows
With fiery sun from solar center.
His loving heart bids all to enter:
"Take upon you, precious child,
Garments of mastery, meek and mild.
Dominion need not bluster,

Yet dominion e'er shall muster
Each required grace
To help the world keep pace
With cosmic legions when facing senile
   moments.[9]
Youth and light appear when facing time's
   election.
Shed, then, all your fears and glow,
Eternal fires of youthful cosmic innocence!"[10]

    On the brink of discovery, we remain your
faithful teachers of light and divine alchemy.

Saint Germain

✠

CHAPTER II

The Highest Alchemy

The sense of reality and the sense of delight with which the student aspiring to create concentrates upon the cloud determines its efficacy. In alchemy, as in all things, doubt and negation destroy; faith and happiness sustain.

Man must come to recognize that space and time are necessary subdivisions of one sole reality, that the limitations which they embody, providing necessary boundaries, can become ladders to boundlessness and a veritable means whereby any electron in space can become a universe or the universe can become any electron. The drawing-in of the sustaining breath of the Holy Spirit and the expelling thereof creates an eddying of consciousness in concentric, rapidly moving rings expanding out to the farthest periphery of manifestation.

The finite mind may find it difficult at first to grasp this principle. To make it easier, let us explain that the consciousness of God that sustains the universe is also within man. Now, if the consciousness of God that sustains the universe is within man, is it unreasonable to suppose that man can also be within the consciousness that sustains the universe?

In the macrocosmic-microcosmic interchange, in the great flow of life, of delight, of boundless joy, man senses the unity of all that lives; and he recognizes that his role as a receiver of benefits from the universe entails the necessary conveyance of benefits from his own creative consciousness back into the universe. There is joy in the construction of the temple of life, for templed order and templed service create in the individual a sense of building when all around him there is a tearing down of values, morals, and faith. But in the temple he finds his constructive role midst the roles of destructivity men have elected for themselves.

Many say, "Let us destruct that we may construct." Let them remember that before they can construct wisely and rightly, all destructive tendencies must be removed from their consciousness; for creative law, as it expands the reality of God into the framework of the natural order, automatically wipes out their imperfect images.

There is no need to hold in consciousness a destructive sense or even a sense of condemnation. Beloved Jesus said, "For God sent not his Son into the world to condemn the world, but that the world through him might be saved."[1] The secret of the Tree of Life is to be found, but the seeker must first surrender his personal sense, his sense of separation from God and from life, so that the universal consciousness can flow into him. Thus the breath of the Great Alchemist shall become his own.

It is not, then, the personal "I" that doeth the work, but the Father in me that worketh hitherto, and I work.[2] The Father that worketh hitherto is the creative effort of the universe that enhances the vision of life's perfection for an onward-moving humanity. The "I" that works is the conscious individuality yoked with the I AM Presence of universal Reality. It is the Son working with the All-Father to produce in and for every man the summation of the glory we knew together before the world was.

If imperfect manifestations defraud the functions of cosmic law, then let it also be remembered that Spirit enhances the quality of life. Through the beautiful bonus of man's acceptance of the reality and the flow of life, he becomes wholly identified with the formless Spirit. He is then able in the form manifestation to create a relative perfection as Above, so below.

As the great Master admonished his disciples, "Be ye therefore perfect, even as your Father which is in heaven is perfect,"[3] so we would disabuse the minds of the would-be alchemists of the idea that form cannot be perfected within a relative framework.

While we acknowledge that according to the patterns of evolution, forms and ideas do transcend themselves in life's great cosmic ongoing, we also see that within a transcendental universe scientists have been able to perfect their methods and inventions through the historical epochs. Thus the dispensations of science have been ordained in the hopes that in relieving mankind of their drudgery, they would use their free time and energy to develop the Christ consciousness that overshadows and transcends the mortal mind and being of man.

The Great White Brotherhood is aware of how destructive trends in music and art can exert enormous influence on young minds. Many of the youth of today have no standard by which to judge that which is fed to them, simply because from early years they have been enmeshed in a web of darkness which seems to them to be a creation of light.

It becomes difficult, then, to extend the wings of the Spirit to these young souls, for the human intellect inciting their rebellious egos has convinced them that free form and the absence of all restrictions is the means through which they will achieve self-realization.

Nothing could be further from the truth, for self-discipline is the requirement of the hour. But these untamed souls would not surrender their human will for anything or anyone, and so it is easy for the prince of darkness to find disciples from among those who have been subverted from their earliest years.

The highest alchemy is the precipitation of the Christ consciousness, and all to whom the breath of life has been given have a solemn obligation to pass on the precepts of holy wisdom before passing the torch of responsibility to the next generation. The ancient proverb "Train up a child in the way he should go: and when he is old, he will not depart from it" becomes, then, life's injunction to all humanity. Seeking a means of improving the strain and the quality of life, they should consider and reconsider its mandates until they are effectively interwoven into the whole structure of striving toward the future.

Immorality, greed, selfishness, and dishonor have never provided for any age any recompense except the destruction of the spirals of the future. Only light can rise, whether in civilization or in individual man. Only light has the power to endow our cloud with the understanding that it is our own future, woven today from the controlled energies of our beings and determinedly endowed with our highest vision and our richest faith, that will produce the fruit of givingness to the universe in the highest creative God-quality.

As I prepare you for more advanced efforts made on your behalf and on behalf of humanity, it is essential that I endow you to the best of my ability through spiritual means with the vision of what God is. Even in our higher octaves, it is impossible for us who are yet in a lesser individualized state to realize the fullness of who and what the Greatest Alchemist is. But we can approach the Holy of Holies; we can draw nigh by transcending ourselves even as he is ever transcending himself, being changed from glory unto glory by the one universal Spirit.

We are never bored and never tired by the changeless effort to change, for we are aware that with each step we take, an infinite leap occurs in the highness of us all. God identifies so beautifully with every part of life that there is a gladness in all creation when the Higher Self makes the giant leap. In the words of the Christ to his disciples of old, "I go before you into Jerusalem."[4]

The City of God, the City of Peace, the cosmic parliament of man—these are the outgrowth of the Father's love, of the idea of the Great Transcendentalist, of the Eternal Alchemist, the Great Spirit, God the Father, Christ the King. He who brings down the mountains and raises the valleys, he who puts down the mighty from their seats and exalts them of low degree,[5] does all things in order to produce the *summum bonum* of ultimate reality for every part of life.

His givingness is beyond reproach, and if his precepts had been heeded in any age by any society, the thorns of that age would have been blunted and broken. The fragrances of the rose would have surrounded the age. The highest

learning, culture, and beauty would have manifested. Pain and suffering would have ended in a
relative sense and, through understanding, the
golden arch would have been seen by all within
the scope of their immediate realization. The
golden door would have ope'd wide, and the
heart of purpose would have been perceived behind it all.

Nature and nature's God conspire to produce universes worlds without end, the great
diurnal magnetism, the universal endowment
that, as male and female, as positive and negative,
as Spirit and Mater, are designed to produce the
wonder of life. Its glaring and awesome beauty
may be everywhere, but to some it is a garish
movement from which they shrink. To others it is
a universal hymn of purpose.

But to those of us who love nothing more
dearly than to guide humanity by word and
deed, it is the opportunity of the eternal Buddha,
the opening bud of the flower of joyous reality
whose fragrance is everywhere. It permeates the
quality of life; it removes the odors of darkness;
it encompasses all. It reveals the meaning and
purpose of love that in sacrificing itself is reborn. What more shall I say as we stand on the
threshold?

I say, I kindle a blaze within your being. Be
the flame tiny or great, may it ever expand and
help you to make for yourself and for the glory
of the Great Alchemist a life full of interest in

taking dominion and in being one with the Great Exemplar.

Oh, let us love together! Let us be together, and let us see together the far-off movement that yearns to draw nigh.

Graciously, I remain

Saint Germain

✠

CHAPTER 12

The Way of
the Tree of Life

The fervor we seek to convey can be assimilated. The fire of our mind and spirit can be absorbed through a simple reading and application of the consciousness, of the heart. We know that man can inductively enter into a higher state. The sincere reading and rereading of our words until they become a very part of the consciousness of the disciple-aspirant can and does create in him a key by which his own alchemical expertise is developed.

So much interest has developed in many of you concerning the creation of the cloud that I wish to expound still further upon it.

The cloud is the means whereby man alters his destiny. I do not say that there are not other methods that can effectively achieve this purpose. Each karmic act has its own recompense. Each deed that men do, each thought that they think makes its imprint upon their lives. But many of these are negatively qualified, hence destructively manifest. They come haphazardly through experiences which men do not govern;

for when men do not govern their worlds, they are governed by the circumstances of the world.

Through the creation of the cloud, then, we seek to transcend time, space, and even karma—short-circuiting many of the old spirals, shortening the time of man's realization of his own God-reality,[1] and helping him to realize in an avant-garde manner the graciousness of the Lord of the Universe.

There are many schools of the Brotherhood. There are many methods of achieving. In our releases through The Summit Lighthouse, we seek to assist our students in expanding their consciousness with facility. We seek to weld together the body of God upon earth by first creating the understanding of both the beauty and the practicality of true alchemy. We are not interested in forming a society of magicians who will go around producing seeming miracles—albeit we acknowledge that the proficient alchemist, even through this course, can do just that.

What we are interested in is the subscribing of our students to a universal brotherhood and body already existing spiritually as the Great White Brotherhood. Being in the invisible, this order, comprising the alchemists of the Spirit, requires a union with embodied humanity. For only through this association can we formulate the most beautiful, sustaining concepts that will enable the entire house of the world to breathe the air of freedom and to be infused with the fires of destiny in its individual and collective aspects.

Man must see and know that as he is and as he does, so others see and do. Thus, in perception and in action, man can endow the pages of history with a revelatory illumination, thereby fulfilling the fiats of God "Take dominion over the earth!" and "Set the example for the age!" With each act of grace, man becomes endowed with more grace. Each step of self-mastery raises him higher in the cosmic peerage, until he is crowned at last through the eternal mysteries with the full realization of his own potential.

Our cloud, then, in answer to some of your questions, can become physically tangible. It need not be so in order to endow you with the highest graces. Through the cloud you can draw to yourselves God's holy witnesses that have lived in all generations, that have called him blessed, that he has blessed.

You can be freed through the light and fire of the cloud from the mediocrity of the present age and from the degradations of past ages and their cumulative effects upon the human psyche. You can, as it were, rend the veil of the Holy of Holies if your purpose be communion with the Most High, as was Moses' in the Sinai Desert. You can realize through the cloud the full perfection of your glorious I AM Presence.

Then through your contact with the I AM Presence, the Presence of all being, you can develop a culture of the Spirit at lower levels that will provide stairways of safety upon which others may climb. There is never any need, regardless of what outer manifestations or vile astral energies may seek entrance to your world, to yield to these depredations. You have the power of the Christ to cast out unwanted states of consciousness.[2]

The Great Alchemist lives within you. You live within him. Therefore, through your conscious experimentations with the cloud, you can surround yourself with the means of producing change.

In our examinations of those who through the ages have worked with the cloud, we have taken note that those who have been convinced of the reality of the cloud, those who have dared to endow their consciousness and being with the very qualities of the cloud itself, have become more and more efficient in its use. For them each daily experiment in creating change has become easier.

I hope that I have conveyed to you in this intermediate course the ideas I have sought to convey. Please understand, however, that the full power and glory can only unfold within the concepts of the total course.

It is my hope, as it was to create this series when I first produced *Studies in Alchemy*, to one day produce for you *Advanced Studies in Alchemy*. We shall then be able to offer humanity a beautiful trilogy—the first section laying the groundwork of ideas[3] through the golden flame of illumination, the second herein pronouncing the love ray that through the cloud of the Holy Spirit endows your ideas with life, and the third section explaining how to make permanent that which you create through the power of the spoken Word.

This trilogy will be especially valuable to those who are not only concerned with "magick," but who also recognize that alchemy is the means of renewing youth, first in the inward parts of man and then throughout his entire consciousness and manifestation. And if this be accomplished, it cannot help but be the means of enhancing individual and world thought.

Now as you ponder the correct experiment for your efforts in alchemy, remember that the stereotypes that abound in the world are not all ugly. In fact, there are many historical and cultural literary masterpieces that embody divine stereotypes, or archetypes as we would call them. It is not necessary for the student in his alchemical experiments to shun all that appears to be of the ordinary. In many cases, rather than ferret out the commonplace, it is more important that you avoid the classification of a condition as trite, for in reality it may be a great idea.

Do not fear to embrace beautiful thoughts because someone else thought of them first. The time will come when you will develop a greater uniqueness. But until you become more proficient with your experiments, it is more important that you go upon a safe highway—that is, if speed combined with exactitude be your desire.

There comes a time when man passes beyond the pale of that which his own experience patterns can teach him. Then the immortals stand ready, even as they do while he is still learning the lessons of earth, to help him expand in every facet of his endeavors, whether human or divine. Progress is never governed as much by what man desires to do or to be, or even by what the world has to offer, as it is by his realization that he can be all that God wants him to be, if he will just accept that simple thought.

Seek not, then, the bizarre; rather be content to be a good man or a good woman. Place yourself in the hands of God, in the hands of the Father of all, who cares for the birds of the air and the fragile flowers that glow for the breath of a moment.

Do you not think that he cares more for you than for the grass of the field that withereth away—he who esteems you enough to give you his consciousness, to create for you a universe, a universal Mother, Nature herself, and to impregnate that Nature with the fires of his own Spirit—all for you, all for you? Yet man is as the grass of the field[4] when he esteems himself so to be, when in mediocrity, selfishness, deceit, and a sense of personal struggle, he strives only for outer recognition.

Let men seek not to be thought great of other men, but to recognize internally the greatness of God that is inherent in all of Life's manifestations. Then their alchemy will hold within it the alchemy of becoming perfected.

I do not say there are not other great mysteries waiting to be revealed in connection with alchemy. I know that there are. I do say that

> The way of the Tree of Life
> Which is the perfect secret
> That God has guarded from the curious
>   and profane
> Remains a penetrable mystery
> To him who is not ashamed
> To wear his wings,
> To him who understands
> The diligence of each day,
> To him who is content to place his hand
> In loving trust that destiny is ours,
> To him who is willing to forsake
> A past that has not produced
> The blossoming beauty he craves,
> To him whose heart reaches up as a cup
> To the highest and sweetest,
> The noblest and best Lord of all
> In the desire to have imparted to himself
> And every part of life
> The best of gifts.
> He speaks in summoned, loving tones
> Of inward communion,
> "O Father, not my will but thine be done!"
> To him there is conveyed the highest crown,
> The word "dominion."

He is the Son, the Alchemist,
The beloved one.
He can divide the loaves and fishes,[5]
Walk upon the waves,[6]
Fulfill his own and others' wishes,
And be the Great Benefactor.
In him the Immortal Spirit prevails,
The ultima Thule is seen.

I sign myself sincerely, your immortal friend,

Saint Germain

Jesus Christ and Saint Germain

Wayshowers of the Aquarian Age

The Ascended Masters Jesus Christ and Saint Germain, passing the torch of the Christ consciousness and the I AM THAT I AM for the Piscean and Aquarian dispensations, stand in the long history of earth and her evolutions as great deliverers of the nations by freedom's fires—and salvation through the resurrection of the soul.

The path of initiation that leads to the soul's reunion with the I AM Presence (the ascension) through the mediator, the Christ Self—the open door to Divine Reality which no man can shut—is exemplified in Jesus, the Piscean Wayshower. The Saviour's fiery baptism of the Holy Ghost is revealed through the Aquarian Master Saint Germain as he delivers to the people of God the dispensation of the seventh age and the seventh ray—the Comforter's all-forgiving violet flame and its application in the balancing of personal and planetary karma through the science of the spoken Word.

Saint Germain is the "voice of the seventh angel" prophesied in Revelation 10:7 who comes to finish the mystery of God "as He hath declared to His servants the prophets." In the eleventh century B.C., he was embodied as Samuel, prophet-priest of the LORD raised up from childhood to be the anointer of kings and judge over Israel. As the sponsor, affectionately called "Uncle Sam," of the United States of America, he is calling the twelve tribes from the four corners of the earth, making known to them their true identity as the light-bearers commissioned to serve with the Ancient of Days[1] to set earth's captives free.

Saint Germain brings to those lost sheep (re-incarnated souls) of the house of Israel the remembrance of the name of the LORD God—I AM THAT I AM.[2] Moreover, he teaches them the power of this lost Word which was given to Moses and the prophets and was also prominent in the Galilean mission of Jesus. Of this Word that was truly made flesh in Jesus, John the Beloved says, "That was the true Light which lighteth *every* man that cometh into the world."[3]

Thanks to the Teachings of Jesus Christ and Saint Germain you, too, can know the LORD through your Christ Self, who is your Real Self prophesied by Jeremiah as THE LORD OUR RIGHTEOUSNESS and by Zechariah as The BRANCH. By this Presence within, every man shall know the LORD (the Word) as he sits in meditation, as Micah observed, under his own vine (Holy Christ Self) and fig tree (the Mighty I AM Presence and causal body).[4]

Jesus Christ and Saint Germain—together with all of the heavenly hosts: Ascended Masters,

Elohim, archangels, angels and servant-sons of God, who comprise the Spirit of the Great White Brotherhood (the multitude of saints robed in white witnessed by Saint John [5])—have come forth from the inner Mystery School at the end of Pisces and the beginning of Aquarius to teach us how to call upon this name of the LORD, alchemical formulas whereby we may put on our individual Christhood even while we overcome personified evil and the *energy veil* of our negative karma, the so-called sins of our past lives.

By the law of transmutation, calling forth God's consuming violet fire in the name of the I AM Presence, students of the Ascended Masters' Teachings all over the world are resolving relationships, transmuting the records of their karma, removing the stain of mortality in the psyche and getting the victory over the 'beast' of the idolatrous self.

This great overcoming of Darkness by Light in the individual encounter with the forces of Armageddon was prophesied by Jesus Christ to his disciple John as he wrote in Revelation 12:11: *And they*—the true saints of East and West—*overcame him by the blood of the Lamb and by the word of their testimony.*

The blood of the Lamb is the essence, or "Spirit," of the Cosmic Christ, His Person and His Teaching, both of which have been withheld from the people for thousands of years by false Christs and gurus, false pastors and prophets—

impostors in every field of endeavor, Church and State and in the governments and economies of the nations. Now, through the Ascended Masters and their Messengers, the knowledge of the LORD and the divine mysteries held in the retreats of the Great White Brotherhood until the appointed time are being brought forth for all to see and know the Truth that shall make them free.[6]

The word of their testimony is their witness unto the Beloved I AM Presence—our God with us—and their exercise through Him of the science of the spoken Word whereby in prayer, meditation, dynamic decrees, and communion with the LORD, His sons and daughters become the effective instruments of the Universal Christ and His sacred labor.

These are they which have the testimony of Jesus Christ,[7] brought to our remembrance by the Holy Spirit in the dictations of the Ascended Masters to the Messengers. The prayers, mantras, and decrees which emanate from the Word—even the sacred AUM (OM), the universal sound and syllable of the Divine Mother—spoken under the dispensation of the Ascended Masters by their unascended disciples, are the means whereby the lightbearers overcome the world tyranny and idolatrous cult of the archdeceivers of mankind (fallen angels embodied in our midst) in these final hours of the twentieth century.

This Great Overcoming following the "Great Tribulation" is decreed by Almighty God as is the coming of the Ascended Masters and their delivery of the Everlasting Gospel to the lightbearers of "every nation and kindred and tongue and people."[8] It is the Teaching of Jesus Christ and Saint Germain that we must make every divine decree, prophecy, and scriptural covenant of the LORD our own and then stand fast to behold the salvation of our God.

As the deliverers of Jew and Christian, Moslem, Hindu and Buddhist, Zoroastrian and Confucian—and the striving ones whose sacred labor is their religion in the Godhead—Jesus Christ and Saint Germain proclaim the Messiah already come in the Person of each one's Holy Christ Self, whose seat of consciousness and authority in the children of God is vested in the threefold flame, divine spark of the Trinity, sealed in the secret chamber of the heart.

Jesus, the Son of man who embodied this nonexclusive/all-inclusive Light of the Son of God, came to teach us the way of the Christ incarnate not in himself alone but as the inheritance of every son and daughter of God. Thus our brother, friend and true saviour of our souls from Death and Hell fulfilled the law and the prophets[9] whose path unfolded the progressive empowerment by the selfsame Word which reached its culmination in the resurrection and ascension of our Lord and all who have followed him on the path of soul regeneration.

In Truth, and in the true science of the religion he taught, all mankind can and shall declare with the blessed Son of God, "I AM—*God in me is*—the Way, the Truth, and the Life," [10] and understand that it is the I AM THAT I AM, the LORD God dwelling in them, who is, was, and forevermore shall be the Way, the Truth, and the Life.

The likenesses of Jesus and Saint Germain were painted by Charles Sindelar, famous American artist and illustrator of the 1920s and '30s. Jesus Christ appeared to the artist on twenty-two consecutive mornings at 2:00 a.m., and the image of the Master would appear throughout the day over both canvas and etching plate, distracting him from his work until he took the advice of a friend to "paint what you have seen."

After five days of continuous work, the portrait was completed. Charles Sindelar was not satisfied with his rendering of the mouth and therefore on the fifth night at 2:00 a.m., Jesus returned until the artist had perfected on canvas the likeness of his Master who stood before him.

The Messengers testify that the portrait of Jesus is the exact likeness of the Master as he has appeared to them both in the retreats of the Brotherhood, in their homes, and on the platform during dictations. They have confirmed that the portrait of Jesus depicts him as he appeared at the

THE ASCENDED MASTER JESUS CHRIST

THE ASCENDED MASTER SAINT GERMAIN

Royal Teton Retreat "in consultation with Saint Germain and the tall Master from Venus."

A number of years after the painting of Jesus was completed, Saint Germain appeared to Charles Sindelar in the presence of Guy Ballard, and the artist completed the portrait as the Messenger served as the anchor point to sustain the forcefield and the Electronic Presence of Saint Germain. Again the Messengers have stated that this likeness of Saint Germain is indeed that of the Ascended Master who is their sponsor and the sponsor of America and every nation on earth.

He has been known to devotees of freedom on the planet earth for over seventy thousand years, and his great love and sacrifice has enabled the evolutions of earth to have the use of the violet flame for the transmutation of all misqualified energies of the human consciousness which stand between the soul and its salvation, *Self-elevation*, through the Christ personified in Jesus, the Saviour, the fullness of the Word incarnate.

The Ascended Masters Jesus Christ and Saint Germain have given their life and their likenesses in these paintings as a glad, free gift for the salvation of earth and her evolutions and "that the earth may be filled with the knowledge of the glory of the LORD (the I AM Presence) as the waters cover the sea."[11] Neither the Masters nor their portraits can be confined to any creed, religion, doctrine, or dogma, nor can their names be invoked for the sealing of anyone's private interpretation of the law or the scriptures.

These blessed Ascended Masters are the intimate friend, guide, teacher, counselor, and comforter on the way of life, walking hand in hand with the lightbearers in this age. All who will call upon them in the name of the I AM THAT I AM will be blessed with an immediate manifestation of their Electronic Presence—the fullness of their tangible light body focalized in time and space within the aura of their disciple.

The devotee may visualize himself with his right hand in the hand of Jesus and his left in the hand of Saint Germain. Calling upon these great wayshowers of the twelve tribes of Israel, the devotee of Truth may know with the certainty of cosmic law, whereby the Call does compel the answer, that these Ascended Masters will never leave him as long as he remains obedient to the principles and practice of Truth, Life, and Love, to the Law of the One, and to the inner God Flame, the I AM THAT I AM.

THE THREEFOLD FLAME OF LIFE

Book Three

A Trilogy

On the
Threefold Flame
of Life

The Alchemy
of Power, Wisdom
and Love

Saint Germain

And now abideth Faith, Hope, Charity,
these three; but the greatest of these is Charity.

CHAPTER I

Power

Gracious Men and Women,

Persistency is recognized as a quality which eventuates in the manifestation of some aspect of perfection. The courage which men externalize by holding fast to a specific momentum in the face of every attempt to prevent its manifestation is a thing of beauty, a joy to every heart, and most wondrous to behold.

The very thought of Power in itself brings delight to the hearts of men. The Power of the universe depicted in the heavens tells men of that seemingly far-off aspect of God for which their souls hunger but unto which it appears impossible to draw nigh. Hope, together with the element of faith, has enabled men to release some degree of Power into their worlds and to subject it to their control.

A. *Power Defined*

Now, Power has taken many forms: abuses have marred its use, whereas virtue has enhanced it. Tyrants have exploited it, and politics and religion have been molded around the star of Power blazing in the firmament of society.

The primary types of Power are physical, mental, emotional, and spiritual energy in various forms. There is electrical, chemical, nuclear, elemental, and cosmic power; and there is temporal power, consisting of social influences and mass pressures, governmental and religious authority. Meanwhile, karmic power affects everyone's status, attainment, and progress.

All Power is interrelated: some is stored, some is static, some is dynamic and subject to a rapid decay rate. All Power is subject to two primary qualifications under the classification of relativity: divine and human, or cosmic-universal and material-transitory.

The Maltese cross, emblem of my dedication to the cause of freedom, is a balanced thoughtform which may be used to illustrate the qualifications of Power. As many realize, a cross symbolizes the meeting of two planes of consciousness—the horizontal bar representing the plane of the human consciousness, the plane of the ego, and the vertical bar representing the energies of God descending from the realm of Spirit into the quadrants of Matter.

The center where the two lines intersect is the point (orifice) where the energies of heaven are released to the earth; and in truth, it is at this point—which is actually the point of the qualification of Power—that great alertness must be maintained by all who use Power in its many aspects, including its organic and inorganic forms.

The Power of speech itself—the Power in the spoken word and the Power of the Word, whether released by pen or edict of sword—changes the course of history and alters the lives of those affected by its release. Whatever its subsequent use or abuse, the tangled threads of Power have always flowed, symbolically and actually, from the orifice of the cross.

The Maltese cross is a symbol of perfect balance—both in the alignment of the four planes of Matter (and the four cosmic forces thereof) and in the inner and outer expression of God's Spirit within the souls of his own.

As such, the Maltese cross illustrates the drawing forth of Light's energy and consciousness from on high (through the north arm) for the manifestation in the world of form of God's omnipotence, omniscience and omnipresence (through the west, south and east arms respectively). And, as we shall soon see, in this cosmic interchange between God and man the Universal Light is beamed forth "as Above, so below" to the right, to the left and in the center in a perfect equilibrium of Power, Wisdom and Love.

Blessed ones, it is easy to complicate that which is simple, but it is often most difficult to simplify that which is really complicated. This I shall attempt to do for you in this study. Bear in mind that when a child first begins the study of arithmetic, he is dealing with simple sums and the concrete; in his world of counting things he can little conceive of the intricate threads of logarithms and abstract equations.

Man should, then, realize that the perfectionment of the soul in God must take into account the training of the child-man and the fact that so-called cradles of 'negation' (e.g., compartments in the world of form) have been created as classrooms or schools of soul testing where transmutation and noble changes can be effected that will result in an expansion of the flame of freedom, raising every son of liberty into the totality of his identity and divine manhood.

In simplifying the understanding concerning the release of Power, it will be shown that the bodies of man, four by definition, are receptacles of that Power. Thus his physical, mental, emotional and etheric 'sheaths of consciousness' are recipients of the charge of Power that is released through the electronic pattern of the Maltese cross.

For the purposes of this study, it is best that we consider the dawn, the beginning of each day, as the arbitrary point of origin for Power's release, when self-conscious awareness once again floods the altar of individuality and men begin again to think and to perceive. For this, too, is an employment of Power, but one which is often abused by neglect.

Few today are aware of the degree of Power which God has conferred upon man through the gift of consciousness. Few are aware that they possess the Power of focalization and intensification in the proper exercise of their attention through individual consciousness; nor do they realize that the interpretive and discriminatory action of the God Self enables them to take firm hold of the reins of Power, to be in control of their lives, and to be less distracted by the social and karmic responsibilities that are daily thrust upon them.

B. *Self-Dominion, Your Reins of Power*

The statement made of old "He that is slow to anger is better than the mighty; and he that ruleth his spirit than he that taketh a city"[1] should be understood. Were it so, more adepts and masters would arise in every generation to take the reins of dominion over themselves and their worlds.

It is an act of utter compassion for universal Law and for universal Love for you to obtain dominion over the finite self. When this happens in your life, and happen it shall as the Law is made known, you will realize that you cannot remain a novice and still be a master. Although you live in the plane of the human consciousness, you must not be subject to its depredations.

Inasmuch as the world is filled with idle minds, and "idling minds," even when housed in a dedicated consciousness, are often tools of the sinister force ("the devil's workshop," as they say), it behooves the student of deeper Truth to recognize that he alone can and must govern his own world through the right use of Power.

In this sphere of cosmic coexistence, where the energies of the macrocosm and the microcosm flow as one, there is a daily release of great Power from the Godhead and a subsequent abuse of that Power by mankind. Some men watch the abuses of others and then respond with an equal or greater abuse of Power; thus they gauge their power train according to the qualifications of Power by individuals and society. This is not action, but reaction.

Others, sometimes consciously and deliberately and at times thoughtlessly or unconsciously, generate discordant thoughtforms and auric emanations from their beings through the triggering action of bad habits and momentums. I would like to list some of these abuses of Power in order that you might perceive how people become the unwitting tools of subtle qualities of negation and how they take in, amplify, and discharge this noxious substance into the planetary atmosphere.

First there is boredom, an indifferent state of mind wherein all seems quite profitless to the individual who cannot see beyond the vanity of this world to the reality of the next. In this disenfranchising state, akin to a vacuum, men denude their souls of vitality.

Then there is dissatisfaction, in which men assess their own progress or lack of it and, by dishonesty in self, or self-deceit, are unwilling to admit their role in fashioning their own weaknesses. Instead, they effect a transfer of responsibility to others, assigning them the blame for their own failures or lack of progress. Often carried on at subconscious levels, this ruse of the carnal mind remains the primary cause of personal stagnation.

Then, too, there are numerous types of fear. One of its most devastating forms which I desire to call to your attention is that which even the sincere sometimes attribute to the Godhead—given men's propensity to fashion their gods after themselves. It is the altogether human quality of whimsy, which stems from a deep-seated insecurity.

Although they themselves have a whimsical nature, they cannot bear the thought of being subject to a whimsical God. Therefore they conclude—for dark and unclear reasons unknown even to themselves—that their lifestreams are not in favor with the universe and that they must withdraw ·therefrom. In this anxious frame of mind they may tend toward aggressive forms of rebellion or their attitude may become one of servility, wherein they easily tolerate feelings of lethargy, depression, and hopelessness.

There is the vibration of doubt which we would also touch upon. Doubt stems from fear and from a lack of real self-knowledge, while self-doubt, as lurking suspicion, colors one's doubts of everyone else. Some, who believe themselves to be fearless and in possession of greater knowledge than they in fact have, may not accept the statement I am making. Nevertheless, I shall affirm its truth; and when in the Light of greater understanding men will have dispelled their own self-ignorance, their doubts, too, will fly out the window.

But men must allow themselves time enough to achieve this. As the Master said, "In your patience possess ye your souls."[2]

Now, there are many other traits and influences that we could go into here, but I do not choose to prolong the enumeration of negatives to which mankind are host. Rather, I would point out, on the basis of a thorough analysis of those I have listed, that mankind's abuses of Power are created primarily as a result of their ignorance and misunderstanding of the laws governing the flow and use of energy.

Moreover, to the great masses inhabiting the planet, from whom even a rudimentary knowledge of the science of karma has been withheld, it is somewhat difficult to explain the cycles of reincarnation that predestine the return of abused Power to the one who has misused it.

The horror with which some who profess to be religious view any doctrine that is not approved by the church of their fathers is a millstone about their necks. How unfortunate! For if they are to be free from the shackles of an ancient dogma, they must open wide the doors of their minds, without fear and without prejudice.

C. *Oneness of Life, Four Lower Bodies*

Now, it must be understood with cherishment that all Life is one, and that an abuse of Power on the part of any member of the world body has its effect upon all. But by a like token, the correct use of Power by anyone upon the planet brings its blessing to all.

Power is energy. Energy stored in the physical body can be measured as the sum total of the energy content of all of the body cells. When this energy is spent, it becomes necessary to in some way reinfuse the cells with energy in order to renew the Power of the body.

To infuse the body cells with new and vital energy when those cells are already clogged with accumulations of negatively qualified substance (residual deposits of Power misused through wrong thought and feeling) is to partially negate the flow of energy in the body. This can cause fatigue, or a loss of Power, which, if unchecked, eventually results in so-called death—the cessation of the flow of Power from the Presence to the physical form.

Consider the value of flushing out these accumulations by spiritual electronics! And then gradually building up the Light in the four lower bodies by the fourfold alchemy of the Maltese cross—and the science of the spoken Word!

Thus it is most necessary to understand the relationship of the four lower bodies as you pursue the rebuilding of the temple of man as a wise masterbuilder.

The mental body interpenetrates the physical body as water interpenetrates a sponge. Having its own reservoir of Power, it is not dependent upon the physical body except as the focal point for the flow and distribution of Power. Yet, the four lower bodies of man are so interrelated that if the mental body is to operate at optimum efficiency, the other three must be in perfect alignment with it and with each other.

The densities that the mental body encounters in the physical body—such as the harmful residue of nicotine, drugs, and impure food, or even the substance of fear, doubt, and mental rebellion accumulated from past lives—clog the brain cells and imprison the light of the atom, effectively impeding the free flow of light to the physical consciousness and thereby impairing the function of the mental faculties.

When misused, the Power of the emotional body becomes the most violent and volatile of the four lower bodies. When agitated by undisciplined feelings, these emotional energies have a tendency to lead men astray in their thinking and in their actions.

The flow of Power to the mental body is also greatly subject to the Power of the etheric, or memory, body. In memory's storehouse, the writings of all past actions in present and previous embodiments stand as an electronic record of considerable weight and influence.

The Power of this record, together with the momentums generated by the misuse of energy, is a subtle pressure that affects the present moment for good or for ill (relatively speaking) unless it is brought under the control of the balancing Power of the great God flame within the heart—the immortal flame of Power, Wisdom and Love.

D. *The Maltese Cross*
Symbol of God-Controlled Power

The Maltese cross, symbol of the perfect balance of the God flame, "as in heaven, so on earth," provides a thought and energy matrix whereby the ill effects of personal and planetary karma can be brought under control and the Power of virtue released in their place, that mankind's use of Power might no longer corrupt life on earth.

It has been said that "power tends to corrupt and absolute power corrupts absolutely."[3] Power can be used as the bow of the Infinite Archer to release an arrow of perfection into the heart of man's goal of happiness. As the pursuit of happiness is an acknowledged treasure, let all who would permanently enjoy it ponder the Maltese cross as a simple thoughtform through which great truths may be revealed for the blessing of all.

Looking at the Maltese cross placed upright before us, we see that the four symmetrical arms extending from the center are triangular in shape, wide at the outside, giving the appearance of a fanning action.

The upper, or north, arm descending to the center resembles the upper vessel of an hourglass. Actually, it is a funnel through which the great energies of God—the Power of God—are descending into the cup (chalice) of being. The wide opening reminds us of the infinite energies of the Source and of God's ability to convey these to man. Therefore we know that we need not accept limitation in any form—whether in receiving or giving the limitless Light of cosmos.

The point of qualification at the center of the cross indicates that you must always consciously determine within your heart and mind to qualify your God-given energy with the purity of the divine intent and with the virtues of your Christ-identity. You need not be weak or weakened when confronted by waves of discordant energy—whether your own or another's. Nor is it necessary for you to be rude in your rebuttal of human error; for it is not the person, but the impersonal energy personally misdirected that must be challenged.

MALTESE CROSS:
FOCUS OF THE DISTRIBUTION OF ENERGY
FROM SPIRIT TO MATTER

Macrocosm—"Day Side of Life"

Energies of Spirit
descend through the

North Arm
White

Orifice
Nexus of conscious being
Point of qualification

As Above, so below

West or
Negative Arm
Power
Blue

East or
Positive Arm
Love
Pink

South Arm
Wisdom
Yellow

Energies of Spirit coalesce as Matter
through the
three lower arms

Microcosm—"Night Side of Life"

Left-Right
"Slingshot" Action

Therefore, establish yourself in a firm, un-yielding consciousness that rejects evil as the lie of man's misqualification; and as you breathe in the essence of the sacred fire, 'flower of Power', determine to strip that lie of its negative Power manifesting as thorns of abuse.

It must be recognized that when the energy-action descends from God to man through the upper arm, narrowing through the funnel to flow into the crucible of being at the point of the cross, it passes through the nexus and fans out into the three lower triangles to manifest as Power, Wisdom and Love in the world of material form.

Thus, the infinite energies of God are molded by the qualifications of man's attention focused at the heart of the cross—the seat of his conscious mind. By this means Power congeals in the physical world, taking the form of the thoughts, the feelings, the acts, and the spoken word of man, the release of its potential being entirely dependent upon the motivation and the will of his consciousness.

The balance between the upper arm, which receives the energies of Spirit; and the three lower arms, through which Spirit's energies coalesce both in and as Matter, provides for the balanced manifestation of God's Power "as Above, so be-low," from the planes of primary causation to the physical effect, as it is taught in the Hermetic science.

If man's qualification of his quotient of spiritual energy released over the crystal cord from the I AM Presence to the heart chakra were retained in purity from the moment it entered the crucible of his consciousness, all that is in manifestation in the microcosm would reflect the perfection of the macrocosm. Think of that!

The energies of the three lower arms, fanning out in a balanced action from the center of the Maltese cross, proceed, then, from the plane of pure Being into the form, or action, phase of the threefold flame. Power by itself (in the left arm) retains the negative polarity unless and until it is qualified with the positive polarity of divine Love (in the right arm). Ponder well this statement!

Now, the left arm of the cross denotes the negative, or minus, charge of spiritual energy qualified by the blue flame of Power. The right arm denotes the positive, or plus, charge qualified by the pink flame of Love. And the lower arm, denoting the central axis of the plus and minus fling, is qualified by the golden flame of illumination, which imbues both the positive and negative poles with Wisdom's God-direction and purpose.

Therefore, all that is below in the microcosm is intended to be a threefold manifestation of the sacred fire that descends from Above in the macrocosm.

The energy released from the Godhead, the Daystar from on high [4]—the lodestone of Power, or the I AM Presence, scintillating in the octaves of perfection—immediately upon entering the lower octaves of Matter assumes the negative pole of being in what is called the night side of manifestation. This is the minus side of Life, where the plus fling of potential released from Spirit enters into material qualification.

The energies garnered in Spirit, when preceded by right thought in the left arm, gain the impetus for God-virtue by the Power of Love's cohesion and attraction as they are released into action through the right arm. This left-right, 'push-pull', action can be illustrated through the principle of the slingshot, wherein the stone in the sling is withdrawn from the Y in a negative pull in order to secure the necessary impetus of Power to drive home the shot through a positive release.

You will recall that it is written in the first chapter of Genesis that the LORD God made "the greater light to rule the day and the lesser light to rule the night."[5] The north arm of the cross represents the day side of being, and the three lower arms the night side.

The left arm of the Maltese cross, being the negative arm of the Trinity *in form*, is itself symbolical of the negative side of Life in which the three lower arms are suspended. Then, too, it is the left arm that denotes the physical nature of man as a cradle, or crucible, into which God pours his Power as a condensation of the fiery intensity of his Light.

This he does in the hope that man will rise above that cradle/crucible and transcend the world of experience which the alchemist perceives as the night side of Life, a temporal densification of Spirit, a laboratory in Matter where he is obliged to prove the scientific laws of being in order to return to the permanent abode of Spirit. It is out of the dense spheres of this world of experience, which the Hindus refer to as the world of maya, that the soul of man must rise, "purified and made white," into the purity of the great God flame of his being.

The Maltese cross has another significance. When the perfect integration of God and man is complete, there is a sunburst effect emitting Light from the dot in the center of the cross. Within the cosmic circle of allness at the dot symbolical of individuality, there is focused the balance of Spirit and Matter, a Divine Oneness of all planes, a union of the Father/Mother God fulfilling the spirals of Alpha to Omega.

Through the sacred heart of the soul wed to the Universal Christ in the alchemical marriage, the Light is come, the Light does shine!

God is in Truth the All-in-all—not only in principle but also in practical application! For this God, Whose Christ, as Paul said, is All and in all, is the All-in-all within the individualized manifestation made in his image and likeness. [6] Thus is the fullness of God's kingdom conferred upon his sons and daughters—thus through the pattern of the Maltese cross is the concept of "Thine is the Power" realized!

God's Power, as his light/energy/consciousness is, then, entrusted to every man. And it is in the right use of this Power in every way—according to the spiritual/physical laws of alchemy which I herewith declare to you *in part*, leaving the rest to your mystical communion with Cosmos—that man can surely come to understand more of the universe and obtain the victory of eternal Life.

I realize that my writings on alchemy were a disappointment to some students because of their faulty levels of expectation. Some actually became obsessed with the idea that I would give them some form of thaumaturgical formula whereby, upon making certain cabalistic signs in the air and reciting *the* secret word or words, precious stones and even money would materialize in their hands as if "out of thin air."

I doubt not that if this were to be conferred upon all, it would be the greatest abuse of Power conceivable, both on my part and on the part of the universe itself; for if men think that they have karmic responsibilities in the use of that Power which they already have, let them consider for a moment what responsibilities they should have if their Power were increased!

Call not so much for an increase of Power, then, as for a better understanding of how to use that Power which you already have, and observe how the universe in all of its great Wisdom, bursting with desire to give you the vital freshness of Being, will confer upon you by direct apprehension those alchemical secrets which will assure you not a continuing *abuse* but a correct and glorious *use* of the Power of God unto salvation for all!

May his peace be with you as I join you in the release of greater understanding concerning your wise dominion of illumination's flame.

Your obedient friend of freedom,

Saint Germain

CHAPTER 2

Wisdom

To the precious disciples of Christ and his mysteries I come bearing the Grail of our Lord. Listen well lest you skip over the unspoken, the unwritten—the principal thing. Therefore in thy Self-discovery know also that we are one.

A. *Wisdom Defined*

Wisdom is derived from the phrase "wise dominion" and it is to God's own flame of holy illumination that we dedicate this portion of our Trilogy. The age-old admonishment "Wisdom is the principal thing; therefore get Wisdom: and with all thy getting get understanding"[1] relates to the acquisition of *divine* Wisdom.

Let me here make a distinction between Wisdom and knowledge. There are men and women who can easily retain the lines of entire series of plays, and they can speak those lines before a sizeable audience with great accuracy and dramatic impact. These same individuals would be at a loss if they were to be called upon to write the play or to assemble the words and ideas which embody its continuity.

Thus, it is not sufficient to possess mere knowledge based on the power of the memory to retain experience. Memory alone does not assure man the proper use or release of stored knowledge at the precise moment when it is needed, nor does it assure mankind the exercise of proper judgment or Wisdom once the facts are made available.

B. *Reembodiment—Keystone in the Arch of Being*

Now, as I have earlier mentioned, it would be most beneficial if the human monad would refrain from prejudgment in matters of cosmic doctrine and even better if he could universally accept the reality of reembodiment. For it is in the acceptance of this fact of life that he will truly discern the Wisdom of the ages and more easily understand his reason for being.

It is most difficult for people in any age, observing in the life span of a comparatively few short years a series of events relative to the personal self, to be able to judge the world in which they live and the society from which they have derived both bane and blessing, and then to be able to perceive matters pertaining to the spirit and properly assess them.

By correctly understanding and accepting his own reembodiment, the individual develops a cosmic sense of the continuity of self—past, present, and future—and is better equipped to see behind the surface effects of today's circumstances the underlying personal causes that stretch back across the dust of centuries.

Simply because men lack conscious memory of a previous existence does not deny the validity of this Truth. Many have experienced the sudden feeling of having done before that which they are doing for the first time in this life. Others recall in a flash of recognition (déjà-vu) that they have seen a face or place before. Then, of course, there is "love at first sight," which is to be explained by soul recognition from past lives or inner-level awareness.

Many have noted with interest the incidence of genius (that some call a "gift" or "talent") in art, music, and science, or other aptitudes that appear at an early age, indicating the soul's resumption of the broken thread of identity. Modern physicians take note of the distinct personality of babies on the day of their birth. And all over the world fascinating stories have been documented concerning people's recall of vivid scenes and experiences from a past life.

Man has been justifiably skeptical of some of this, yet Truth reveals itself not as a pseudo-science but as the very science of Being without end. Think how glorious, how full of hope life can be to all who therefore see before them not death but only self-transformation as the alchemy of positive change!—to all who see in the law of reembodiment an opportunity for the slow learners and the rebellious to recover in new dignity from error's stains, rising at last from the astral sea of identity, the personal morass of mortality, into the morning of eternal hope and the crown of victorious Life!

A world fabricated to be the platform for billions of lifestreams, all created as mere moths destined to fall into the flame and be consumed, a world that is a kaleidoscope of changing scenes and ideas drifting, sans stability, in an endless sea of spinning nebulae and swirling gases, holds no promise for the children of the Sun other than to eat, drink and be merry, and to die like mortals. [2]

What marvel that men have accepted any religion at all when the factor of reembodiment is denied by the religions and many of their leaders! You see, it was by removing this teaching from the so-called mysteries of the early Church that there came into existence the very grave distortions of life's purposes in both Church and State that have challenged society to the present day.

When the Wisdom of God is imparted to man, it makes him aware of the fact that the sum total of all that he is—whether he likes it or not—is the result of his own doings. He sees on the instant the need, as well as the Power, to change his ways and to draw himself into alignment with cosmic law.

Faith in God mounts up; for hope joins hands with faith, and the personal mistakes of the past appear to be possible of present rectification. The understanding of current failures reveals them to be the result of wrongful acts, human error, rather than a deliberate resistance to Life. And men and women are enabled once again to enter the main-stream of Life and to participate in a cosmic drama wherein divine Wisdom eventuates in a union of such celestial dimension as to stagger the imagination.

The greatest of rockets, ancient and modern, have a platform or launching pad from which they thrust off into the heavens. So it is with men and women in their search for cosmic Truth. From the platform of present existence they must seek and find the threads of cosmic light that will lead them through the golden door and beyond to etheric realms where blazes illumination's flame. Thus, from Wisdom's fount as well as inner study, the seeking, striving ones must learn to see God in action in themselves and summon him to take command of their affairs on earth.

How great is the suffering that Christians have endured through the elimination of this one point of spiritual Truth! By denying reembodiment they have denied their souls the keystone in the arch of being.

You see, there are certain fine points of cosmic law that in a relative sense are not as important as this one. Man can deny some specifics without suffering too much damage, but to deny the Truth of the continuity of his own being—its span of previous existence and its future glorious destiny—is to cut himself off from the basic premise of Life!

C. *The Eternal Now—Doorway to the Future*

The Eternal Now is more important than either the past or the future. It is the doorway into the future even as it is memory's link to all that passes through the heart of man's experience.

Beloved ones, eternal Life *is* divine Wisdom, for by the acquisition of many fragments of eternal Life (segmented as lifetimes) man has stored up for himself treasures in the heaven of Being.[3]

Accordingly, the guidelines of the Ascended Masters' universities for the training of souls in the way of personal adeptship are firmly fixed, based on the great law of experience—the cumulative record in the Great Causal Body of the universe. These guidelines are drawn not only from the life events of one individual and the many, but from the net gain of empirical knowledge (as well as the gnosis) derived from the experiences of all who have mastered the three-fold flame in the time/space continuum and ascended to higher dimensions.

One of the most important features of the world's universities is that they are repositories for the many doings of mankind—records of the historical stream and the thought evolution of the race—and by their faculties and libraries they possess the means of communicating this treasury of codified knowledge so that it becomes a part of the mental wealth of their students and the forward movement of the planet.

Now consider, the entire universe is, in fact and configuration, a depository of cosmic law; and the most wonderful thing about this cosmic university is that all who will may attend and drink of its storehouse of knowledge!

In the retreats of the Great White Brotherhood one of the first lectures the Masters give their 'freshmen' classes, by way of correcting the misconceptions resulting from a common doctrinal error, is on the false belief that all things terminate at death.

If death or illness were to be permanent, if human discord, sin, and unhappiness were to remain as an unremovable stain upon the soul, the master of a man's destiny, and their influences could not be broken here or hereafter, if life's opportunity were to cease by the calamity of sudden and untimely death—no further chapters to be written in the book of life—then individual man could never assimilate the wondrous blessings held in store for all by the Mind of God. Such a cruel turn of fate could not be conceived by the God of Love whose mercies endure beyond the grave.

Through the soul's reincarnation, her return to the plane of cause and effect where she has accounts to settle, imbalances to resolve—more Power, Wisdom, and Love to release from her heart for the blessing of many lifestreams—the God of Mercy extends opportunity to try and try again, and to prove that all death and sorrow, sin and stain *can* be dissolved in the sacred fires of the Holy Spirit. By right choice and his gracious violet flame, with a working knowledge of the alchemy of the spoken Word, souls born again may live to love again and forge and win their immortality.

In their classes the Masters point out, then, that the first and greatest contribution of God to man is *the gift of Life as a continuum*—identity preserved through the divine spark, the threefold flame of Life. And the second, which is like unto it, is *the gift of free will* in the exercise of Power, Wisdom, and Love—choosing step by step eternal Life.

Alas, the densities and opacities of the world of form, spread over the human mind as a mask of imperfection, have for untold generations robbed mankind of this his birthright of spiritual Wisdom and experience unto the glories of the endless Day!

D. *The Etheric Realm—Upper and Lower Strata*

Let me take you, then, into new levels of awareness where we will confront certain facts as yet little known by people at large. Many have thought about the existence of other worlds and other civilizations. Some have speculated concerning the penetrability of Matter and the simultaneity of forcefields in time and space whereby other worlds might co-occupy the position of this blessed earth, yet in other dimensions.

When the laws of frequencies and wave emanations are better understood by the scientists of the world, the facts of this reality will be revealed. At this writing it is my intent to speak briefly of the etheric realm.

Upon departing from the physical world and drawing their last allotted breath, the spirits of men are often taken into the etheric realm (a higher octave of the Matter plane corresponding to their more refined, or 'finer', etheric body), which to them has the solid appearance of the physical.

Here are scenes of nature, the beauty of earth, sea, and sky as well as towns and buildings constructed like those on earth—verily an entire band of frequencies in the similitude of that to which these departed souls have been accustomed on earth—created for their comfort and the continuity of their sense of self, as well as their eventual transition to worlds beyond.

The etheric octave has many strata, or levels, of consciousness. Some who reach it may be said to live on split levels, for they move from one sphere to another, whereas others become anchored to a specific sector.

I do not deny that in the lower etheric realm, which overlaps the denser astral plane, the negative forces have created focuses which are largely responsible for much of mankind's current and past distress. From these mass entities, tentacles of sinister thoughtforms and demons reach out to control mankind, including the children of the Light, with elements of human discord, seducing them by addiction, astral enslavement and sheer viciousness, which are further amplified and manipulated against people's own best interests by the false hierarchy of the planet (brothers of the shadow, impostors who oppose the legions of Light).

Bear well in mind that man and woman are also responsible for this, their own untoward creation. Due to their original departure from the voice of Truth in the garden of God—a freewill choice for which they alone are accountable—they began to weave cause/effect sequences outside the circle of Oneness. And ever since, their children and their children's children have reaped unhappy situations and deleterious conditions which affect their souls, their livelihoods and families—most distressingly when they ever so often make contact with this lower etheric, or 'memory', level where old, untransmuted evils gather as floating grids and forcefields of mankind's negative momentums.

Such contacts are triggered by many situations common to everyday life: everything from family arguments to violence on TV, horror movies, rock music, drug usage and astral connections through addictions, gambling, cavorting with spirits, dabbling in witchcraft or making UFO personalities and science fiction their gods.

Although considered harmless as innocent fun or 'pastimes', these activities as well as mankind's endless fascinations with symbols of death and sex—favorite topics of the tabloids, the soaps, subliminal advertising and thriller novels—do hold their energies captive to the astral plane and the adepts of control who, in or out of embodiment, make the lower etheric their territory.

Attention is the key; for where man's attention goes, there goes his energy, and he himself can only follow.

Children of Earth's first godparents, attention! If you would rise in spiritual attainment and in the God-mastery of your life, you must go to the mountain of God and fast from all of these distractions to your true Selfhood which derives from the Universal One.

If you would self-transcend the planes of human suffering in order to aid your fellow creatures, you must also be willing to part with painful pleasures which *you know*—deep down inside—are destroying your very soul by your own freewill consent. And place your attention on your I AM Presence!

The Ascended Masters beckon the compassionate ones to confront the astral *e-veil* (energy veil) that besets the unwary who are daily falling before the four horsemen.⁴ The deadly illusions and adepts of the black arts to which the race have fallen prey must be challenged by the alert alchemist and spiritual benefactors of the race whom I have called to world service as Keepers of the Flame and organized under the fraternal order bearing my sponsorship.

You may wonder why I bring all these things to your attention. It is because your souls have cried out for freedom and the God of very gods has sent me to tell you that you will find it only by your acceptance of the whole Truth and holy Wisdom. Therefore, consider well my words in this little book, for the hour is late and another may not come to knock again upon the door of your heart.

Now, if all of the etheric levels were manifesting absolute perfection, do you not think, blessed ones, that this perfection, being as close as your own memory and the memory of the planetary body, would not long ago have changed the world of effect so much so that only perfection could manifest on earth!

Therefore, to accomplish the realignment of the soul with the living Spirit of the LORD, there is a need to make continuous corrections of a kind that adjust the set of the sail by the compass of Life—self-corrections of major and minor deviations from Life that devour bit by bit the spirit of a man and his helpmeet and their offspring. And it is the better part of holy Wisdom that I reveal it here, in order that you may participate in the re-creation of worlds within and without by the science of the spoken Word, in partnership with the heavenly hosts.

Let the extremes of Light and Darkness, Absolute Good and the Evil One, hold no terror for any, for one moment before I spoke to you or you read these facts, they were still in existence and had been for centuries. Our concern is that by Christ illumination the mists of error shall not remain as a controlling or dominant force in your life in the world of form, but that the chains of all such binding human deviltry shall be broken and replaced by divine direction from the highest reaches of your own immortal God-free being.

These facts concerning astral focuses of human discord (already fully known by you at subconscious levels) which I now bring to your waking attention must keep you on guard mentally, spiritually, physically and emotionally. Of course, there are also radiant celestial focuses of divine harmony almost without number. These are presently accessible to the sweet children of the Light and sons and daughters of God in the highest etheric levels. Wondrous temples of music exist where celestial tones, unknown, unheard today upon the entire planet, resound from advanced instruments possessing the capacity for almost infinite harmony.

There are temples of beauty presided over by Paul the Venetian and other Ascended Masters, some from other systems of worlds. Paintings, tapestries, statuary, artistic forms, and planetary records on exhibit, also from this and other systems, are preserved in these great temples, museums, and universities of the Spirit on the etheric levels of this planet.

And by now I think you have guessed that there are also treasuries of Wisdom, including the inventions and scientific achievements preserved from earth's past golden ages, stored in these halls of learning and spiritual centers where responsive and responsible souls may study either between embodiments to prepare for a future mission in the next life, or presently through soul travel out of the body during sleep or samadhi. (The latter subject I have reserved for the Keepers of the Flame lessons, for your exercises in soul travel require our close attention and guardian action.)

But let us now face certain facts of man's being, fundamental to the quest for the Grail of self-knowledge in the etheric octave. For by determined self-mastery in the first steps he may arrive at the portal of opportunity for world service.

E. *Wisdom's Way by the Threefold Flame*

The mere acquisition of knowledge, without the Wisdom to discriminate in its use, as we have noted, is not productive of the right kind of fruit but often becomes a wholly ego-centered activity. Wherefore, when the flame of Wisdom is utilized by a lifestream, invoked from the heart of his own beloved God Presence, and the dross of wrong thinking colored by human emotion is burned out of the cells of the mind and the lower mental body, then the way is cleared for a flow of great Wisdom into man's consciousness and use. To tap the resources of the cosmic universities, men need pure hearts!

We do not deny that the violent rebels against the Cause of Almighty God have taken heaven "by force,"[5] as has been said, piercing the veil by psychic means, drugs, Satanic rite and the black arts. They have penetrated beyond the strata of the ordinary, at times employing various chemicals, herbs and human pharmacopoeia in order to escape the realm of the present self and present karmic responsibilities, yet finding but temporal reward for their stealing of forbidden fruit—for the Law does not allow them to keep their ill-gotten gains.

Let me point out that the way to paradise lost, the way to the Garden of Eden and the Tree of Life[6] can be found by legitimate and wholesome means whereby the satisfactions of soul-mastery and personal integrity (integration with the Whole) are achieved each step of the way. This is a part of holy Wisdom. For merely to acquire Power without understanding the meaning of justice and mercy, as I have long stressed, is an error for which the lifestream is fully accountable, both here and hereafter.

Inasmuch as mankind's karma holds them accountable for so much already, I see no reason why they should further complicate matters by acquiring Power without acquiring the Wisdom to properly apply it and the Love to restrain its selfish abuse. And therefore, I choose to make certain suggestions here and now that I believe will afford souls of Light and alchemists on the Path entrée into a higher spiritual realm, as well as their proper use of God's energy here and now to the blessing of all in this perilous physical octave.

Some of you are aware of the fact that the threefold flame, which is being interpreted in part in this Trilogy, is only one-sixteenth of an inch high within the average human heart. It is made up of a blue plume, a yellow plume, and a pink plume of radiant, God-charged, electronic light. Each plume is a manifest focus of God-qualities.

The blue plume of spiritual Power relates to faith, goodwill, and the divine intent. The yellow plume of divine Wisdom relates to illumination and to the right use of knowledge, the expansion of the intelligence of the Godhead into the chaliced heart and mind of the earnest aspirant to godliness.

The pink plume of divine Love is the crown of Life which provides a permeation of the qualities of mercy, compassion, justice, and creativity. Divine Love as radiant Light is also the crown of God's happiness which he sheds forth by his mighty light rays throughout the universe, whether the universe is aware of it or not.

Let me point out that the sunshine yellow plume, or sunburst of divine illumination that is within everyone (released through the south arm of the Maltese cross as the pivot between the positive and negative arms of the cross), is the secret key by which man can unfold his own Wisdom flame.

This central plume of the tripartite flame of Life must be consciously expanded within heart and mind through invocation to the I AM Presence. For, as the animating principle of God's own Mind, it is given freely for the use of all who will make the call in the name of the Christ.

By visualizing its golden yellow radiance passing through one's four lower bodies many times daily, the devotee initiates the process of burning out the accretion of negation and density, purifying the mind, feelings, and memory, reinforcing therein the revitalizing electronic Power of vital Truth.

As he joyously assimilates Wisdom's fires, these displace and consume the dross of erroneous thoughts and feelings previously assembled in the human mind that prevent the flow of light through the human consciousness and, until transmuted, remain the enemy of every man seeking God-illumination.[7]

Jesus said, "A man's foes shall be they of his own household,"[8] and no more motley household has ever been assembled than a man's own wrong thoughts! It is not necessary to pull up the weeds of those wrong thoughts all at once, for the wheat may easily be removed along with the tares.⁹ However, it is essential to recognize that some degree of reappraisal and self-examination is *constantly* necessary—if one is to retain the true alchemist's objectivity and standard of perpetual progress on the Path.

Because it was announced years ago that a number of black magicians had been removed from the planet, some students were of the opinion that the world was then completely freed of the emanation of embodied evil. When cosmic unity and harmony exist everywhere, when criticism, condemnation, and judgment have ceased, when celestial happiness penetrates the world and all strife is ended, I may agree.

But, for the time being, the presence of many more black magicians who by free will have chosen the left-handed path is apparent in the outplaying of atrocities on a world scale alongside of pleasure cults and rituals of Darkness tempting psychic suicide. All this in fast motion as you read my very words. So goes the world à la *1984!*¹⁰

"By their fruits ye shall know them"¹¹ is the criterion to be applied to the international scene as well as to the individual. People may hide for a while behind a mask of perfection, but the great, unfailing Light of God penetrates behind all masks and brings each one to judgment. There is no escape from evil karma except to turn from it and do well.

Let every man be aware, then, that it is his duty and responsibility to nurture self-concern; for by concern for himself as to what thoughts he shall admit to his mind (and what motives and feelings he shall allow to tarry in the chamber of his heart), he is able to purify that mental world of his and to guard it by purity's flame in such a manner as to be of greater benefit and service to others.

Indeed, can the blind lead the blind? As the Master Jesus said, "Shall they not both fall into the ditch?"[12]

By a forthright will and willingness reinforced by the decree of your word, remove, then, all barriers in your being and consciousness that *you know* impede the flow of the God flame of illumination. Use the violet/purple flame of freedom. Welcome it into every atom and cell of your world. Each day ask your God Presence for greater Wisdom and for an increase of the flame of illumination and its right use.

In the name of the Christ and by the threefold flame within your heart, demand of your great God Self a balanced flow of Power, Wisdom and Love—and see what Life will do for you!

F. *Balanced Achievement—The Way of Mastery*

Imbalance—where giantism occurs in one aspect of the threefold flame, causing it to be out of proportion to the others—prevents the achievement of daily goals as well as the goal of individual Christ-mastery.

As the tangible, balanced flame of illumination expands from within your consciousness, it gradually enfolds your being until God, as holy Wisdom, is enthroned upon the altar of your heart. But with each increase of Wisdom, the Power and Love plumes must also rise by the fiat of your devotion to goodwill, else Wisdom's gain will not be retained. Likewise, with each getting of Power there must come the attainment of Wisdom and Love in perfect complement; so, too, Love is actualized only through an equivalency of Power and Wisdom.

Recognizing that balance is the golden key to Christhood, you will understand that you cannot know for yourself nor bring into manifestation that which you have not first realized within the realm of your outer or inner experience in God. Such experiences become ultimately meaningful, beautiful, when woven through the rhythm of the balanced threefold flame.

This accounts for the differences expressed in men's employment of the faculties of mind and heart. While some have denied themselves the graces of heaven, others, the so-called ignorant or uneducated, are not necessarily bereft of the blessings of holy Wisdom; neither do the learned always receive them "as a little child." For holy Wisdom is imparted not only through study in an outer sense, but also through attunement in an inner sense with the great spiritual powers of Light, God-free beings and circles of initiates who live and move and breathe the sacred fire breath in the higher octaves.

Masters of the Far East and those who have risen from ancient temples of Lemuria and South America frequent the retreats of the Great White Brotherhood on the highest etheric planes, receiving, as the Law allows, those who mount the spiral staircase of the degrees to seek and find their abode of the Spirit. That men need not wait until they have passed from the screen of life to obtain greater divine Wisdom should be a source of great happiness to all who read these words.

It is true, in fact, that for those who do not successfully attain the goal of the ascension at the close of this embodiment, their succeeding incarnation will be enriched through present diligence to precepts herein imparted; and let me assure you that for those who do attain the goal, whatever is done in God's name today is the achievement of eternity.

Nothing divine is ephemeral, nor can it be taken from anyone. All divine blessings are permanent, and this is their wondrous inherent quality.

With all thy getting, let it not be the mere fretting away of the hours. With so many waiting at the portals of birth, yearning to breathe the planetary air (even though polluted!) and to bask in the sunlight here, let those who have this opportunity to right all wrong, to obtain entrance into the eternal kingdom, to overcome error, to enthrone the rightful Deity, and to challenge every false opinion accept from the Godhead the scepter of their own Wisdom's dominion.

None can obtain who will not try; none can obtain who lack faith. All who will can summon the holy energies and glorify God in that feeling of infinite happiness that comes to those who cherish the outpouring of Light's radiance in its balanced, threefold flame of Power, of Wisdom, and of Love which abideth forever.

Most graciously, I AM

Saint Germain

✠

CHAPTER 3

Love

Precious Seekers for Your Own Freedom,

Know that the full Power of the three-times-three is the mighty momentum of the stream of Love that issues from God's heart! Filling the universe with abundant joy, it flows forth into thine own heart. This is the cosmic fount of pure Love that springs up as the crowning radiance of each manifestation in nature, in the angelic hosts, and in man.

It is to this Love of God that we must pay tribute whenever we drink in the floral fragrances of the blossoms of natural beauty nodding in the sunlight and the gentle wind. This Love is also the motivating Power behind all angelic action. Therefore, those who would draw very close to the angelic hosts, that they might receive their protection, radiance, and blessing, will be most wise to keep harmonious at all times and to shun all forms of human discord.

The greatest Love ever to be found in man is the Love which lays down its life daily to keep the well-being of its friend.[1] What greater service can be rendered unto life than simply to manifest Love?

Remember, true Love is the great magnet that draws forth the Power of God's heart charged with his holy Wisdom. The secret of the evocation of Power, then, really lies within the heart of Love. It must be acknowledged here that men and women of the first ray who so successfully invoke Power do so by turning to the great Power of Love and drawing therefrom the Power of God.

A. *Love's Labor Lost in Human Compromise*

Unfortunately, some among our readers out of sheer ignorance, and sometimes bigotry, look to find a flaw in our teaching and our released concepts. Now, the human mind can be very tricky and stubborn. If individuals determine that they are going to find a flaw or contradiction in our words, be assured that they will.

Then, too, the sleuths inspecting for fallacy in the Logos itself can always find a false answer or wrong conclusion by the same systems of human logic which at their bidding will support or justify their own ends according to the premise taken.

I regret that such as these are moved by their vacuums of self-knowledge and a desire for self-righteousness, but I cannot be moved to undue concern for them. One day they will humbly seek Truth.

However, I am concerned for the sincere and would therefore mention the law of relationships involved in the polarizations of the human consciousness—as opposed to the law of the divine polarity inherent within every attribute, or 'be-attitude', of the Godhead.

Some of you are aware that the study of the relationship of opposites in the planes of relativity is reflected in the dialectic of the nineteenth-century German philosopher Georg Hegel, who theorized that man's thought process and all historical change result from the interplay of three elements: thesis, antithesis, and synthesis. According to this observer of life's forces, every thesis generates its opposite, or antithesis, and the interaction of the two produces a synthesis which transcends both. The emerging synthesis in turn becomes a new thesis and the entire process is repeated again and again.

Thus, in the Hegelian dialectic all progress is brought about through the inevitable conflict of opposing forces—a principle Karl Marx turned upside down in his "dialectical materialism," wherein he replaced Hegel's idealism with economic materialism. Whereas Hegel supported the value of the state and saw in the dialectical process the unfoldment of spiritual principle, Marx branded the state a mechanism of exploitation and claimed that all progress arises from conflicts involving the economic means of production.

You who understand the premise of the Ascended Masters' teachings to be the Law of the One do not always take into account this law of relativity governing relative good and evil, perceived by psychologists, scientists and the worldly philosophers. Moreover, in the world of maya, where good and evil are always 'relatively' in opposition, we must also reckon with the negative misqualification of the Absolutes of Power, Wisdom and Love upon which we have been discoursing. Therefore we would touch upon both the human and the divine equations.

The Law of the One, based on the unity of Being, also functions within the framework of human reason and human events and when it comes full circle in the individual's experience supports Truth and exposes error.

But in the human 'two-eyed' perception of the world acquired after the departure from the Edenic self-knowledge in and as the One—when the world view of man and woman was no longer single in the immaculate all-seeing eye of God but the same as that of the band of seducing fallen angels called serpents—there were unalterably two sides to every human equation, with the pendulum swing hot/cold, left/right, always just waiting to happen.

Not so in the divine equation. Here the true Divine Polarity of Alpha and Omega, the plus/minus of the Godhead, and of each member of the Trinity are the Masculine/Feminine counterparts of Being. These are complementary, not opposing, always fulfilling the Law of the One as the Divine Whole. But in the human condition,

just as there is a positive pole, so there is a negative pole to a given situation. These are opposing
forces, rivalrous in nature and mutually destructive. For example, if the thesis be human love,
its antithesis will be some form of love's polar
opposite—human hatred, fear, suspicion or even
mild dislike. Their synthesis will be a watered-
down version of both with no commitment either
to one or the other.

This is the lukewarm state of mediocrity
which Jesus spurned when he said, "Because thou
art lukewarm, and neither cold nor hot, I will
spue thee out of my mouth.[2] And this is precisely
why the economic evolution of mankind according to Marx and Lenin can never lead to the divine
conclusion: self-transcendence according to the
Law of Love, the Law of the One which self-con-
tains the true Trinity—Power, Wisdom and Love—
as the triad of every man and woman's being.

Apart from the double-minded who are unstable in all their ways,[3] divine Truth stands still
as a Sun of Love to melt the most brittle human
concepts and to unveil the Law of the One!

B. *The Original Premise and Polarity of Love*

Now hear the word of the LORD.

In the original premise of the Godhead,
Power, or the will to be, is the thesis. Wisdom is
the antithesis and Love is the synthesis. As Wisdom magnetizes the intelligence inherent in the
Power of God, drawing it out into the Word of all

ideation now expressed, the twain become One, displaying the glorious revolution of Love as the grand synthesis of Power and Wisdom. Love as the consummation of the essence of Power/Wisdom then becomes the new thesis which embodies the fullest realization of Itself in the Work of the LORD—incarnating the Three-in-One in every manifest action!

This true synthesis of the Divine Attributes reveals that Love, Wisdom and Power are in reality the One indivisible/individed Whole which can never be divided or divisive—their atoms chanting as they chart the spheres: "We are One, We are One, We Are One..."

But this is not all. The cosmic white fire of the Universal Mother now enters. Born out of the unity of the Divine Triad, She whom I like to call the 'Luminous One' steps forth out of her latency in the fiery nucleus of the threefold flame to become the antithesis, or divine polarity, of this thesis of the Trinity. And out of *this* union there is produced the synthesis of many manifestations of the Whole—sons and daughters of God, each one a new premise embodying the Fourfold Attributes, Father, Son, Holy Spirit, and Mother!

Each Self-expression of the Whole uniquely synthesizing their qualities by ultimate free will in freedom's flame—not by some damnable inevitability of historical or economic forces successively enslaving the race, but by Union in the Law of the One—and then the Three, girded by the

Fourth, the Blessed Mother. She manifesting her complementary nature as the Shakti of each Person of the Trinity, releasing out of the white lily center of each plume, from the masculine(+) polarity of Power, Wisdom and Love, the feminine(–) manifestation in the worlds of form.

As these four become the pillars in the temple of twin flames, foundations in their mighty work of the ages, they themselves become pillars in the temple of our God.⁴ And no other foundations or false premises or synthetic conclusions can be laid, for Man as the offspring of the Highest contains the original thesis, antithesis and synthesis as the trilogy of the threefold flame within his heart.

He is also child-man of the Mother, containing her seed-atom and her sacred fire within himself. And none other can displace this fourfold foundation of his Being—unless he himself succumb by choice to the lie and the liars who lead the pack of the international capitalist/communist conspirators spawning their pseudometaphysical cults of materialism and the dialectic on planet earth.

Now let us see how Love is in Truth defined by the Divine Lovers.

The path of fiery Love, which is God's all-consuming sacred fire, consumes even the force of Anti-Love, the Absolute Evil of reprobate angels against the Godhead, for Divine Love is more than Love—it is Power and Wisdom self-contained all in One—and then some. And herein lies Love's mystery. Love is more than effect or lesser causation, it is First Cause and the point of Light beyond all light and darkness. Love is all Love excelling beyond Love's visible expressions and interchanges. Love is the unbeatable cosmic force!

True Love, divine Love, in its very magic can still be known by twin flames dwelling in the twilight zone of adulterated love. For Love is always pure and does not contain within itself any self-polluting, self-mutilating force such as fear of failure, fear of Truth, fear of Life, fear to be Love. No interplays or power plays of human psychology can mar true Love, but these can and do mar human love in incubation waiting, tending the flocks of consciousness until the angel of the LORD should trouble the waters of the mind and raise a single drop to the Sun whereby the whole fabric of human love surrenders in the embrace of the Divine.

True Love is always understanding, yet not necessarily always understood. It speaks with the Shepherd's voice of authority, never the petty tyrant; it chastens, peeling away by its caressing flames the layers of self-deception of child-man. Love as discipline has the hardness of the diamond-shining Mind of God that alone can bind the tyrant ego and set the captive free. From Christ's heart of true Love, then, the words "Father, forgive them; for they know not what they do"[5] are easily uttered.

Love has no imitators, for God alone is Love. You see, in the human sense of love there is love's thesis and antithesis self-contained. Thus, humanly speaking, that which has the capacity for human love also has the capacity for human hatred. And this is precisely the source of life's tragicomedy. But the Divine is not so.

In the Absolute—where self-disintegration is not, where the law of human synthesis does not neutralize the plus and minus of the divine magnet—the attributes of God's Power, Wisdom and Love are always personified in the polarity of twin flames representing the Divine Whole of the Father-Mother God. In the Hindu tradition these divine incarnations of the male and female Principles of each plume of the Trinity are given names and are cherished as emanations of the Deity.

In this relationship of the Divine Absolutes, Father is thesis, Mother is antithesis, and the whole of their creation, including the fruit of their Christ Consciousness, is the synthesis—their reason for Being and for being the Divine Incarnation.

What happens when the Divine Lovers meet in the Divine Embrace of the T'ai Chi—the Great Causal Body of God—is their net contribution to Cosmos. So it is when twin flames return to the white fire ovoid of their Origin. Only in this ultimate Union (the celebration of the Holy Communion of Alpha and Omega) can the creative purpose of their Being be fully realized.

Thus, the Divine Lovers fulfilling the plus/

minus *interchange* of the attribute of Power are identified as Brahma and Sarasvati, who exemplify the masculine and feminine embodiment of the Cosmic Force. (Notice the word I use to describe this yin and yang is not *synthesis*, for if either half of the Whole were to lose the magnetism of this polarity of cosmic forces, the worlds of form would collapse; hence *interchange*, or *exchange*, yes! *synthesis*, no!)

In the Hindu view Brahma as Father-figure, the First Person of the Trinity, is described as the Immense Being—the Creator, Supreme Ruler, Lawgiver, Sustainer, and Source of All Knowledge—while Sarasvati represents eloquence, the Mother who articulates the Wisdom of the Law. She is Mother/Teacher to those who love the Law as God's will revealed by Brahma. Thus she is the Power of volition, the will and motivation to be the Law in action, the Source, the river and the riverbed, for the flow of universal knowledge as appreciation for the Law of the Creator self-contained in every particle of the creation.

Likewise, the pair in polarity who comprise the Law of the One in the attribute of Wisdom are known and loved as real personalities—Vishnu and Lakshmi, embracing the circle of qualities attributed to one or the other, yet lovingly shared and divinely surrendered in the whirling sphere of their Oneness.

Thus, in heaven two equals One individed Whole; on earth two in one often sacrifice their true identity to the human synthesis which becomes the new thesis—the distinction of the two parts of the original premise neutralized in the moving stream of relativity. For you see, relativity has no fixed polarity. And therein lies its mutability.

But above in the shining splendor of the Sun, Vishnu—the immortal Son—stands the embodiment of Cosmic Christ Wisdom, whose essence is duration, the enduring quality, the very continuity of the consciousness of God. He is cohesiveness personified, bonding by Wisdom's Love the cosmic forces conceived in the Universal Mind; his way is liberation by Self-knowledge in the Highest God Self.

Vishnu, whose more famous incarnations have been Rama and Krishna, always Hari in manifestation, is the all-pervading Protector—protecting, by God-awareness of the anti-Self (and then the annihilation thereof) that would steal that True Self before it is born in his little ones. This Second Person of the Trinity is the Preserver of the divine design conceived in Wisdom's flame out of Power's lawful Presence. He is the Restorer of the universe by Wisdom's all-healing Light, the true Power of illumination's alchemy of Love.

Vishnu's consort, Lakshmi, is eternally identifiable as the polarity of all that he is, her Wisdom revealed in blessings of prosperity, the precipitation of abundance by the science of Prakṛti and Puruṣa and the control of the four cosmic forces.

She bears a cornucopia of good fortune by the 'eye-magic' of the all-seeing eye of her Beloved. She teaches the mastery of karmic cycles on the cosmic clock, and multiplicity and beauty—the One, and the many out of the Beautiful One—by mirroring the image of Wisdom's God.

So, too, the Holy Spirit comes alive in the charming personages of Shiva and his Shakti. Each one a sphere yet simultaneously a half of the other, these divine complements of Love stand as living proof before all souls in Love that the opposite of Divine Love is not hatred but the balance, whether of masculine or feminine charge, of compassion, of kindness chastening with firmness, giving and receiving gratitude as active and passive modes of the same verb, "to love."

The dual nature of Shiva, the Lord of Love, himself the Destroyer/Deliverer, is complemented by his consort who in manifold form is both demon slayer and child saver. Parvati is the name of the benign "daughter of the mountain," the beneficent, gentle Mother and Wife. The face of Durga is that of the fierce defender of her children, terrible and menacing to her enemies—the "Goddess Beyond Reach"—while Kali, another metamorphosis of Shiva's feminine nature, represents the supreme night of the Mother that swallows up the grid of karma and the time/space worlds that contain it. She complements Shiva's Power in the destruction, by Love, of the energy veil (illusion). She is the Mother who lays down her life for the

Cause of her consort and her children. Her dread appearance is the symbol of her boundless Power.

Thus the spherical embodiment of Absolute Love by Cosmic Twin Flames consumes the forces of Absolute Evil in the form and personages of Anti-Love arrayed against It. This force is embodied by the original betrayers of Love, the fallen angels, who would, if they could, transfer it to Love's own. Remember, then, always to differentiate between Love's self-contained pure polarity of Being and Love diametrically opposed by a force alien to and outside of Itself—and never make the mistake of confusing the two.

The law of perversion by misqualification of the original Principle in the practice of the black arts by adepts of the left-handed path, we see, is all confused and mixed up with the adaptation of the Hegelian synthesis to the Communist world view. In order for their theory to come out, they must insert seeds of corruption in every thesis they desire to swallow up by the creation of a synthetic (trumped up) antithesis.

If Christ Truth be the premise of the abundant Life on earth, the lie of anti-Christ as opposition to all that Christ Truth is and stands for will be set up as antithesis to tear down, break up, compromise, and destroy. And the devil's delight is to hold up his red pajamas and say: See me! See my way of merry mediocrity, see my synthesis of two opposing systems that won't work without my intercession and expertise!

But oil and water do not mix, nor bond and free, nor the ways of heaven and hell. There is no human solution or dissolution to the Divine Thesis. The cosmic honor flame stands alone, all-one, as the flaming two-edged sword to keep the way of every man's tree of life.[6] Its purity all consuming is its only response to every synthetic, antithetical assailant of its Divinity untouchable.

And the divine alchemist knows the harmony of his elements and which admixture will cause explosion and injury to life, which is the universal solvent and which will change base metals into gold—and how to heal the flaws of gemstones, and the gemstone of the heart.

For my thoughts are not your thoughts, neither are your ways my ways, saith the Lord.[7] And the twain shall not be forced to meet by devils disguised in philosopher's robes bearing their synthetic white stone and their compromise solution which shall be their own dissolution in the end.

C. *The Rock That Is Higher Than I*

Therefore, in Love you must come up higher. You must meet Love's standard. For divine Love will not be compromised nor can it suffer dissimulation. Love is the Rock that David knew to be higher than the I.

"Lead me to the Rock that is higher than I," he implored.[8] Thus, contrary words of criticism and condemnation, words of harsh or hypocritical judgment—words of malintent—do not spontaneously spring forth from a heart such as his, accustomed to attunement, yea that lives and breathes God's mighty flame of Love.

Have we not heard as John heard, "He that loveth not his brother whom he hath seen, how can he love God whom he hath not seen?"[9] This maxim still speaks Truth when made to read, "If you do not see God and sense his Love, you cannot truly love your brother." So Christ commanded his own "that he who loveth God love his brother also."[10] Therefore let your own actions be your index to your attainment on this path of the third ray. For they do speak. And speak they shall, more than to thyself.

You see, the true Love that inspired the universes can be drawn only from God's heart, the center of all Being—the Great Source of Life (Power), Truth (Wisdom), and Love and every benign quality that springs therefrom. I would say, then, that inasmuch as there is no other source for Love but God, and so many have for so long been "absent from the LORD,"[11] verily they have lost even the spiritual mechanism within themselves to understand that which they no longer possess.

Now, if any find that he is unable to summon Love for his brethren, or compassion for the world and its problems, let him consider that this problem indexes a state of spiritual dryness. To be sure, this is a serious shortcoming in the aspirant on the Path which may stem from mental rigidity and hardness of heart, products of fear and self-hatred.

But Perfect Love casts out *all* fear and *all* torment that fear begets.[12] And thy soul hath need to be infused with eternal Love by a mighty invocation—fervent in the Holy Spirit.

He that fears evidences that he is not yet made perfect in Love.[13] He belies the fundamental principle of his relationship with God and, concomitantly, with his beloved twin flame. Without faith in this relationship there can be no other lasting Love, for, as Paul says, "Without faith it is impossible to please God."[14] Without faith in Love it is impossible for us to be pleased with ourselves or with any of our relationships, all of which come under the canopy of the firstfruits of our Love/trust with our Father/Mother God and our divine counterpart.

As Christ spake to his disciples: "Cast the net on the right side of the ship and ye shall find!"[15] so let all who would manifest more Love recognize their need for greater attunement with Almighty Love through the record in heaven of the Father, the Word and his Holy Spirit;[16] for even those who do not feel the mighty heartbeat of Universal Love and who have been unsuccessful in amplifying its release on behalf of all life upon earth can through the heavenly Trilogy correct their deficiency—which, I might add, is not to be taken lightly.

Unless you, alchemist of the sacred fire, would-be adept of the mysteries, continually enkindle Love—Love as compassion and kindness,

Love as tolerance and tactfulness, Love as appro-
bation and support, patience, long-suffering and
forbearance, Love as gratefulness and merciful
forgiveness—and actively expand it as a flame
flower, a many-splendored rose whose tender pet-
als unfold all of these qualities and so many
more—the law of balance as God's Justice will
cause the Wisdom and Power aspects of the threefold flame to be reduced to the lowest common
denominator of your externalized Love plume.

I cannot honestly say that I marvel at the
number of spiritual seekers who desire Power over
themselves—for mastery—and over other parts of
Life—for control—while ignoring the Great Law
that requires man to express a true and lasting
Love toward God and self and brother before he
can possess both the Wisdom and the Power of
that very Love which gave birth to the creation.

Remember that just as God cannot be invoked
in part, the "unfed flame"*—the fullness of the tripartite flame of Power, Wisdom and Love—must
be invoked in its totality and completeness from
the Father, the Son, and the Holy Spirit revealed
by Jesus Christ. For *it is* their focus of the Divine
Whole—the creative spark of God's desiring within
you; and no partial manifestation can generate the
cutting action of the Whole that arrests Light's
antithesis, the Darkness that would clutch thee to
itself—torment, enslave, and possess thy soul.

Only thy faithfulness to the Father and Son,
thy hopefulness and charity in the Spirit of the

*synonym for the threefold flame—perpetually burning, unfed by any human
source

perpetual Helper, will set free thy captive heart and release both Light and spirit of the seeker from the dungeons of self-division and the divisive ones. Thus, day unto day does the glory and power of God's kingdom expand from within the three-fold flame of the heart—rarest of all immortelles.

D. *Divine Love Defined*

We must acknowledge that there are many types of feelings which are called Love but which, in Reality, are not. In releasing our Trilogy here, we slant our words not wholly to the advanced initiate nor wholly to the beginner, but to a median state where both shall derive the benefit.

Therefore, again, let us define Love. As the worlds were framed by Love, Love is both sagacious and potent; for each part of the unfed flame is complementary to every other part and to the Whole. Yet Love in essence is the very inmost being of God! For Love in manifest action is God in *manifest-ation!*

"For God so loved the world, that he gave his only begotten Son, that whosoever believeth in him should not perish, but have everlasting Life." [17] This Love of God to us is fully expressed in the gift of the Father's Presence with us, in his gift of the Son whom we know and love in Jesus Christ, in the Emmanuel of our Christ Self—and in the gift of the Holy Spirit.

Everyone who loves is born of the Spirit [18] and finds Love's fulfillment in this Trinity and in its expression in every part of Life. Thus, it can be said and truly that he who loves not has not yet come unto Life, for he knows neither self nor neighbor in the image and likeness of Love.

This God who is Love, then, sent forth to us the divine spark, the threefold flame whose threefold attributes of Power, Wisdom and Love are all Love's kindling Light, the engrafting and engrafted Word [19] that alone can raise us to the Source who is this Love beyond all Love expressed.

Truly, beloved, Love is the LORD's holiness with us. And in his name we say, HOLINESS UNTO THE LORD. [20]

Love is penetrating and expansive; Love is enfolding and transmutative; Love is forgiveness and understanding. Love is wisdom and strength. Love is virtue and purity. Love is dedication and constancy. Love is all of the qualities of God combined with an added ingredient not yet fully known to unascended man and woman—which, for many reasons, we here can neither define nor unveil, except to say that the fullness of Love is the very secret of Life!

Love's Secret Obedience

Power and Wisdom garner Love's intent
The fullness of God-guidance
    in the twig, that bent,
Inclines its ear to hear Love's call
That shapes the tree of life
    so straight and tall.

As spires rise to clouded heights,
The Power of Love's obedient Light,
The diadem of Life, does shine,
Its Grail-like motif making all divine.

'Tis Love's excelling mortal plans,
Enforcing by obedience Love's demands,
That breaks the deathly sod
And, gazing upward, sees the face of God.

John experienced the Truth he wrote, that "he that dwelleth in Love dwelleth in God and God in him." [21] Truly, beloved, this is the perfect equation of God in man and man in God—the consummation of your Oneness in the Universal Christ.

But John also commented on your perfecting of this Love. Only the challenge of Antichrist before his very soul could have quickened these words: "Herein is our Love made perfect, that we may have boldness in the day of judgment." [22] This judgment is the dividing of the way between the Real and the unreal within you—your restoration to Love's original premise. But it is also the climactic cleaving asunder of Light and Darkness on apocalyptic scale by Love's two-edged sword. Indeed! Armageddon is the day of your divine choosing to be your Real Self in the midst of the world wars of the gods.

Your boldness to proceed with this walk in Love's aloneness, when all around you fools scatter

and shatter Love's creation, must be based on aeons
of faith established through trust in Almighty
Love. To challenge the Adversary within and
without fearlessly, in the defense of the unity of
Love, this is indeed the initiation that must precede, as requirement, the alchemical marriage. To
pass it you need the intercession of Chamuel and
Charity, the LORD's angels of Love. And He shall
send them to your side in answer to your call.

Divine Love, then, is the courage to defend
Love against all enemies and to know that Only
Love, and Love All-One, will sustain thee. Having
so said and so done, enter thou into the joy of the
LORD! [23]

E. *Self-Love, Family Love and Human Relationships*

Now let us peer within the domain of the self
of each individual, e'en of thine own Self, and
perceive the meaning of Self-love. And row by
row we shall without fear separate the tares from
the wheat (and the tears as well) and step by step
in Love's own mastery you shall mount the spiral
stairs of Love's degrees.

Selfish love is not Self-love. That which seeks
not that it may share with every other part of
God's Life but that it may possess this Life unto
itself, holding people, things and ideas imprisoned in the domain of exclusivity, is but selfish
love. This is the idolatrous adornment of the ego.

That which seeketh not its own but another's good, drawing forth abundance that it

may expand the glories of Life and share them with the many, is a manifestation of truest Love. This is true Self-love—the love of the True Self in all.

Self-love, or the love of the Real Self, does not generate disrespect or aloofness; on the contrary, it regenerates man's faith in the inherent Good of all and teaches him, even while admitting the possibility of human error, that error is no part of the Real Self.

When human mistakes, which are but temporary recordings on the chart of man's experience, are cleared by noble deeds and the violet flame, and all inequities are righted by service to Divine Justice, the fruit of unselfish action will manifest on an altar swept clean of all inordinate desire.

For the threshing floor of the heart made pure will provide a suitable altar upon which the unfed flame will more than flicker. Its rising pulsations will expand in the rhythm of Life to elevate all whom it contacts, commencing with the aspirant himself.

True Self-Love is the foundation of all other relationships.

Now, there are many forms of human love and these relate principally to man's contact with other parts of Life. There is the love of father and mother for one another and their children, and the love of the offspring for its parents. The love of siblings, relatives, neighbors, the servant and his lord, the disciple and Master.

There is the love of angels for the lowly and of God for his highest creation. There is the Love of the Guru and the One Sent for every chela of goodwill. And there are chelas loving one another and the Guru positioned in every sector of cosmos singing praises unto the God-free beings who rule the spheres.

And everywhere is Love unfolding the mysteries of Life.

Patterning and filling in the pattern of the Whole of Love, the Great Law has seen fit to charge the parents of this world with the responsibility for bringing into manifestation the children of the Most High who represent the third point of the Life triad. It follows, then, that maternal and paternal influences are destined, and were so intended, to be divinely sponsored matrices.

The father person, representing the positive, masculine polarity of the Godhead, has a wonderful and kingly responsibility for each offspring, whereas the mother, who nurtures and guards the young child from the period of conception through gestation and birth, has a very close responsibility in bearing Wisdom's lotus flame throughout the life of the incoming child.

While we are on this subject, it is my earnest wish to clear up for all time certain misconceptions concerning childbearing in the world of form and the use of the vital and generative force by our sons and daughters on the Path.

First let me say that unless there be some

lightbearers who are aware of the frightful opposition to high souls seeking birth on this planet, who are willing in each era to offer themselves as vehicles for the incoming holy and advanced lifestreams, it would prove most difficult for us to assist in giving them the proper training from an early age which the Great Law requires in order for them to fulfill their mission to this darkened world (although it is now somewhat lightening and en-lightening by devotees' decrees to the violet flame and thus soon-to-be recognized as freedom's star!).

In the name of heaven, beloved ones, the guarding of the body, mind, soul and energy levels of an incoming holy child is an awesome responsibility! It is for this very reason that many desire to sponsor such holy children at inner levels and to act as their spiritual guardians, some being themselves beyond the age of childbearing. While they may elect to stand, as it were, as godfather or godmother for incoming lifestreams—a good and necessary service—let me point out that to the present hour the natural process of childbirth continues on earth; and consequently there is a desperate need for dedicated fathers and mothers.

It is true that there are a number of studies being given attention at higher levels to alter the present system of giving birth, to cause the entire process to be painless and more immaculate, raising earth's evolutions into a new Christ era. Yet we must be most practical and admit to the

Power of God's Love to flow forth through his embodied sons and daughters both to generate and to regenerate all life upon earth.

Now, you cannot deny, for all around you the evidence stands, that side by side with the lightbearers the planet is filled with children who are obviously rebellious spirits. Many of these have been released by the Lords of Karma to reembody in recent years, some of them having been detained for a considerable period in the compound* (some since the sinking of Atlantis), others having been held in special spheres of assistance in healing temples, awaiting rebirth.

The opportunities and restrictions governing the life of each incoming child are determined by their own karma and reviewed by the Karmic Board to determine what dispensations of mercy may be granted. Each soul receives the approval and seal of the Lord Maha Chohan and beloved Mother Mary prior to entering the etheric birth canal.

Remember, it is simply not possible for us to set aside cosmic law because someone knocking at the portals of birth deems himself wiser than he is. Therefore the law will always act according to God's Justice both toward souls awaiting their turn for another opportunity to make things right on earth and toward those who pray for the opportunity to have them—as well as toward those who, mutually bound by difficult

---

*compound: place on the astral plane where recalcitrant souls are detained to defer reembodiment until a more propitious period for their evolvement.

karma, have no choice but to play their parts and play them well.

The sacred use of God's vital energy for procreative purposes by those who wish to sponsor a family dedicated to constructive purposes is not only admirable but commendable. I do not say that all will or necessarily should elect to pursue this path. Certainly free will must govern all matters of marriage and procreation, for much is at stake and the commitment is large. By a like token, do not think it vanity that desires to house and to nurture a grand lifestream—whether that lifestream be a karma-free being or one of considerable attainment on the Path or a great benefactor of Life—but let both parents acknowledge the pure desire to be simply and humbly the LORD's instruments.[24]

Remember, dear ones, that at the time when an advanced soul comes into embodiment there is always a scene of parting at higher levels and the full awareness that the mission of that one may or may not be successful. When entering a veil of flesh, there is never any guarantee that that individual will not, through some form of contention, become involved in a karmic situation necessitating a round of unpleasant experiences.

Simply because an individual is highly evolved or a Christed one, as was beloved Jesus, does not insure against failure. There is always a risk, the eventuality that one's friends who had intended to be his guardians and the guardians of his Light will betray that Light. Then, too, there is the possibility that associates will misinterpret his motives, discount his good intents or ignorantly strive to force him from the ranks of God's service through impugning his character, and in other regrettable manners fail to assist his holy purposes through misunderstanding and indifference aggravated by the opposition of the sinister force.

Let all recognize that upon the earth body in this present hour there are children of Light and children of mammon. Although Jesus said, "The children of this world are in their generation wiser than the children of Light," [25] let all realize that the children of Light *must* become wiser than the children of mammon!

I do not deny that some of the children of mammon have behaved as children of Light and that some children of Light have behaved as children of mammon. This does not prove that the law is wrong. It simply proves the tenacity of the element of human discord, vanity, and sin on the one hand and on the other the Power of the Creator's inherent goodness that seeks to raise all life.

It also proves that laggard qualities are contagious and that vigilance is required to hold an immaculate concept regardless of what appearances may be involved and to guard the heirs of the promises from the astral contagions of modern life and bad examples parading everywhere. Certainly virtuous motherhood such as Mother Mary offered is yet the requirement of the hour!

Inasmuch as I am dealing here with interrelationships between people, I want to point out that in the case of employer and employee, there ought never to exist any form of slavery or tyranny. It is as much the responsibility of the employee as the employer to see that this slavery does not exist. Therefore, "Let brotherly love continue." [26]

The Word of the LORD recorded in the second chapter of Genesis brings to mind Love's enduring tribute to the creation of twin flames in the white fire ovoid and their divine Love which endures unto the blessing of all other human relationships: "It is not good that the man should be alone; I will make him an help meet for him." [27] Where the karma of twin flames does not allow their togetherness in a given life, soul mates as partners on the Path brought together for a special service also provide the polarity for the cosmic wholeness to be nurtured on earth in the complementary roles of Alpha and Omega.

This statement from Genesis concerning man's aloneness has also been correctly interpreted as meaning "It is not good for the manifestation to be all one; therefore, I will make individual parts of my all-oneness," or, as the LORD promised Abraham, "I will multiply thy seed as the stars of the heaven, and as the sand which is upon the sea shore." [28]

And so, let the love of the individual parts for one another and for the Whole exceed self-love and excel unto an expansion of Love within the creation in honor of the Creator, finding thereby reunion with the one Life which is All and in all.

F. *Christ Love*

The great and awesome Power of creativity that floods forth myriad and wondrous forms in nature and in man, that creates cosmic beings and angel messengers of fire, holds in cosmic Mind the Truth that a love not wholly integrated with the allness of the cosmos in the oneness thereof would not be God, would not be Good.

Inasmuch as Goodness requires some objective manifestation of itself in order to love, the great creative will of God was and is to create many Self-expressions in form: the wondrous design of twin flames descending from the Sun to unveil in flesh the faces of Alpha and Omega in so many ways—sons and daughters of the Most High, children of the One basking in the Love play of angels and elementals, guarded by nature spirits, luminous presences and mighty beings of the Elohimic spheres, all in one grand hierarchical order, that each one, from an electron to a star, might, in receiving his Love, return that Love not only to the Central Sun and the Creator but also to all creatures he has made, dwelling now in the peripheral worlds of time and space.

Few have reached the level of Saint Francis of Assisi in their comprehension of this concept concerning the multifaceted parts of the one individed Whole. I would, therefore, call to your attention the great depth of compassion and the true scientific understanding of the psychology of the soul, far in advance of his time, which your blessed Kuthumi externalized in his embodiment as dear Francis and which remain to the present hour in his ascended state the outstanding qualities of his service with beloved Jesus in the office of World Teacher.

Truly his life was a message of God's Love borne in the chalice of the fiery heart of the saint for all Life's expressions:

Dear Francis' love for creatures great and small
  Compassed the sea, the sky, and all.
His love the outbreathed universe did frame
  As stars ensoul compassion's flame
On path where every open heart did sing
  And hopes did rise like bird on wing.
O Love, thy flame shall bear one yet on high!
  O Love that lives and cannot die,
To cross the bar and then become a part
  Of God's own fiery beating heart!
For where I AM in shining knowing free,
  I feel the power of Truth fill me.
What thrills me most as cup runs over now
  Is this great truth: That I AM Thou!

How great was his example! Yet, the great example need not be anyone with whom you are familiar, or it may be anyone with whom you are familiar. In the history of Christendom the great

338 BOOK THREE · CHAPTER 3   Love

example finds its purest form and expression in
the figure and divinely human personality of
Jesus. And yet I do not blaspheme when I say that
many men and women in embodiment today
have, through their devotion to Jesus and to the
great God Self, received the same sacred love
tokens from God's heart that the Almighty imparted unto Jesus.

The dove of the Holy Spirit has rested upon
their heads and its snow-white radiance of purity
has flowed from their hearts. Though not always
well known, the divine gifts of healing, of miracles
and of teaching and preaching the Word of God
have been given unto them also.[29]

Some have founded no new religion, all have
supported holy endeavors and sought to be examples of God's purity. Over the centuries mature
sons and daughters of God of considerable accomplishment in many fields—prophets, teachers,
reformers and not a few great lights—have bright-
ened the planetary corner with their Presence.
And by their balanced expression and generous
sharing of their developed threefold flame—to
which the Saviour by his grace has added his momentum—they have been wayshowers of the path
of individual Christhood ordained by God not for
one son alone but for all heirs of His Light.

For unto all who believe in the reality of the
Christ-flame in Jesus, the Master has the Power to
make them—by Love's enkindling Power, by the
engrafting of the Word—*to make them*, I say,

more the Son of God. Thus it is written (John 1:12) and thus the Ascended Master Jesus Christ initiates his disciples today by the heart-to-heart impartation of his flame unto those who work his Works and embody his Word.

I would, therefore, offer this plaudit on their behalf, this acknowledgment in Freedom's name that the world is not so poor as it sometimes considers itself to be in the manifestation of this great God-essence of Love but that it already possesses a great wealth of divine Love—a Love all too often unrecognized even when seen!—a Love that commemorates Jesus' devotion to his fold and upholds the standard he set for those who would follow him in deed.

To them he also paid tribute with the words: A new commandment I give unto you, That ye love one another *as I have loved you.* By this shall all men know that ye are my disciples, if ye have love one to another.[30] Greater love hath no man than this, that a man lay down his life for his friends. Ye are my friends, if ye do whatsoever I command you.[31]

This Love, as Life's essential ingredient, flows not only from God on high to the hearts of known and unknown manifestations of himself below, but also from holy men and women in embodiment, whose Love as devotion and service to every part of God's Life becomes day by day more like unto the Father and the Son in their mutual adoration.

Man's penetration of the holy substance of

God's essential Love provides him, through the power of the Maha Chohan, with an infusion of that élan which makes the world go round. That it does not spin faster, that it does not more swiftly throw off its discord, can be attributed to the impediments to divine Love sustained by the masses who yet know not what they do.[32]

Those hearts—and many of them yearn to know the Truth and to be free[33]—who pursue a dyed-in-the-wool path of their own misguided wills and spew out hatred against men of goodwill whom they do not understand, do indeed place their feet in ruts of stumbling upon the mountain of attainment.

And although the great connecting link, the lifeline from on high, as a giant skein of Light and Life dropped down to earth, continually pulls man forward, the traction created by the pulling back of these people (the recalcitrance of a stiff-necked generation), compounded by the sheer weight of their numbers exercising free will in opposition to (as the antithesis of) the Divine, does in effect prevent the universal manifestation of God's kingdom upon earth!

G. *Harmony, the Fulfilling of the Law of Love*

In the holy name of Love we would speak in a practical manner on the great need for keeping and maintaining one's personal harmony not only in one's feelings but also in one's thoughts. For harmony is not only the Law of Love, it is the epitome of Love, the sign of Love's true conquering heroes.

Now, as many of you know, when the thought desires to go to the right and the feelings pull to the left, most often it is the feelings that win out and the thought, by rationalization, will gravitate in their direction. And in many cases, unless, of course, the feelings are motivated by purest Love, this is not the fulfillment of the law of harmony; rather it is very often a compromise made by the soul caught between the mental and feeling worlds. And it can result in that peace without honor which, because it is not based on Principle, cannot provide the permanent solution to the problem.

In all his noble efforts to precipitate substance alchemically, man will find no higher alchemical key than the purity of divine Love flowing forth from his consciousness as God's thoughts and feelings—winged messengers of Light delivering blessings, attracting more of their kind and returning to the alchemist the blessings of the abundant Life.

The Love of God made manifest in the threefold flame scintillates with immortal brilliance. Its vibrant, radiant, all-enfolding Light comprises the sun flame centers of all interrelated macrocosmic/microcosmic energy systems in material and spiritual manifestation. Withdraw the Power of Love from any of these and their eventual collapse is certain.

Every system of worlds, planetary or starry body that has ever been dissolved, whatever the apparent or scientific reason, has collapsed from within due to the withdrawal of the Love charge from the sun center. The lapse from the moment of withdrawal to the moment of dissolution may range from thousands to even millions of years as men reckon time; or it may consist of a few microseconds—or the pause between them. But the decay of every system begins with the withdrawal of Love's 'lodestone' from its center. Love, then, is truly the cohesive Power of the universe.

One of the most dreaded diseases upon earth today manifests as a result of mankind's hatred toward one another, which, when it returns to the sender, drives the Love element from the cells, thereby causing a perversion of their function. Through invasion and metastasis, the disease eventually spreads throughout the body; and death ensues when the form, whose cells have lost the cohesive power of Love, can no longer magnetize enough light to sustain the bodily functions. Though the cause may be ancient, having lain dormant for lifetimes, the karma comes due. Only flood tides of Love and oceans of violet fire can bring permanent resolution to the festering hatred that lodges in the psyche of man.

Yet to this day some have vowed to bear world karma in their members. Saints without blemish are these who take into their bodies the world sin of human hatred. Thus, judge not the infirm, but help them! uphold them! heal them! by Love. In healing the many types of cancer and other physical, mental, or emotional disorders, the invocation to divine Love is essential. And the healer must be all Love in action.

Jesus' compassionate response to the cry of the two blind men, "Thou son of David, have mercy on us," was a personal action of divine Love. He touched their eyes and said, "According to your faith, be it unto you."[34]

The Master's healing of the woman who touched his garment without his knowledge was an example of the impersonal action of divine Love. His response, "Who touched me? for I perceive that Light hath passed from me to her . . .," showed that the Impersonal Christ had healed her through him without his foreknowledge.[35]

Divine Love as the living Christ, the Son behind every son of man, is both personal and impersonal; and it is fulfilled measure for measure, as ye are able, in every one of you through the cycles of the law of your Being, the law that is ever Love in manifestation. When you exercise it, the Law of Love unites the purity of justice, mercy, and freedom in perfect balance through the threefold flame within your heart.

Let those who will, discount the law as Love and deny its corrective measures as an action of Love. I charge you to remember the words "Whom the LORD loveth he chasteneth, and scourgeth *every* son whom he receiveth."[36]

In closing this Trilogy, then, I say unto all, let not selfish love carry you into the byways of delusion, far and apart from your brothers and sisters and those other parts of Life whom God has made. Remember, too, that those who have chosen to embody elements of evil ever seek to divide the children of the Light by subtlety, flattery, hypocrisy, money schemes, sexual entanglements, etc.—you yourself can name the rest; whereas true Love would unify the sons and daughters of God in the very essence of holiness and world service.

To pay tribute to Love is to pay tribute to the great drawing Power of God's own tripartite flame. Love is God's flame of Being in manifestation. One day the scientists of the world, through special instruments, will be able to measure a portion of the Love flame and its radiant energies, but never will an instrument be made that has a scale great enough to measure the all-encompassing Power of infinite Love.

Infinite Love can best be expressed as the manifestation of God. The manifestation of God can occur in everyone. It is the destiny of man that shakes from man his dust. Love, then, is the fullness of God as he manifests man. I tell you there is no limit to the degree of God's Love which anyone who will may manifest. Anyone who wills to invoke it, to be it, and to share it may be the answer to Love's call and calling.

Here in the realm of divine Love is the City

of God, the foursquare city described by beloved John [37] as the place of conscious attainment where the fullness of your aspirations may find unhampered expression. Here your soul looks out upon the great wide-open spaces of the creation.

Love has unlimited new worlds to conquer. Love is the Promised Land where the strength of the lion's nature is given to the heart of the lamb, and the Good Shepherd of the Eternal Covenant seals all in the victory of the expanding Three-in-One Flame of God-Good, worlds without end.

For thine is the Kingdom—the consciousness of God, his Wisdom; thine is the Power—the unlimited, inexhaustible strength to be and to fulfill your fiery destiny; and thine is the Glory—the crowning Light of Love's diadem of perfection—forever and forever. Amen.

Thy God hath willed it so.

I AM faithfully in Freedom's cause
and service,

Saint Germain

✠

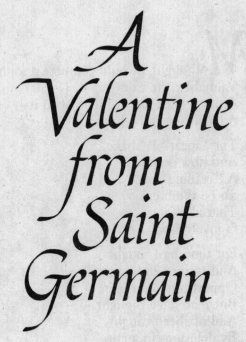

A
Valentine
from
Saint
Germain

Methought I would compose a sonnet
Valued by the world,
A poem with light of love upon it—
A challenge to be hurled.

The "spear" I "shake"
And now do make,
A "Willing" of "I AM,"*
To be the break
That all may take
O lovely God, I AM.

For thou hast sought
And to men brought
Opportunity and plan,
But men have thought
And oft been caught
By delusions in a jam.

Now if the power
Of Truth this hour
Earth's freedom course must chart,
There must be men,
O valiant men,
To rally from the start—

*Will-i-am Shake-speare

To see behind
The shams of men
The fraud they have created,
Attacking Truth
And Sons of Light
Whom they have oft berated.

Now, I might add
This "not so bad"
Assessment of our friends
Is bad enough
Through lacking Love—
How they have underrated!

But we who've been
A part of earth
And felt the lash
Of tyrants bold—
For freedom's sake
We now do make
A call to hearts of gold.

Stand stalwart, then,
And let your heart
Be framed by fragrant flowers,
Not earthly substance
That will fade—
Choose immortelles
From heaven's bowers.

And see thy heart
As altar chalice,
Loved by God and man,

And holding forth forevermore
Tripartite Flame
... 'Twill exalt the plan.

You are never alone
But always one
With us who love you now,
And as all came
From Central Sun
Our Love's eternal, vowed.

May I, on this occasion, speak of the heart to those of you who are perhaps familiar with the subject. And at the same time, inasmuch as many new souls are joining the ranks of those who read and love the Pearls of Wisdom, may I say to all that your heart is indeed one of the choicest gifts of God.

Within it there is a central chamber surrounded by a forcefield of such light and protection that we call it a 'cosmic interval.' It is a chamber separated from Matter and no probing could ever discover it. It occupies simultaneously not only the third and fourth dimensions but also other dimensions unknown to man. This central chamber, called the altar of the heart, is thus the connecting point of the mighty silver cord of light that descends from your God Presence to sustain the beating of your physical heart, giving you life, purpose, and cosmic integration.

I urge all men to treasure this point of contact that they have with Life by giving conscious recognition to it. You do not need to understand by sophisticated language or scientific postulation the how, why, and wherefore of this activity.

Be content to know that God is there and that within you there is a point of contact with the Divine, a spark of fire from the Creator's own heart called the threefold flame of Life. There it burns as the triune essence of Love, Wisdom, and Power.

Each acknowledgment paid daily to the flame within your heart will amplify the power and illumination of Love within your being. Each such attention will produce a new sense of dimension for you, if not outwardly apparent then subconsciously manifest within the folds of your inner thoughts.

Neglect not, then, your heart as the altar of God. Neglect it not as the sun of your manifest being. Draw from God the power of Love and amplify it within your heart. Then send it out into the world at large as the bulwark of that which shall overcome the darkness of the planet, saying:

I AM the Light of the Heart
Shining in the darkness of being
And changing all into the golden treasury
Of the Mind of Christ.

I AM projecting my Love
Out into the world
To erase all errors
And to break down all barriers.

I AM the power of infinite Love,
Amplifying itself
Until it is victorious,
World without end!

With this gift of infinite freedom from God's own heart this Valentine season, I close this epistle with a never-ending promise to assist you to find your immortal freedom as you determine never to give up and never to turn back. Remember that as long as you face the Light, the shadows are always behind. And the Light is there, too, to transmute them all.

Keep your gaze toward "the City" and be not overcome of evil but overcome evil with Good.

For the freedom of all mankind,

Lovingly, I AM

Saint Germain

✠

Book Four

The
Alchemy
of the Word

Stones for the
Wise Masterbuilders

Mark L. Prophet
Elizabeth Clare Prophet

In the beginning was the Word . . .

Glossary

Words set in italics are defined elsewhere in the glossary.

Adept. A true adept is an initiate of the *Great White Brotherhood* of a high degree of attainment, especially in the control of *Matter*, physical forces, nature spirits, and bodily functions; fully the alchemist undergoing advanced initiations of the *sacred fire* on the path of the *ascension*.

Akashic records. All that transpires in an individual's world is recorded in a substance and dimension known as akasha (Sanskrit, from the root *kāś* 'to be visible, appear', 'to shine brightly', 'to see clearly'). Akasha is primary substance, the subtlest, ethereal essence that fills the whole of space; "*etheric*" energy vibrating at a certain frequency so as to absorb, or record, all of the impressions of life. These records can be read by *adepts* or those whose *soul (psychic)* faculties are developed.

Alpha and Omega. The Divine Wholeness of the Father-Mother God affirmed as "the beginning and the ending" by the Lord *Christ* in Revelation. Ascended *twin flames* of the Cosmic *Christ consciousness* who hold the balance of the masculine-feminine polarity of the Godhead in the Great

Publications and cassettes cited for further teaching on topics in this glossary are available from Summit University Press, Box 5000, Livingston, MT 59047-5000. Telephone: (406) 222-8300. For prices and information on postage charges, see pp. 464–69.

Central Sun of *cosmos.* Thus, through the Universal Christ, the *Word* incarnate, the Father is the origin and the Mother is the fulfillment of the cycles of God's consciousness expressed throughout the *Spirit-Matter* creation. *See also* Mother.

(Rev. 1:8, 11; 21:6; 22:13. Compare the Hindu Puruṣa and Prakṛti.)

Angel. Divine spirit, herald, forerunner; messenger sent by God to deliver his Word to his children. Ministering spirits sent forth to tend the heirs of *Christ*—to comfort, protect, guide, strengthen, teach, counsel, and warn. Cohorts of *Light* in the service of the Christed ones, the *sons and daughters of God,* throughout cosmos. An 'angle' of God's consciousness—an aspect of his Self-awareness; a being fashioned by God out of his own flaming Presence to minister unto his Life in form. "And of the angels he saith, 'Who maketh his angels spirits and his ministers a flame of fire.'" The angelic hosts comprise an evolution set apart from mankind by their flaming selfhood and their purity of devotion to the Godhead and to the *Archangels* and hierarchs under whose command they serve. Their function is to concentrate, accelerate, and amplify the attributes of God on behalf of his creation. They minister to the needs of mankind by magnetizing Light to their auras, intensifying feelings of hope, faith, and charity, honor, integrity, courage, truth and freedom, mercy and justice, and every aspect of the crystal clarity of the Mind of God. Because of the blessedness of their unseen presence, the author of Hebrews said, "Be not forgetful to entertain strangers: for thereby some have entertained angels unawares"—and in so saying made a point for the case that angels do take embodiment and move among us as our best friends and helpers, even when total strangers.

Metaphorically speaking, angels are electrons revolving around the Sun Presence that is God—electrons who have elected, by his will innate within them, to expand his consciousness in every plane of being. Angels are electrons who have been 'charged' with the light/energy/consciousness of the Great *Central Sun* to be 'electrodes', i.e., pillars of God's fiery presence acting as 'step-down transformers' of the ineffable Light, that his children might receive some hope of the glory that is to come midst the dark night of their karmic condition upon earth. Angels can assume human form or that of 'rods' and 'cones' or spirals and coils of concentrated energy that can be released for personal and planetary healing in answer to the call of the Christed ones as a literal transfusion of the Body and Blood of the Cosmic Christ wherever and whenever there is a need. There are angels of healing, protection, love, comfort and compassion, angels attending the cycles of birth and death, angels of the All-Seeing Eye of God who wield the flaming sword of Truth to cleave asunder the Real from the Unreal. There are types and orders of angels who perform specific services in the *cosmic hierarchy*, such as *seraphim* and *cherubim*, and angel *devas* who serve with the nature spirits and *elementals* of fire, air, water, and earth.

The fallen angels are those who followed *Lucifer* in the Great Rebellion and whose consciousness therefore "fell" to lower levels of vibration and awareness as they were by law "cast out into the earth" at the hand of Archangel Michael—constrained, by the karma of their disobedience to God and his Christ and their blasphemy of his children, to take on and evolve through dense physical bodies. Here they walk about, as Peter said,

seeking whosesoever souls and minds and bodies
they may devour, sowing seeds of unrest and the
Luciferian rebellion among the people through the
subculture of rock music and drugs, the media, and
their Babylonian cult of idolatry. They are known
variously as the fallen ones, Luciferians, Watchers,
Nephilim, "giants in the earth," Satanists, Serpents,
sons of Belial, etc.

(Ps. 104:4; Heb. 1:7; 13:2; Rev. 12:9; Gen. 6:1–7. See Elizabeth
Clare Prophet, *Forbidden Mysteries of Enoch: Fallen Angels and
the Origins of Evil*, containing all the Enoch texts, including the
Book of Enoch and the Book of the Secrets of Enoch.)

Angel deva. *See* Deva.

Angel of the LORD. The presence of the Deity in
angelic form. The Seven *Archangels* and their
Archeiai ministering on the *seven rays* together with
the five of the secret rays and the hierarchs of the
thirteenth are the Angels of the LORD that "stand in
the Presence of God" and are "sent from God" as
his messengers to transmit the *Light (Christ consciousness)* of that I AM THAT I AM to his sons
and daughters for the accomplishment of those
dispensations that they announce. Unto Moses was
revealed the *I AM Presence* through "the angel of
the LORD who appeared unto him in a flame of
fire," which was the actual presence and personification of the I AM THAT I AM by Archangel
Michael. This truth confirms the initiation conferred by God upon certain beings advanced in the
heavenly *hierarchy* to actually bear in their person—
in their *chakras* and auric field—the weight of God's
Presence. Even so have his prophets, *messengers* and
Christed ones borne this "burden" of the LORD, as
they were called to be his visible evangels in form,
taking embodiment to minister with the *angels*,

Archangels, *cherubim*, and *seraphim* on behalf of souls evolving in the earth planes.

(Luke 1:19; Exod. 3:2; Jer. 23:30–40; Zech. 9:1; 12:1; Hab. 1:1; Mal. 1:1.)

Antahkarana. (Skt. for "internal sense organ.") The web of life. The net of *light* spanning *Spirit* and *Matter* connecting and sensitizing the whole of creation within itself and to the heart of God.

Antichrist. *n.* When capitalized, the specific embodiment of Absolute *Evil*, the Evil One. The planetary *dweller-on-the-threshold*. "Little children, it is the last time: and as ye have heard that Antichrist shall come, even now are there many antichrists; whereby we know that it is the last time." The term is also applied to such as *Lucifer, Satan,* the Watchers, Nephilim, and other fallen *angels* who "kept not their first estate," who stand in opposition to Absolute Good. These betrayers of the *Word* have sworn allegiance to the powers of Death and Hell and vowed to destroy God incarnate in his Church, his saints and his little ones. When lowercased, a person or power antagonistic to the *Christ,* or *Light,* in *Jesus* and his own. *adj.* Having the characteristics of Antichrist, denying the Christ potential in the children of God, destroying *souls* by the perversion of the Person and Light of Christ.

(I John 2:18, 22; 4:3; II John 7; Gen. 6:1–7; Jude 6.)

Archangel. Hierarch of angelic hosts; the highest rank in the orders of *angels.* Each of the *seven rays* has a presiding Archangel who, with his divine complement, an *Archeia,* embodies the *God consciousness* of the *ray* and directs the bands of angels serving in their command on that ray. The Archangels and

Archeiai of the rays and the location of their *retreats* are as follows: First Ray, blue, Archangel *Michael* and **Faith**, Banff, near Lake Louise, Canada. Second Ray, yellow, Archangel **Jophiel** and **Christine**, south of the Great Wall near Lanchow, north central China. Third Ray, petal pink, deep rose and ruby, Archangel **Chamuel** and **Charity**, St. Louis, Missouri, USA. Fourth Ray, white and mother-of-pearl, Archangel **Gabriel** and **Hope**, between Sacramento and Mount Shasta, California, USA. Fifth Ray, green, Archangel **Raphael** and *Mary*, Fátima, Portugal. Sixth Ray, purple and gold, ruby, Archangel **Uriel** and **Aurora**, Tatra Mountains, south of Cracow, Poland. Seventh Ray, violet and purple, Archangel *Zadkiel* and *Holy Amethyst,* Cuba.

(See *Vials of the Seven Last Plagues: The Judgments of Almighty God Delivered by the Seven Archangels.* Archangel Gabriel, *Mysteries of the Holy Grail.* "The Class of the Archangels," in *Pearls of Wisdom,* 1981, vol. 24, Book I, nos. 4–15; 8-audiocassette album. "The Healing Power of Angels," in *Pearls of Wisdom,* 1986, vol. 29, Book I, nos. 25–34; Book II, nos. 51–57; 2 videocassette albums, 2 cassettes each; 2 audiocassette albums, 12 cassettes each. Elizabeth Clare Prophet, "Self-Healing Workshop with the Healing Power of Angels," 3 audiocassettes; "On the Healing Power of Angels: Christ Wholeness—the Seven Rays of God," 2 videocassettes; 3 audiocassettes.)

Archangel Michael. *See* Michael, Archangel.

Archangel Zadkiel. *See* Zadkiel, Archangel.

Archeia (pl. **Archeiai**). Divine complement and *twin flame* (feminine polarity) of an *Archangel.*

Arhat. A Buddhist monk who has attained nirvana; one undergoing the initiations of the *Buddha.*

Ascended being. *See* Ascended Master.

Ascended Master. One who, through *Christ* and the putting on of that Mind which was in Christ *Jesus*, has mastered time and space and in the process gained the mastery of the self in the *four lower bodies* and the four quadrants of *Matter*, in the *chakras* and the balanced *threefold flame*. An Ascended Master has also transmuted at least 51 percent of his *karma*, fulfilled his *divine plan*, and taken the initiations of the Ruby Ray unto the ritual of the *ascension*— acceleration by the *sacred fire* into the *Presence* of the I AM THAT I AM. An Ascended Master is one who inhabits the planes of *Spirit*, the kingdom of God (God's consciousness), and may teach unascended souls in an etheric *retreat* or in the etheric cities on the *etheric plane* (the kingdom of heaven). (Phil. 2:5.)

Ascension. The ritual whereby the *soul* reunites with the *Spirit* of the Living God, the *I AM Presence*. The ascension is the culmination of the soul's God-victorious sojourn in time and space. It is the reward of the righteous that is the gift of God after the last judgment before the great white throne in which every *man* is judged "according to their works." The ascension was experienced by Enoch, of whom it is written that he "walked with God: and he was not, for God took him"; by Elijah, who went up by a whirlwind into heaven; and by *Jesus*, although his ascension did not take place on the occasion when scripture records that he was taken up into a cloud into heaven. The Ascended Master El Morya has revealed that Jesus made his ascension from *Shamballa* after his passing in Kashmir at the age of 81 in A.D. 77. The reunion with God in the ascension, signifying the end of the rounds of *karma* and rebirth and the return to the LORD's glory, is the goal of life for the *sons and daughters of God*. Jesus said, "No man hath ascended up to heaven but he that came down from heaven, even the Son of man." By the salvation, 'Self-elevation', the conscious raising up of the **Son of God** within her temple, the soul puts on her wedding garment to fulfill the office of the **Son** (Sun, or *Light*) **of manifestation.** The soul is made worthy by Jesus' grace to be the bearer of his cross and his crown. Following the initiatic path of Jesus, she ascends through the *Christ Self* to her LORD, the I AM Presence, whence she descended.

(Rev. 20:12, 13; Gen. 5:24; II Kings 2:11; Luke 24:50, 51; Acts 1:9–11; John 3:13. See Serapis Bey, *Dossier on the Ascension.* Elizabeth Clare Prophet, A *Retreat on the Ascension—an Experience with God,* 8-audiocassette album.)

Aspirant. One who aspires; specifically, one who aspires to reunion with God through the ritual of the *ascension.* One who aspires to overcome the conditions and limitations of time and space to fulfill the cycles of *karma* and one's reason for being through the *sacred labor.*

Astral. *adj.* Having or carrying the characteristics of the *astral plane. n.* A frequency of time and space beyond the physical yet below the mental, corresponding with the *emotional body* of man and the collective unconscious of the race. Because the astral plane has been muddied by impure human thought and feeling, the term "astral" is also used in a negative context to refer to that which is impure or "psychic." *See also* Psychic.

Astral body. *See* Emotional body.

Astral plane. The repository of the collective thought/ feeling patterns, conscious and unconscious, of mankind. The pristine purpose of this band, or frequency, is for the amplification of the pure thoughts and feelings of God in man. Instead it has been polluted with the impure records (vibrations) of the race memory multiplied ad infinitum by an evolution caught in the riptides and repetitive cycles of its own negativity.

Atlantis. The island continent that existed where the Atlantic Ocean now is and that sank in cataclysm (the Flood of Noah) approximately 11,600 years ago as calculated by James Churchward. Vividly depicted by Plato; 'seen' and described by Edgar Cayce in his readings; recalled in scenes from Taylor Caldwell's *Romance of Atlantis*; scientifically explored and authenticated by the late German scientist Otto Muck, who fixed the time and date of her destruction (by an asteroid that plunged into the Bermuda Triangle with the force of 30,000 hydrogen bombs) at 8 p.m. June 5, 8498 B.C.! In his dialogues, Plato recounts that on "the island of Atlantis there was a great and wonderful empire" that ruled Africa as far as Egypt, Europe as far as Italy, and "parts of the continent" (thought to be a reference to America, specifically Central America, Peru, and the Valley of the Mississippi). It has been postulated that Atlantis and the small islands to its east and west formed a continuous bridge of land from America to Europe and Africa. (James Churchward, *The Lost Continent of Mu* [1931; reprint, New York: Paperback Library Edition, 1968], p. 226. Otto Muck, *The Secret of Atlantis* [New York: Pocket Books, 1979]. Ignatius Donnelly, *Atlantis: The Antediluvian World* [New York: Dover Publications, 1976], pp. 11, 23, 173, 473. For lectures on Atlantis delivered by Elizabeth Clare Prophet, based on the Teachings of the Ascended Masters and *A Dweller on Two Planets* by Phylos the Tibetan, send for a Summit University Press catalog.)

Aura. A luminous emanation or 'electromagnetic' field surrounding the physical body, often equated with the *astral body*. A halo or nimbus associated with the saints, originating in the *soul* and soul blueprint, which mirrors by *free will* the heavenly or the earthly patterns. The distinctive radiation of sentient life and inorganic objects as captured in Kirlian photography. Breath or atmosphere surrounding and interpenetrating the *four lower bodies* of man and his *chakras* upon which the impressions, thoughts, feelings, words, and actions of the individual are registered, including his *karma* and the records of past lives. The highly charged circle of *sacred fire* surrounding *Christ*, an *Ascended Master*, *angel*, *Elohim* or *Cosmic Being*, transferable as 'grace' to whomsoever they will it. A spiritual corona, referred to as the L-field or Life-field (*astral/ etheric* sheath) surrounding mankind and organic life that both regulates and reflects the health, vitality, and longevity of the *physical body* or organism. (See Kuthumi, *Studies of the Human Aura*, and Djwal Kul, *Intermediate Studies of the Human Aura*; both published in *The Human Aura*. Elizabeth Clare Prophet, *The Control of the Human Aura through the Science of the Spoken Word*, 2-audiocassette album.)

Avatar. (Skt. *avatāra* 'descent', from *avatarati* 'he descends', from *ava-* 'away' + *tarati* 'he crosses over'.) The incarnation of the *Word*; the descent or crossing-over of the Universal *Christ* from the plane of *Spirit* to the plane of *Matter*. The avatar of an age is the Christ, the incarnation of the Son of God (Vishnu), the Second Person of the Trinity. The avatar, with his divine complement, Shakti, or *twin flame*, "outpictures" and "outplays" in consciousness and in the *four lower bodies* the archetypal pattern of the Father-Mother God for the evolution of *souls* in a two-thousand-year cycle. The principal avatars of an age are two in number—the masculine and feminine prototypes who embody and show by their example the path of initiation designated by the solar hierarchies responsible for the lifewaves moving toward the center of the Cosmic Christ through the Open Door (the Teacher and Teaching) of that two-thousand-year dispensation. According to mankind's *karma*, the evolutionary status quo of the children of God (their soul progress or lack of it in previous dispensations), and the requirements of the Logos, the *Manus* may designate numerous Christed ones—those endued with an extraordinary *Light*—to go forth as world teachers and wayshowers. The Christed ones demonstrate in a given epoch the Law of the Logos, stepped down through the Manu(s) and the avatar(s) until it is made flesh through their own Word and Work—to be ultimately victorious in its fulfillment in all souls of Light sent forth to conquer time and space in that era.

Ballard, Guy W. *Messenger* for the *Great White Brotherhood* from the late 1920s to the year 1939, when he made his *ascension* on December 31. Now the *Ascended Master* Godfre, he ensouls the consciousness of God-obedience. He was embodied as Richard the Lion-Hearted and as George Washington. In his final embodiment, with his wife and *twin flame*, Edna Ballard (who ascended February 12, 1971), he founded the I AM movement under the direction of the Ascended Master *Saint Germain*. His pen name was Godfré Ray King, hers Lotus Ray King. Their most important works are *Unveiled Mysteries*, *The Magic Presence*, and *The "I AM" Discourses*.

Bodhisattva. A Sanskrit term meaning literally a being of bodhi (or enlightenment), a being destined for enlightenment, or one whose energy and power is directed toward enlightenment. A Bodhisattva is one who is destined to become a *Buddha* but has foregone the bliss of nirvana with a vow to save all children of God on earth. In the Mahayana school of Buddhism, becoming a Bodhisattva is the goal of the *Path*. The path of the Bodhisattva is generally divided into ten stages, called *bhumis*. The Bodhisattva strives to progress from one stage to the next until he obtains enlightenment.
(See the following by Elizabeth Clare Prophet: "Lord Maitreya: The Coming Buddha Who Has Come" and "The Path of the Bodhisattva: The Historical Maitreya," in *Pearls of Wisdom*, 1984, vol. 27, Book I, pp. 1–76; Book II, pp. 1–74. "The Path of the Bodhisattva: Confession," 1 videocassette; 2 audiocassettes. "The Path of the Bodhisattva: The Guru-Chela Relationship—Marpa and Milarepa," 3 audiocassettes. "The Age of Maitreya," 1 videocassette; 2 audiocassettes. "The Buddhic Essence," two 1-hr. TV shows on video; 4 audiocassettes.)

Bodies of man. The four lower bodies are four sheaths consisting of four distinct frequencies that surround the *soul*—the physical, emotional, mental, and etheric—providing vehicles for the soul in her journey through time and space. The etheric sheath, highest in vibration, is the gateway to the three higher bodies, which are the *Christ Self*, the *I AM Presence*, and the *Causal Body*. *See also* Chart of Your Divine Self, Etheric body, Mental body, Emotional body, and Physical body.
(See Mark L. Prophet and Elizabeth Clare Prophet, *Climb the Highest Mountain*, 2d ed., pp. 164–73; *The Lost Teachings of Jesus I*, softbound, pp. 224–26; or pocketbook, Book Two, pp. 66–69.)

Body elemental. A being of nature (ordinarily invisible and functioning unnoticed in the physical octave)

that serves the *soul* from the moment of its first incarnation in the planes of *Mater* to tend the *physical body*. About three feet high and resembling the individual whom he serves, the body elemental, working with the guardian *angel* under the regenerative *Christ Self*, is the unseen friend and helper of man. *See also* Elementals.
(See Mark L. Prophet and Elizabeth Clare Prophet, *Climb the Highest Mountain*, 2d ed., pp. 455–64.)

Brahma/Vishnu/Shiva. The Hindu Trinity of Creator, Preserver, Destroyer/Deliverer. Brahma (God the Father) is seen as the Creator, Vishnu (God the Son) is seen as the Preserver, and Shiva (God the Holy Spirit) is seen as the Destroyer of Evil, hence the Deliverer of souls.
(See *Saint Germain On Alchemy*, pp. 316–20.)

Brotherhood. *See* Great White Brotherhood.

Brothers and Sisters of the Golden Robe. An order of *ascended* and *unascended beings* dedicated to the illumination of mankind through the flame of wisdom, headed by the *Ascended Master Kuthumi*, with retreats on the *etheric plane* in Shigatse and Kashmir.
(See Kuthumi, "The 'Second Coming' of the Saints," in *Pearls of Wisdom*, 1989, vol. 32, pp. 781–82, 786.)

Buddha. (From Skt. *budh* 'awake', 'know', 'perceive'.) Buddha means "the enlightened one." It denotes an office in the spiritual *hierarchy* of worlds that is attained by passing certain initiations of the *sacred fire*, including those of the *seven rays* of the *Holy Spirit* and of the five secret *rays*, the raising of the Feminine Ray (sacred fire of the Kundalini), and the "mastery of the seven in the seven multiplied by the power of the ten."
(See Djwal Kul, *Intermediate Studies of the Human Aura*, chap. 10; also published in *The Human Aura*.)

Gautama attained the enlightenment of the Buddha twenty-five centuries ago, a path he had pursued through many previous embodiments culminating in his forty-nine-day meditation under the Bo tree; hence he is called Gautama, the Buddha. He holds the office of *Lord of the World*, sustaining, by his *Causal Body* and *threefold flame*, the divine spark and consciousness in the evolutions of earth approaching the path of personal Christhood. His aura of Love/Wisdom ensouling the planet issues from his incomparable devotion to the Divine *Mother*. He is the hierarch of *Shamballa*, the original *retreat* of *Sanat Kumara* now on the *etheric plane* over the Gobi Desert. On April 18, 1981, the beloved Gautama Buddha established his *Western Shamballa* in America's wilderness at the northern border of Yellowstone National Park at the Inner Retreat of the Royal Teton Ranch. *See also* Lord of the World, Shamballa.

(See Gautama Buddha, "Quietly Comes the Buddha," in *Pearls of Wisdom*, 1975, vol. 18, nos. 17–29; *Pearls of Wisdom*, 1983, vol. 26. Elizabeth Clare Prophet, "The Message of the Inner Buddha," in *Pearls of Wisdom*, 1989, vol. 32, nos. 28–30; *A Message of Perfect Love from the Heart of Gautama Buddha*, 3-audiocassette album; *Peace in the Flame of Buddha*, 2-audiocassette album; *The Buddha and the Mother*, 6-audiocassette album; *The Buddhas in Winter*, 16-audiocassette album; "Insatiable Desire: The Enemy Within" and "The Eightfold Path of Self-Mastery," two 1-hr. TV shows on video; 2 audiocassettes.)

Lord Maitreya, the Cosmic *Christ*, has also passed the initiations of the Buddha. He is the long-awaited Coming Buddha who has come to the fore to teach all who have departed from the way of the Great Guru, *Sanat Kumara*, from whose lineage both he and Gautama descended. In the history of the planet, there have been numerous Buddhas who have served the evolutions of mankind through the steps and stages of the path of the *Bodhisattva*. In the East *Jesus* is referred to as the Buddha Issa. He is the World Saviour by the Love/ Wisdom of the Godhead. *See also* Lord Maitreya, Bodhisattva.

(See the following by Elizabeth Clare Prophet: *The Lost Years of Jesus.* "Lord Maitreya: The Coming Buddha Who Has Come" and "The Path of the Bodhisattva: The Historical Maitreya," in *Pearls of Wisdom,* 1984, vol. 27, Book I, pp. 1–76; Book II, pp. 1–74. "The Path of the Bodhisattva: The Historical Maitreya," 2 audiocassettes.)

In the 1960s, nine unascended *lifestreams* who had passed the initiations of the Buddha volunteered to embody to assist the evolutions of earth during their difficult and dangerous transition into the age of Aquarius. Their world service will be recognized when they have reached the age of the Christic and Buddhic example, age thirty-three to thirty-six. On January 1, 1983, Gautama Buddha announced that nine Buddhas who had been in nirvana for nine hundred years were descending the shaft of light to enter the hearts of nine individuals upon this planet and, by their Electronic Presence, to enter the forcefield of thousands of dedicated hearts. Gautama also released the dispensation that every prayer, mantra, and chant of devotees of Christ and Buddha from that time on would be multiplied by the power of the heart of Gautama and the nine Buddhas.

Carnal mind. The *human ego,* the human will, and the human intellect; self-awareness without the *Christ;* the animal nature of man, called mechanization man and the mechanization concept by the Master R; called the *dweller-on-the-threshold* in esoteric tradition. For the apostle Paul, "the carnal

mind is enmity against God: for it is not subject to
the law of God, neither indeed can be."
(Rom. 8:7. See Elizabeth Clare Prophet, "The Lost Teachings
of Jesus: On the Enemy Within," 2 audiocassettes. *Pearls of
Wisdom,* 1983, vol. 26, pp. 50, 383–91, 429–54; 1985, vol. 28,
Book I, pp. 84, 85–93, 97; 1986, vol. 29, Book I, pp. 199, 203,
210–12.)

Causal Body. The body of First Cause; seven concentric spheres of *light* and consciousness surrounding
the *I AM Presence* in the planes of *Spirit,* whose
momentums, added to by the Good—the LORD's
Word and Works manifested by the *soul* in all past
lives—are accessible today moment by moment as
we need them. One's spiritual resources and creativity—talents, graces, gifts and genius, garnered
through exemplary service on the seven *rays*—may
be drawn forth from the Causal Body through
invocation made to the I AM Presence in the name
of the *Christ Self.* The Causal Body is the place
where we "lay up treasure in heaven"—the storehouse of every good and perfect thing that is a part
of our true identity. In addition, the great spheres
of the Causal Body are the dwelling place of the
Most High God to which *Jesus* referred when he
said, "In my Father's house are many man-
sions. . . . I go to prepare a place for you . . . . I will
come again and receive you unto myself; that
where I AM [where I, the incarnate Christ, AM in
the I AM Presence], there ye may be also." The
Causal Body is the mansion, or habitation, of the
Spirit of the I AM THAT I AM to which the soul
returns through Christ Jesus and the individual
Christ Self in the ritual of the *ascension.* The
Causal Body as the star of each man's individualization of the God Flame was referred to by Paul
when he said, "One star differeth from another

star in glory." *See also* Chart of Your Divine Self. (Matt. 6:19–21; John 14:2, 3; I Cor. 15:41.)

Cave of Symbols. *Etheric* as well as physical *retreat* of the Master *Saint Germain* located at Table Mountain in the Rocky Mountains in the environs of Wyoming. Here initiates of the Seventh *Ray* are taken in their finer bodies to prepare for the *ascension*. Those who qualify receive teachings directly from the Master Alchemist in the sacred mysteries of Christhood as well as the science and technology of the new age. In the chemical and electrical laboratories of this retreat, scientists are perfecting formulas and inventions that they have been permitted to take from hermetically sealed cities at the bottom of the Atlantic Ocean, which have been protected since the sinking of *Atlantis*. Saint Germain is the guardian of the records of advanced scientific and spiritual achievements of ancient civilizations that will be brought forth in the *golden age* of Aquarius—to which Saint Germain and his studies in alchemy open the door. Three focuses at the Cave of Symbols designed to assist souls in the ascension process are the Atomic Accelerator, the Crystal Mirror, and the Sphere of Light.
(See *Pearls of Wisdom*, 1977, vol. 20, pp. 184, 192.)

Central sun. A vortex of energy, physical or spiritual, central to systems of worlds that it thrusts from, or gathers unto, itself by the central sun magnet. Whether in the *microcosm* or the *Macrocosm*, the central sun is the principal energy source, vortex, or nexus of energy interchange in atoms, cells, man (the heart center), amidst plant life and the core of the earth. The **Great Central Sun,** also called the **Great Hub,** is the center of *cosmos*; the point of integration of the *Spirit-Matter* cosmos;

the point of origin of all physical-spiritual creation; the nucleus, or white fire core, of the *Cosmic Egg*. (The God Star, Sirius, is the focus of the Great Central Sun in our sector of the galaxy.) The **Sun behind the sun** is the spiritual Cause behind the physical effect we see as our own physical sun and all other stars and star systems, seen or unseen, including the Great Central Sun. The Sun behind the sun of cosmos is perceived as the Cosmic *Christ*—the *Word* by whom the formless was endowed with form and spiritual worlds were draped with physicality. Likewise, the Sun behind the sun is the Son of God individualized in the *Christ Self*, shining in all his splendor behind the *soul* and its interpenetrating sheaths of consciousness called the *four lower bodies*. It is the Son of man—the 'Sun' of every *man*ifestation of God. The Sun behind the sun is referred to as the "Sun of righteousness," which does heal the mind, illumine the soul and light all her house, and as "the glory of God," the *Light* of the *City Foursquare*. (Mal. 4:2; Rev. 21:23.)

Chakra. (Skt. for "wheel," "disc," "circle.") Term used to denote the centers of *light* anchored in the *etheric body* and governing the flow of energy to the four lower *bodies of man*. There are seven major chakras corresponding to the *seven rays*, five minor chakras corresponding to the five secret *rays*, and a total of 144 light centers in the body of man. The seven major chakras, their rays, Sanskrit names, and colors are as follows: First Ray, **throat**, Vishúddha, blue; Second Ray, **crown**, Sahasrāra, yellow; Third Ray, **heart**, Anāhata, pink; Fourth Ray, **base-of-the-spine**, Mūlādhāra, white; Fifth Ray, **third eye**, Ājñā, green; Sixth Ray, **solar plexus**,

Maṇipūra, purple and gold; Seventh Ray, **seat-of-the-soul**, Svādhishthāna, violet.

(See Djwal Kul, *Intermediate Studies of the Human Aura*, also published in *The Human Aura*. Mark L. Prophet and Elizabeth Clare Prophet, *The Lost Teachings of Jesus I*, softbound, pp. 261–91, color plates following p. 260; or pocketbook, Book Two, pp. 114–55. Elizabeth Clare Prophet, *Mother's Chakra Meditations—From My Heart to Buddha*, 8-audiocassette album; *Saint Germain's Heart Meditation I*, audiocassette.)

Chamuel. *See* Archangel.

Chart of Your Divine Self. There are three figures represented in the Chart, which we will refer to as the upper figure, the middle figure, and the lower figure. The upper figure is the *I AM Presence*, the I AM THAT I AM, the individualization of God's presence for every son and daughter of the Most High. The Divine Monad consists of the I AM Presence surrounded by the spheres (color rings) of light that make up the body of First Cause, or *Causal Body*. These spheres are the many mansions of the Father's house where we lay up for ourselves "treasures in heaven." Our treasures are our words and works worthy of our Creator, positive thoughts and feelings, our victories for the right, and the virtues we have embodied to the glory of God. When we judiciously exercise our *free will*, the energies of God that we harmoniously qualify automatically ascend to our Causal Body. These energies are deposited in the spheres of light that correspond to the seven *chakras* and the seven color *rays* we use in our creative activities. They accrue to our *lifestream* as "talents," which we may increase as we put them to good use lifetime after lifetime.

The middle figure in the Chart is the Mediator between God and man, called the Holy *Christ*

Self, the *Real Self*, or the *Christ consciousness*. It has also been referred to as the Higher Mental Body or one's Higher Consciousness. This Inner Teacher overshadows the lower self, which consists of the *soul* evolving through the four planes of *Matter* using the vehicles of the *four lower bodies* (the *etheric*, or memory, *body*; the *mental body*; the *emotional*, or desire, *body*; and the *physical body*) to balance *karma* and fulfill the *divine plan*.

The three figures of the Chart correspond to the Trinity of Father, who always includes the *Mother* (the upper figure), Son (the middle figure), and *Holy Spirit* (the lower figure). The latter is the intended temple of the Holy Spirit, whose *sacred fire* is indicated in the enfolding *violet flame*. The lower figure corresponds to you as a disciple on the *Path*. Your soul is the nonpermanent aspect of being, which is made permanent through the ritual of the *ascension*. The ascension is the process whereby the soul, having balanced her karma and fulfilled her divine plan, merges first with the Christ consciousness and then with the living Presence of the I AM THAT I AM. Once the ascension has taken place, the soul, the nonpermanent aspect of being, becomes the Incorruptible One, a permanent atom in the Body of God. The Chart of Your Divine Self is therefore a diagram of yourself— past, present, and future.

The lower figure represents the son of man or child of the Light evolving beneath his own 'Tree of Life'. This is how you should visualize yourself standing in the violet flame, which you invoke daily in the name of the I AM Presence and your Holy Christ Self in order to purify your four lower bodies in

CHART OF YOUR DIVINE SELF

The Threefold Flame of Life:
Your Opportunity to Become the Christ

preparation for the ritual of the alchemical marriage—your soul's union with the Beloved, your Holy Christ Self. The lower figure is surrounded by a *tube of light*, which is projected from the heart of the I AM Presence in answer to your call. It is a cylinder of white light that sustains a forcefield of protection twenty-four hours a day, so long as you guard it in harmony. The *threefold flame* of Life is the divine spark sent from the I AM Presence as the gift of life, consciousness and free will. It is sealed in the secret chamber of the heart that through the Love, Wisdom and Power of the Godhead anchored therein the soul may fulfill her reason for being in the physical plane. Also called the Christ Flame and the liberty flame, or fleur-de-lis, it is the spark of a man's Divinity, his potential for Christhood.

The silver (or crystal) cord is the stream of life, or "lifestream," that descends from the heart of the I AM Presence to the Holy Christ Self to nourish and sustain (through the chakras) the soul and its vehicles of expression in time and space. It is over this 'umbilical' cord that the energy of the Presence flows, entering the being of man at the crown and giving impetus for the pulsation of the threefold flame as well as the physical heartbeat. When a round of the soul's incarnation in Matter-form is finished, the I AM Presence withdraws the silver cord, whereupon the threefold flame returns to the level of the Christ, and the soul clothed in the *etheric* garment gravitates to the highest level of her attainment, where she is schooled between embodiments until her final incarnation when the Great Law decrees she shall go out no more.

The dove of the Holy Spirit descending from the heart of the Father is shown just above the head of the Christ. When the son of man puts on and becomes the Christ consciousness as *Jesus* did, he merges with the Holy Christ Self. The Holy Spirit is upon him and the words of the Father, the beloved I AM Presence, are spoken, "This is my beloved Son in whom I AM well pleased."

(Matt. 3:17. See the Keepers of the Flame Lessons. Mark L. Prophet and Elizabeth Clare Prophet, *Climb the Highest Mountain; The Lost Teachings of Jesus I*, softbound, pp. 205–59, 267–68; or pocketbook, Book Two, pp. 43–110, 126–27. Elizabeth Clare Prophet, *The Astrology of the Four Horsemen*, chap. 37.)

Chela. (Hindi *celā* from Skt. *ceṭa* 'slave', i.e., 'servant'.) In India, a disciple of a religious teacher or guru. A term used generally to refer to a student of the *Ascended Masters* and their teachings. Specifically, a student of more than ordinary self-discipline and devotion initiated by an Ascended Master and serving the cause of the *Great White Brotherhood. See also* Discipleship.

(See El Morya, *The Chela and the Path: Meeting the Challenge of Life in the Twentieth Century*.)

Cherub (pl. **cherubim**). Member an order of angelic beings devoted to the expansion and protection of the flame of love, wielding the sword and the judgment of the Ruby Ray and the *Holy Spirit*. Hence the LORD God "placed at the east [gate] (the gate of the *Christ consciousness*) of the garden of Eden Cherubims and a flaming sword which turned every way, to keep the way of the *Tree of Life*." Even so the LORD instructed Moses to fashion cherubim of gold as focuses of these true angelic guardians of the mercy seat of the ark of the covenant. Traditionally, God dwelt between

the cherubim and spoke to Moses from the mercy
seat—the altar of the *I AM Presence*, whose Law,
engraven on tablets of stone, was carried in the
ark from place to place in their wilderness wander-
ings. David describes the LORD riding upon a
cherub, flying upon the wings of the wind. Ezekiel
portrays the cherubim as four-winged, four-faced
creatures accompanied by whirling wheels. The
cherub may be identified with the winged *karibu*,
"intercessor" in Mesopotamian texts, portrayed
as a sphinx, griffin, or winged human creature.
Throughout *cosmos*, the wise and strong cherubim
are found in manifold aspects of service to God and
his offspring.
(Gen. 3:24; Exod. 25:17–22; II Sam. 22:11; Ezek. 1, 10.)

Chohan. Lord or master; a chief. Each of the *seven rays*
has a Chohan who focuses the *Christ consciousness*
of the *ray*, which is indeed the law of the ray
governing its righteous use in man. Having en-
souled and demonstrated this law of the ray
throughout numerous incarnations, and taken initiations both before and after the *ascension*, the
candidate is appointed to the office of Chohan by
the *Maha Chohan*, "Great Lord," who is himself
the representative of the *Holy Spirit* on all the rays.
The names of the Chohans of the Rays (each one
an *Ascended Master* representing one of the seven
rays to earth's evolutions) and the locations of
their physical/*etheric* focuses are as follows: First
Ray, *El Morya,* Retreat of God's Will, Darjeeling,
India. Second Ray, **Lanto,** Royal Teton Retreat,
Grand Teton, Jackson Hole, Wyoming, USA.
Third Ray, **Paul the Venetian,** Château de Liberté,
southern France, with a focus of the *threefold flame*
at the Washington Monument, Washington, D.C.

Fourth Ray, **Serapis Bey,** the Ascension Temple
and Retreat at Luxor, Egypt. Fifth Ray, **Hilarion**
(the apostle Paul), Temple of Truth, Crete. Sixth
Ray, **Nada,** Arabian Retreat, Saudi Arabia. Seventh Ray, **Saint Germain,** Royal Teton Retreat,
Grand Teton, Wyoming; *Cave of Symbols,* Table
Mountain, Wyoming. Saint Germain also works
out of the *Great Divine Director's* focuses—the
Cave of Light in India and the Rakoczy Mansion
in Transylvania, where Saint Germain presides as
hierarch.

(See "Messages from the Seven Chohans of the Rays," in *Pearls
of Wisdom,* 1968, vol. 11, nos. 1–7. The Seven Chohans, the
Maha Chohan, and the World Teachers, "The Opening of the
Temple Doors," in *Pearls of Wisdom,* 1973, vol. 16, nos. 10–19.
Mark L. Prophet and Elizabeth Clare Prophet, *Lords of the
Seven Rays; The Lost Teachings of Jesus II,* softbound, pp. 149–
226; or pocketbook, Book Three, pp. 105–200. Elizabeth Clare
Prophet, "Lords of the Seven Rays on Crystals, with Chakra
Initiations," 4 audiocassettes; "Lords of the Seven Rays: Find
the Perfect Master and Crystal for You," two 1-hr. TV shows
on video.)

Christ. (From the Gk. *Christos* 'anointed'.) **Messiah**
(Heb., Aram. 'anointed'); '**Christed one**', one fully
endued and infilled—anointed—by the *Light* (the
Son) of God. The *Word,* the Logos, the Second
Person of the Trinity, "And the Word was made
flesh and dwelt among us (and we beheld his glory,
the glory as of the only begotten of the Father), full
of grace and truth. . . . *That was the true Light
which lighteth every man that cometh into the
world.* He was in the world, and the world was
made by him, and the world knew him not." In the
Hindu Trinity of *Brahma, Vishnu, and Shiva,* the
term "Christ" corresponds to or is the incarnation
of Vishnu, the Preserver; Avatāra, God-man, Dispeller of Darkness, Guru.

The **Universal Christ** is the mediator between the planes of *Spirit* and the planes of *Matter;* personified as the *Christ Self,* he is the mediator between the Spirit of God and the *soul* of *man.* The Universal Christ sustains the nexus of (the figure-eight flow of) consciousness through which the energies of the Father (Spirit) pass to his children for the crystallization (Christ-realization) of the *God Flame* by their souls' strivings in the cosmic womb (matrix) of the *Mother* (Matter). This process is called materialization (*Mater*-realization), "The Descent." The process whereby the soul's coalesced energies of the Mother pass through the nexus of the *Christ consciousness* to the Father is the acceleration called spiritualization (*Spirit*-realization), "The Ascent." Another name for the process whereby the soul's energy returns from Matter to Spirit is sublimation (sublime action), or transmutation. The consummation of this process is experienced by the soul, now one with the Son, as the *ascension*—union with the Spirit of the *I AM Presence,* the Father. The ascension is the fulfillment in heaven of *Jesus'* promise on earth: "At that day ye shall know that I am in my Father, and ye in me, and I in you. . . . If a man love me, he will keep my words: and my Father will love him, and we will come unto him, and make our abode with him."

The fusion of the energies of the positive and negative polarity of the Godhead in the creation takes place through the Universal Christ, the Logos without whom "was not any thing made that was made." The flow of light from the *Macrocosm* to the *microcosm,* from the Spirit (the I AM Presence) to the soul and back again over the figure-eight spiral, is fulfilled through this blessed mediator, who is Christ, the LORD, the true incarnation of the I AM THAT I AM. Because Jesus Christ is that embodied Word he can say, "I AM [the I AM in me is] the Open Door (to heaven and earth) which no man can shut" and "All Power is given unto me [through the I AM in me] in heaven and in earth" and "Behold, I AM [the I AM in me is] alive forevermore—as Above, so below—and have the keys of the kingdom of heaven and the keys of hell and death, and to whomsoever the Father wills I give it, and it is given in his name." This which is affirmed even today by the *Ascended Master* Jesus Christ is also affirmed in your behalf by your beloved Christ Self. Thus the Universal Christ of the one Son and the many does indeed mediate the Presence of the I AM to you through your very own beloved Holy Christ Self. This is the true Communion of the Cosmic Christ whose Body (Consciousness) was 'broken', shared, individualized, for every child of the Father's heart. The Sons of God hold the Maxim Light in trust for the babes in Christ.

The term "Christ" or "Christed one" also denotes an office in *hierarchy* held by those who have attained self-mastery on the *seven rays* and the seven *chakras* of the *Holy Spirit*. Christ-mastery includes the balancing of the *threefold flame*—the divine attributes of *Power, Wisdom, and Love*—for the harmonization of consciousness and the implementation of the mastery of the seven rays in the chakras and in the *four lower bodies* through the Mother Flame (raised Kundalini). At the hour designated for the ascension, the soul thus anointed raises the spiral of the threefold flame from beneath the feet through the entire form for the transmutation of every atom and cell of her being, consciousness, and world. (See p. 376.) The saturation and acceleration of the four lower bodies and the soul by this transfiguring light of the Christ Flame takes place in part during the initiation of the transfiguration, increasing through the resurrection and gaining full intensity in the ritual of the ascension.

The individual Christ Self, the personal Christ, is the initiator of every living soul. When the individual passes these several initiations on the path of Christhood, including the "slaying of the *dweller-on-the-threshold*," he earns the right to be called a Christed one and gains the title of *son or daughter of God.* Some who have earned that title in past ages have either compromised that attainment altogether or failed to manifest it in subsequent incarnations. In this age the Logos requires them to bring forth their inner God-mastery and to perfect it on the physical plane while in physical embodiment. Therefore, to assist the sons and daughters of God in making their manifestation commensurate with their inner Light, the Masters of the *Great White Brotherhood* have released their teachings through the Ascended Masters and their *Messengers* in this century. And *Saint Germain* founded the *Keepers of the Flame Fraternity* providing graded monthly lessons to the members of this order, dedicated to keep the flame of Life throughout the world. Prior to the successful passing of the initiations of *discipleship*, the individual is referred to as a child of God in contrast to the term "Son of God," which denotes full Christhood wherein the soul in and as the Son of man is become one in the Son of God after the example of Christ Jesus.

Expanding the consciousness of the Christ, the Christed one moves on to attain the realization of the Christ consciousness at a planetary level and is able to hold the balance of the Christ Flame on behalf of the evolutions of the planet. When this is achieved, he assists members of the heavenly hierarchy who serve under the office of the *World Teachers* and the planetary Christ. *See also* Chart of Your Divine Self, Jesus.

(John 1:1–14; 14:20, 23. Compare Rev. 3:8; Matt. 28:18; Rev. 1:18.)

Christ consciousness. The consciousness or awareness of the self in and as the *Christ*; the attainment of a level of consciousness commensurate with that which was realized by *Jesus*, the Christ. The Christ consciousness is the realization within the *soul* of that Mind which was in Christ Jesus. It is the attainment of the balanced action of *Power, Wisdom, and Love*—of Father, Son, and *Holy Spirit*—and the purity of the Mother through the balanced *threefold flame* within the heart. It is Faith perfected in the desire to do God's Will, Hope in the salvation of Christ Jesus by the path of his righteousness performed in us, and Charity's excellence in purest Love of giving and receiving in the LORD.

(Phil. 2:5.)

Christ Self. The individualized focus of "the only begotten of the Father full of grace and truth." The Universal *Christ* individualized as the true identity of the *soul*; the *Real Self* of every man, woman, and child to which the soul must rise. The Christ Self is the mediator between a man and his God. He is a man's own personal Teacher, Master, and Prophet who officiates as High Priest before the altar of the Holy of Holies (*I AM Presence*) of every man's temple made without hands. The advent of the universal awareness of the Christ Self in God's people on earth is foretold by the prophets as the descent of THE LORD OUR RIGHTEOUSNESS, also called the BRANCH, in the Universal Age at hand. When one achieves the fullness of soul-identification with the Christ Self, he is called a Christed, or anointed, one, and the Son of God is seen shining through the Son of man.

(John 1:14; Isa. 11:1; Jer. 23:5, 6; 33:15, 16; Zech. 3:8; 6:12. See Mark L. Prophet and Elizabeth Clare Prophet, *Climb the Highest Mountain*, 2d ed., pp. 148–60, 340–41, 368–69; *The Lost Teachings of Jesus I*, softbound, pp. 240–45; or pocketbook, Book Two, pp. 86–92. Elizabeth Clare Prophet, *The Astrology of the Four Horsemen*, pp. 53–57, 479–86, 494–98; "Jesus Christ, Avatar of the Ages," 1 videocassette; 2 audiocassettes.)

City Foursquare. The New Jerusalem; archetype of *golden-age, etheric* cities of *light* that exist even now on the *etheric plane* (in heaven) and are waiting to be lowered into physical manifestation (on earth). Saint John the Revelator saw the descent of the Holy City as the immaculate geometry of that which is to be and now is in the invisible realms of light: "And I John saw the holy city, new Jerusalem, coming down from God out of heaven." Thus, in order that this vision and prophecy be fulfilled *Jesus* taught us to pray with the authority of the *spoken Word*, "Thy kingdom come on earth as it is in heaven!" Metaphysically speaking, the City Foursquare is the mandala of the four planes and the quadrants of the *Matter* universe; the four sides of the Great Pyramid of *Christ's consciousness* focused in the Matter spheres. The twelve gates are gates of Christ's consciousness marking the lines and the degrees of the initiations he has prepared for his disciples. The twelve gates are the open doors to the twelve qualities of the Cosmic *Christ* sustained by the twelve solar hierarchies (who are emanations of the Universal Christ) on behalf of all who are endued with the Spirit's all-consuming fiery Love, all who would in grace "enter into his gates with thanksgiving and into his courts with praise."

Unascended *souls* may invoke the mandala of the City Foursquare for the fulfillment of the Christ consciousness, as Above, so below. The City Foursquare contains the blueprint of the solar (soul) identity of the 144,000 archetypes of the *sons and daughters of God* necessary to focus the Divine Wholeness of his consciousness in a given dispensation. The Light of the city is emitted from the *I AM Presence*; that of the Lamb, the Cosmic Christ, from the *Christ Self.* The jewels are the 144 focuses and frequencies of Light anchored in the *chakras* of the Cosmic Christ.
(Rev. 21:2, 9–27; Ps. 100:4.)

Color rays. *See* Seven rays.

Cosmic Being. (1) An *Ascended Master* who has attained *cosmic consciousness* and ensouls the *light/ energy/consciousness* of many worlds and systems of worlds across the galaxies to the Sun behind the Great *Central Sun.* (2) A being of God who has never descended below the level of the *Christ*, never taken physical embodiment, made human *karma* or engaged in *sin* but has remained a part of the *Cosmic Virgin* and holds a cosmic balance for the return of *souls* from the vale (veil) of sorrows to the Immaculate Heart of the Blessed *Mother.*

Cosmic Clock. The science of charting the cycles of the *soul's karma* and initiations on the twelve lines of the Clock under the twelve hierarchies of the Great

Central Sun. Taught by Mother Mary to Mark and Elizabeth Prophet for *sons and daughters of God* returning to the Law of the One and their point of origin beyond the worlds of form and lesser causation. (See Elizabeth Clare Prophet, "The Cosmic Clock: Psychology for the Aquarian Man and Woman," in *The Great White Brotherhood in the Culture, History and Religion of America,* chap. 15; *The ABC's of Your Psychology on the Cosmic Clock: Charting the Cycles of Karma and Initiation,* 8-audiocassette album; "Seminar on the Cosmic Clock: Charting the Cycles of Your Karma, Psychology and Spiritual Powers on the Cosmic Clock," 2 audiocassettes and accompanying packet of study materials.)

Cosmic consciousness. (1) God's awareness of himself in and as the *cosmos.* (2) Man's awareness of himself as he lives, moves, and has being within the spheres of God's cosmic Self-awareness. The awareness of oneself fulfilling the cycles of the cosmos in and through the Great *God Self;* the awareness of the self as a part of God in cosmic dimensions; the attainment of initiations through the blessedness of the Cosmic Christ leading to God Self-realization in the Universal One.

Cosmic Egg. The spiritual-material universe, including a seemingly endless chain of galaxies, star systems, worlds known and unknown, whose center, or white fire core, is called the Great *Central Sun.* The Cosmic Egg has both a spiritual and a material center. Although we may discover and observe the Cosmic Egg from the standpoint of our physical senses and perspective, all of the dimensions of *Spirit* can also be known and experienced within the Cosmic Egg. For the God who created the Cosmic Egg and holds it in the hollow of his hand is also the God Flame expanding hour by hour within his very own sons and daughters. The Cosmic Egg represents the bounds of man's habitation in this cosmic cycle. Yet, as God is everywhere throughout and beyond the Cosmic Egg, so by his Spirit within us we daily awaken to new dimensions of Being, soul-satisfied in conformity with his Likeness.

Cosmic hierarchy. The universal chain of individualized God-free beings fulfilling the attributes and aspects of God's infinite Selfhood. Included in the cosmic hierarchical scheme are Solar Logoi, *Elohim*, *Sons and Daughters of God*, *ascended* and unascended *Masters* with their circles of *chelas*, *Cosmic Beings*, the twelve solar hierarchies, *Archangels* and *angels* of the *sacred fire*, children of the *Light* and nature spirits, called *elementals*, and *twin flames* of the Alpha-Omega polarity sponsoring planetary and galactic systems. This universal order of the Father's own Self-expression is the means whereby God in the Great *Central Sun* steps down the Presence and Power of his Universal Being/Consciousness in order that succeeding evolutions in time and space, from the least unto the greatest, might come to know the wonder of his Love. The level of one's spiritual/physical attainment—measured by one's balanced self-awareness "hid with *Christ* in God" and demonstrating his Law, by his Love, in the *Spirit-Matter cosmos*—is the criterion establishing one's placement on this ladder of life called hierarchy.

In the third century, Origen of Alexandria set forth his conception of a hierarchy of beings, ranging from angels to human beings to demons and beasts. This renowned scholar and theologian of the early Church, who set forth the chief cornerstone of Christ's doctrine and upon whose works subsequent Church fathers, doctors, and theologians built their traditions, taught that souls are assigned to their respective offices and duties based on previous actions and merits, and that each one has the opportunity to ascend or descend in rank. Many beings of the heavenly hierarchy are named in the Book of Revelation. Apart from the false hierarchy of Antichrist, including the reprobate angels, some of the members of the *Great White Brotherhood* accounted for by *Jesus* are *Alpha and Omega*, the Seven Spirits, the angels of the seven churches, the Four and Twenty Elders, the four beasts, the saints robed in white, the Two Witnesses, the God of the Earth, the Woman clothed with the Sun and her Manchild, *Archangel Michael* and his angels, the Lamb and his wife, the one hundred and forty-four thousand who have the Father's name written in their foreheads, the angel of the Everlasting Gospel, the seven angels (i.e., the Archangels of the seven rays) which stood before God, the angel clothed with a cloud and a rainbow upon his head, the seven thunders, the Faithful and True and his armies, and him that sat upon the great white throne. *See also* Elohim.

(Rev. 1:4, 8, 11, 20; 2:1, 8, 12, 18; 3:1, 4, 5, 7, 14; 4:2–10; 5:2, 6, 11; 6:9–11; 7:1, 2, 9, 13, 14; 8:2; 10:1, 3, 7; 11:3, 4; 12:1, 5, 7; 14:1, 3–6, 14–19; 15:1; 16:1–4, 8, 10, 12, 17; 17:1; 18:1, 21; 19:4, 7, 11–17; 20:1; 21:6, 9; 22:13. See Elizabeth Clare Prophet, *The Great White Brotherhood in the Culture, History and Religion of America*, pp. 83–101. Origen, *On First Principles*.)

Cosmic law. That law which governs mathematically, yet with the spontaneity of mercy's flame, all manifestation throughout the *cosmos* in the planes of *Spirit* and *Matter*.

Cosmic Virgin. The Divine *Mother*, specifically in her immaculate awareness (*cosmic consciousness*) of our Divine Wholeness maintained on behalf of us all— we who are the children of her Sun Presence swimming in her cosmic womb. The Omega whose

sound, "Om," leads to the soundless Sound behind
all creation.

Cosmos. The universe conceived as an orderly, harmonious system; a complex orderly self-inclusive system. All that exists in time and space including spectra of *light*, forces of bodies, cycles of the elements—life, intelligence, memory, record and dimensions beyond physical perception—mathematically calculated as the evidence of things not seen as yet, but which do appear in the *Spirit* cosmos that coexists with and interpenetrates the *Matter* cosmos as a grid of light. Our Mother's Matter cosmos consists of the entire physical/astral creation of universes known and unknown. Our Father's Spirit cosmos all around us veils the inner blueprint and motion of First Cause and causation by which worlds are framed and hung by his Universal Mind and the planes of effect *(karma)* in which we abide are sustained for a season.

Darjeeling Council. A council of the *Great White Brotherhood* consisting of *Ascended Masters* and unascended *chelas* headed up by *El Morya*, its chief, headquartered in Darjeeling, India, at the Master's etheric *retreat*. Members include *Mother Mary*, *Kuan Yin*, *Archangel Michael*, the *Great Divine Director*, *Serapis Bey*, *Kuthumi*, Djwal Kul and numerous others whose objective is to train *souls* for world service in God-government and the economy, through international relations and the establishment of the inner *Christ* as the foundation for religion, education, and a return to *golden-age* culture in music and the arts.

Decree. *n.* a foreordaining will, an edict or fiat, an authoritative decision, declaration, a law, ordinance or religious rule; a command or commandment. *v.* to decide, to declare, to determine or order; to ordain, to command or enjoin; to invoke the presence of God, his light/energy/consciousness, his power and protection, purity and perfection.

It is written in the Book of Job, "Thou shalt decree a thing, and it shall be established unto thee: and the light shall shine upon thy ways." The decree is the most powerful of all applications to the Godhead. It is the "Command ye me" of Isaiah 45:11, the original command to *Light*, which, as the "Lux fiat," is the birthright of the *sons and daughters of God*. It is the authoritative Word of God spoken in man by the name of the *I AM Presence* and the living *Christ* to bring about constructive change on earth through the will of God and his consciousness come, on earth as it is in heaven—in manifestation here below as Above. The dynamic decree offered as praise and petition to the LORD God in the science of the *spoken Word* is the "effectual fervent prayer of the righteous" that availeth much. The dynamic decree is the means whereby the supplicant identifies with the Word of God, even the original fiat of the Creator "Let there be light: and there was light." Through the dynamic decree spoken with joy and love, faith and hope in God's covenants fulfilled, the supplicant receives the engrafting of the *Word* and experiences the transmutation by the *sacred fire* of the *Holy Spirit*, the "trial by fire" whereby all *sin*, disease, and death are consumed, yet the righteous *soul* is preserved. The decree is the alchemist's tool and technique for personal and planetary transmutation and self-transcendence. The decree may be short or long and is usually marked by a formal preamble and a closing or acceptance.

(Job 22:28; Gen. 1:3; James 1:21; 5:16; I Cor. 3:13–15; I Pet. 1:7.
See Mark L. Prophet and Elizabeth Clare Prophet, *The Science
of the Spoken Word.* Jesus and Kuthumi, *Prayer and Meditation.
Prayers, Meditations and Dynamic Decrees for the Com-
ing Revolution in Higher Consciousness,* Sections I and II.
Elizabeth Clare Prophet, *The Astrology of the Four Horsemen,*
chaps. 38–40. Mark L. Prophet and Elizabeth Clare Prophet,
*The Science of the Spoken Word: Why and How to Decree
Effectively,* 4-audiocassette album. Elizabeth Clare Prophet,
*"I'm Stumping for the Coming Revolution in Higher Conscious-
ness!"* 3-audiocassette album. For audiocassettes of decrees,
songs, mantras and rosaries, including decrees to Archangel
Michael, El Morya and Lord Lanto and violet flame decrees,
see pp. 465–66.)

Desire body. *See* Emotional body.

Deva. (Skt. for "radiant being.") Member of an order of
angelic beings who serve with the elemental forces
of nature, assisting them to perform their various
functions. *Angel* devas are the guardian spirits of
the mountains and the forests. They also ensoul
and hold the matrix for the *Christ consciousness*
to be outpictured by the people of a particular
locale—city, state, nation, or continent—or for a
particular race, nationality, or ethnic group.

Diamond Heart. A concentration of the *sacred fires* of
the will of God that coalesce as a diamond matrix
in the hearts of devotees of God's will, his *divine
plan* and his inner *(etheric)* blueprint for all life.
Hence, a term used to describe the heart of the
Ascended Masters, angel *devas,* and *chelas* who
embody the will of God; often associated with
El Morya and Mary the Mother of *Jesus.* The
Diamond Heart of God possesses the quality of the
diamond, its hardness resisting every sinister strat-
egy of the anti-Self and the anti-Will. At the same
time it reflects the brilliance of Love/Wisdom

throughout the creation—magnifying and projecting the prismatic virtues and charismatic powers of
the *Holy Spirit* embodied by the ascended and
unascended *sons and daughters of God*.

(See Jesus and Kuthumi, *Corona Class Lessons,* pp. 90–91.
Mother Mary, "The Order of the Diamond Heart," and Jesus,
"The Hour of Thy Victory Draweth Nigh," in *Pearls of Wis-
dom,* 1987, vol. 30, pp. 629, 633–37, 640–46, 237 n. 9.)

Discipleship. The state of being an adherent of the
Christ and of the Teachings of the *Great White
Brotherhood*; the process of attaining self-mastery
through self-discipline in the initiations of the *Buddha*, the *World Teachers*, and the *Ascended Masters*.

Steps of initiation in discipleship under the Living
Word: (1) **Student:** Under this phase the individual
studies, becomes a student of the writings and the
teachings of the Master. He is free to come and go
in his community, enjoying fellowship with his
followers and the fruits of their dedication but has
declared no particular responsibility to the person
of the Master. He has taken no vows, made no
commitment, but may be studying to "show himself approved" in order to be accepted as a servant,
or co-server (otherwise known as *"chela"*), sharing
the joy of the Master's world mission. (2) **Disciple**
(chela): The individual desires to enter into a bond
with the Master—to be taught directly by the Master rather than through his published writings
alone. The disciple answers the call of the Master
to leave his nets of karmic entanglements and
worldly desire and follow him: "Come leave your
nets, I will make you fishers of men." The disciple
receives the initiations of the Cosmic Christ in the
course of his service to the Master. His heart,
mind, and *soul* have begun to unfold a greater love

as appreciation and gratitude for the teachings received in the previous level of student. This love is translated into action as self-sacrifice, selflessness, service, and surrender to the Person of the Christ, the Sun behind the Son of man of the Master; when this step has been accelerated to the level of the "acceptable offering," and the chela is engaged in balancing his *threefold flame* and his *karma*, he may be considered for the next step. (3) **Friend:** Those counted as friend of the Master enter by invitation—"Henceforth I call you no more servants but friends"—into a relationship as companion and co-worker, bearing increased responsibilities for the Master's path as world saviour. The friend bears the cross as well as the burden of *Light* of the Master; he demonstrates the qualities of friendship as in the life of Abraham and other chelas who have risen to a level of understanding the very heart and the experience of the Master— providing comfort, consolation, advice, and support out of loyalty to both the purposes and the person of the Master. (4) **Brother:** The degree of brother is the level where the oneness of the Guru-chela, Alpha-Omega relationship is complete through the horizontal figure-eight exchange heart-to-heart; the Guru has actually made his disciple a part of his own flesh and blood and offered to him the full momentum of his attainment and portions of his mantle and authority in preparation for the Master's *ascension* and the disciple's assuming of the part or whole of the Master's office. This is the love relationship exemplified between *Jesus* and John, his *Mother, Mary,* and perhaps his own flesh-and-blood brother (or cousin) James. (5) **Christ,** or **Christed one:** the Anointed of the Incarnate Word.

(II Tim. 2:15; Matt. 4:19; Mark 1:17; John 15. See Jesus and Kuthumi, *Corona Class Lessons*, chaps. 25-30.)

Divine Ego. Awareness of true selfhood in and as the *Christ Self*, the God Self, or the *I AM Presence*; the Higher Consciousness; the Source or Origin of *man*. One's sense of selfhood at the point of origination; Divine Monad.

Divine Manchild. The Manchild born to the Woman clothed with the Sun is the incarnation of the Universal *Christ* for the Aquarian age in the one and the many *sons and daughters of God* whose destiny it is to focus the *Christ consciousness* to the evolutions of earth. Lowercased, the term "manchild" refers to the child who has the *Holy Spirit* from his mother's womb, e.g., John the Baptist and *Jesus.* (Rev. 12.)

Divine Monad. *See* Chart of Your Divine Self.

Divine Mother. *See* Mother.

Divine plan. The plan of God for the soul's individualization of the God Flame ordained in the beginning when the blueprint of life was impressed upon the white fire core of the individual *I AM Presence.* The divine plan determines the limits of the individual expression of *free will.* As the acorn is destined to be the oak, so each individual *soul* is destined to realize the fullness of his preordained (but not predestined) potential drawn by free will from the *Tree of Life*—the I AM Presence and the *Causal Body.* What that potential is and how it is to be self-realized in this life is known of God and can be released to the outer consciousness through application to the individual *Christ Self*, the I AM Presence, and the *Great Divine Director.*

Dweller-on-the-threshold. A term sometimes used to designate the anti-self, the not-self, the synthetic self, the antithesis of the Real Self, the conglomerate of the self-created ego, ill-conceived through the inordinate use of the gift of *free will*, consisting of the *carnal mind* and a constellation of misqualified energies, forcefields, focuses, animal magnetism comprising the subconscious mind. Man's contact with the reptilian anti-magnetic self—that is the enemy of God and his *Christ* and the *soul's* reunion with that Christ—is through the desire body, or *astral body*, and through the solar-plexus *chakra*. The dweller-on-the-threshold is therefore the nucleus of a vortex of energy that forms the 'electronic belt', shaped like a kettledrum and surrounding the *four lower bodies* from the waist down. The serpent head of the dweller is sometimes seen emerging from the black pool of the unconscious. This electronic belt does contain the cause, effect, record, and memory of human *karma* in its negative aspect. Positive karma, as deeds done through the divine consciousness, registers in the *Causal Body* and is sealed in the electronic fire-rings surrounding each one's own *I AM Presence*. When the sleeping serpent of the dweller is awakened by the presence of Christ, the soul must make the freewill decision to slay, by the power of the I AM Presence, this self-willed personal *anti-Christ* and become the defender of the Real Self until the soul is fully reunited with Him who is the righteous LORD, THE LORD OUR RIGHTEOUSNESS, the true Self of every *lifestream* on the path of initiation.

The dweller appears to the soul on the threshold of conscious awareness where it knocks to gain entrance into the 'legitimate' realm of self-acknowledged selfhood. The dweller would enter to become the master of the house. But it is Christ and only Christ whose knock you must answer—him only must you bid enter. The most serious initiation on the path of the disciple of Christ is the confrontation with the not-self. For if it is not slain by the soul who is one in the Christ Mind, it will emerge to devour that soul in the full-vented rage of its hatred for the *Light*. The necessity for the Teacher on the *Path* and for the Guru *Sanat Kumara* with us, physically manifest in the *Messenger* of *Maitreya*, is to hold the balance both spiritually and in the physical octave for each individual initiate on the Path as he approaches the initiation of the encounter—face-to-face with the dweller-on-the-threshold. The planetary dweller-on-the-threshold is personified in the forces of *Antichrist*.

(See Jesus Christ, "The Awakening of the Dweller-on-the-Threshold," and Elizabeth Clare Prophet, "Christ and the Dweller," in *Pearls of Wisdom*, 1983, vol. 26, nos. 36, 38. *Pearls of Wisdom*, 1985, vol. 28, Book I, pp. 84, 85–93, 97; 1986, vol. 29, Book I, pp. 199, 203, 210–12; 1988, vol. 31, Book II, pp. 422, 456–57. Elizabeth Clare Prophet, "The Lost Teachings of Jesus: On the Enemy Within," 2 audiocassettes.)

Elementals. Beings of earth, air, fire, and water; nature spirits who are the servants of God and man in the planes of *Matter* for the establishment and maintenance of the physical plane as the platform for the soul's evolution. Elementals who serve the fire element are called salamanders; those who serve the air element, sylphs; those who serve the water element, undines; those who serve the earth element, gnomes. *See also* Body elemental.

(See Mark L. Prophet and Elizabeth Clare Prophet, *Climb the Highest Mountain*, 2d ed., pp. 444–70, 548–55. *Saint Germain On Prophecy*, Book Three. Jesus and Kuthumi,

Corona Class Lessons, pp. 371–76. *Violet Flame for Elemental Life—Fire, Air, Water and Earth 1* and *2*, audiocassettes of decrees and songs.)

El Morya. The *Ascended Master.* Lord *(Chohan)* of the First *Ray* of God's Will, Chief of the *Darjeeling Council* of the *Great White Brotherhood*, founder of *The Summit Lighthouse*, teacher and sponsor of the *Messengers* Mark L. Prophet and Elizabeth Clare Prophet. The Master's extraordinary devotion to God's Word and Work is a powerful stream that runs throughout his soul's incarnations on earth as he has stood staunch in the role of Advocate, Teacher, and Exemplar before our spirits soaring unto Love.

As the Rajput prince El Morya Khan, he worked closely with *Kuthumi*, Djwal Kul, *Serapis Bey*, *Saint Germain* and others to found the Theosophical Society in 1875. He was Abraham, the ancient patriarch who emerged from Ur of the Chaldees to become the prototype and progenitor of the twelve tribes of Israel. Returning as Melchior, one of the three wise men of the East, he followed the star that portended the birth of the best of his seed who would fulfill all the promises of God unto his spiritual descendants.

As Arthur, king of the Britons, he summoned knights of the Round Table and ladies of the court of Camelot to quest the Holy Grail and to attain through initiation the inner mysteries of *Christ*. Appearing again on Britain's soil as Thomas Becket as well as Thomas More, both martyred, he twice played the role of defender of the Faith and challenger of King Henry—also twice born (Henry II and VIII), and twice the oppressor. In the sixteenth century, his *soul's* journey took him to the East in the person of Akbar, greatest of Mogul emperors, and in the nineteenth to Ireland to be her poet laureate Thomas Moore. In 1898 the renowned "Mahatma of the Himavat," El Morya Khan, ascended to the heart of God.

During the 1920s and 1930s the Ascended Master El Morya worked with Nicholas and Helena Roerich, who set forth his writings in numerous published works. In 1958 he called Mark L. Prophet to disseminate the Teachings of the Ascended Masters as *Pearls of Wisdom*, published by the newly founded Summit Lighthouse. With Saint Germain and *Mother Mary*, he also trained Elizabeth Clare Prophet as his *Messenger*. Through the embodied Messenger he delivers the Teachings of the Universal *Christ* for the Aquarian age and conducts retreats on practical spiritual techniques for meeting the personal and planetary challenges posed by the prophecies of Saint John's Revelation. El Morya's musical keynote, capturing the frequencies of his Electronic Presence, was set forth in part by Sir Edward Elgar in his *Pomp and Circumstance*.

(See the following works by El Morya: *The Chela and the Path*; *The Sacred Adventure*; *Morya: The Darjeeling Master Speaks to His Chelas on the Quest for the Holy Grail*; *Ashram Notes*; *Ashram Rituals*, booklet and 2 audiocassettes; *El Morya: Chohan of the First Ray*, 2-audiocassette album. Mark L. Prophet and Elizabeth Clare Prophet, *Lords of the Seven Rays*, Book One, chap. 1; Book Two, chap. 1. *El Morya, Lord of the First Ray: Dynamic Decrees with Prayers and Ballads for Chelas of the Will of God 1–4*, audiocassettes. *Hail to the Chief! A Salute to El Morya*, songs on CD and audiocassette.)

Elohim. (Plural of Heb. '*Eloah*,' God.) One of the Hebrew names of God, or of the gods; used in the Old Testament about 2,500 times, meaning "Mighty One" or "Strong One." *Elohim* is a uni-plural noun referring to the *twin flames* of the Godhead that comprise the "Divine Us." When speaking specifically of either the masculine or feminine half, the plural form is retained because of the understanding that one half of the Divine Whole contains and is the androgynous Self (the Divine Us). The Seven Mighty Elohim and their feminine counterparts are the builders of form; hence, Elohim is the name of God used in the first verse of the Bible, "In the beginning God created the heaven and the earth." Serving directly under the Elohim are the four beings of the elements, "the Four Cosmic Forces," who have dominion over the *elementals*— gnomes, salamanders, sylphs, and undines.

The Seven Mighty Elohim are the "seven Spirits of God" named in Revelation and the "morning stars" that sang together in the beginning, as the LORD revealed them to his servant Job. There are also five Elohim who surround the white fire core of the Great *Central Sun*. In the order of *hierarchy*, the Elohim and *Cosmic Beings* carry the greatest concentration, the highest vibration, of Light that we can comprehend in our state of evolution. They represent, with the four beings of nature, their consorts and the elemental builders of form, the power of our Father as the Creator (the blue *ray*). The Seven *Archangels* and their divine complements, the great *seraphim*, *cherubim*, and all the angelic hosts represent the love of God in the fiery intensity of the Holy Ghost (the pink ray). The Seven *Chohans* of the *Rays* and all *Ascended Masters*, together with unascended *sons and daughters of God*, represent the wisdom of the Law of the Logos under the office of the Son (the yellow ray). These three kingdoms form a triad of manifestation, working in balance to step down the energies of the Trinity. The intonation of the sacred sound "Elohim" releases the tremendous power of their God Self-awareness stepped down for our blessed use through the Cosmic Christ.

Following are the names of the Seven Elohim, the rays they serve on, and the locations of their etheric *retreats:* First Ray, **Hercules and Amazonia,** Half Dome, Sierra Nevada, Yosemite National Park, California, USA. Second Ray, **Apollo and Lumina,** western Lower Saxony, Germany. Third Ray, **Heros and Amora,** Lake Winnipeg, Canada. Fourth Ray, **Purity and Astrea,** near Gulf of Archangel, southeast arm of White Sea, Russia. Fifth Ray, **Cyclopea and Virginia,** Altai Range where China, Siberia, and Mongolia meet, near Tabun Bogdo. Sixth Ray, **Peace and Aloha,** Hawaiian Islands. Seventh Ray, **Arcturus and Victoria,** near Luanda, Angola, Africa.
(Rev. 1:4; 3:1; 4:5; 5:6; Job 38:7. See *Spoken by Elohim, Pearls of Wisdom,* 1978, vol. 21. The Seven Mighty Elohim, "The Chalice of Elohim," in *Pearls of Wisdom,* 1989, vol. 32, nos. 9–15; 5 audiocassettes. *The Seven Elohim in the Power of the Spoken Word,* 4-audiocassette album.)

Emotional body. One of the four lower *bodies of man,* corresponding to the water element and the third quadrant of *Matter;* the vehicle of the desires and feelings of God made manifest in the being of man. Also called the *astral body,* the desire body, and the feeling body.

Etheric. Of or relating to the highest plane of the *Matter cosmos,* i.e., the heaven world. The etheric frequency and its correspondent plane of consciousness is the repository of the fiery blueprint of the entire physical universe.

Etheric body. One of the four lower *bodies of man*, corresponding to the fire element and the first quadrant of *Matter*; called the envelope of the *soul*, holding the blueprint of the *divine plan* and the image of *Christ*-perfection to be outpictured in the world of form. Also called the memory body. *Sanat Kumara* announced on New Year's Day 1985 that the earth received a new *etheric* sheath containing the record and blueprint of the planet's original divine plan and that the opportunity for the world to renew the *golden age* had never been greater.

(See Sanat Kumara, "The Turning Point of Life on Earth: A Dispensation of the Solar Logoi," in *Pearls of Wisdom*, 1985, vol. 28, Book I, pp. 60–61.)

Etheric plane. The highest plane in the dimension of *Matter*; a plane that is as concrete and real (and more so) as the physical plane but that is experienced through the senses of the *soul* in a dimension and a consciousness beyond physical awareness. The plane on which the *akashic records* of mankind's entire evolution register individually and collectively. It is the world of *Ascended Masters* and their *retreats*, *etheric* cities of *light* where souls of a higher order of evolution abide between embodiments. It is the plane of reality, free from the sordid, sin/sick society men and devils have made of the earth planes. Here the *golden age* is in progress, Love is the fullness of God's presence everywhere, and *angels* and *elementals* together with God's children serve in harmony to manifest *Christ's* kingdom in the Universal Age, worlds without end. As such it is the plane of transition between the earth/heaven realms and the kingdom of God, *Spirit*, or the Absolute. The **lower etheric plane** overlaps the *astral*/mental/physical belts. It is contaminated by these lower worlds occupied by the false hierarchy

and the mass consciousness it controls, including
its matrices and emotions of the mass consciousness (i.e., e-motions, "energies in motion").
(See Elizabeth Clare Prophet, "On Dealing with Death, Discarnates and Malevolent Spirits, Part III," 4 audiocassettes.)

Evil. *Energy-veil*; the veil of misqualified energy that
man imposes upon *Matter* through his misuse of
the *sacred fire*; maya, illusion. The consciousness
of relative good and evil, embodied by *lifestreams*
moving against the current of God's will, is the
consequence of the *freewill* experiment adopted by
souls who chose to descend in plane and consciousness below the level and frequency of the Christ
Mind. Absolute Evil, embodied by fallen *angels*, is
the state of those who declared war against Almighty God, his *Christ* and his offspring in the
Great Rebellion, who have not ceased their warfare
against the seed of the Divine *Mother*, will not bend
the knee before the *Light* and will be defeated in
Armageddon by the LORD's Judgment through his
hosts—the forces of Absolute Good, God-identified
in heaven and earth. As a consequence of the
victory of Light over Darkness, souls who have lost
the Edenic bliss may be saved from all evil and the
Evil One by conscious freewill election in Christ to
return to his reign under the Law of God.
(See Elizabeth Clare Prophet, *Forbidden Mysteries of Enoch:
Fallen Angels and the Origins of Evil*; "Keys from Judaism: The
Kabbalah and the Temple of Man," Part 4: "The Origin of
Evil," 1-hr. TV show on video.)

Four lower bodies. *See* Bodies of man, Physical body,
Mental body, Emotional body, and Etheric body.

Free will. The freedom to create; the option to choose
the right- or the left-handed path, Life or Death,
the positive or the negative spirals of consciousness.

Having the gift of free will, the *soul* may choose to dwell in the plane of the relative, where good and *evil* are relative to one's perspective in time and space; or she may choose the plane of the Absolute, where Good is real and Evil is unreal and the soul beholds God as living Truth "face-to-face." Free will means that the individual may accept or reject the *divine plan*, the laws of God, and the opportunity to live in the consciousness of Love.

God's gift of free will carries with it a certain span of consciousness known as the life span, a series of embodiments, and the "bounds of man's habitation." The soul, therefore, is not only confined to time and space during the period of her experimentation with free will, but she is also limited to a certain number of life cycles. At the end of this opportunity (compartmentalized in days, years, and dimensions), the use that the soul has made of the gift of free will determines her fate. The soul that has chosen to glorify the *Divine Ego* (Reality) ascends into the Presence of the I AM THAT I AM. The soul that has chosen to glorify the *human ego* (unreality) passes through the second death, her Self-denying consciousness permanently self-canceled; and all of her energies, simultaneously passed through the *sacred fire*, are returned to the Great *Central Sun* for repolarization. (Rev. 20:6, 11–15; 21:8; Acts 17:26.)

Gabriel. *See* Archangel.

Gautama Buddha. *See* Buddha.

Goal-fitting. A term used by *El Morya*, *Chohan* of the First *Ray*, to describe the fitting of the evolving *soul* consciousness for the goal of reunion with God; a process of discipline and initiation through

service and application of the *sacred fire* that souls
preparing for the *ascension* undergo under the loving direction of the *Ascended Masters*.
(See *The Chela and the Path* for the Master's fundamentals on goal-
fittedness for meeting the challenges of the twentieth century.)

God consciousness. The consciousness, or awareness,
of one's true self as the manifestation of God; the
awareness of the I AM THAT I AM, or the *I AM
Presence*, in and through and beyond oneself in
universal manifestation; the ability to maintain this
conscious God Self-awareness—omnipotent, omniscient and omnipresent—wherever oneself, as
Being, is and declares in the fullness of the *Light*,
"Lo, because Thou art, I AM." The state of God
Self-mastery whereby one maintains this vibration
in Divine Wholeness of the *Alpha-Omega* principle in the planes of *Spirit-Matter*. The plane of
God's consciousness is the kingdom of God. And
all who dwell therein (beyond the earth/heaven
realms) are truly extensions of God's own consciousness—only his in the highest expression of
Love. *See also* Cosmic consciousness.
(Ps. 82:6; John 10:34.)

Goddess of Justice. *See* Portia.

Goddess of Liberty. The *Ascended* Lady *Master* who
holds the *God consciousness* of liberty for the earth.
While embodied on *Atlantis*, she erected the Temple of the Sun where Manhattan Island now is.
With the sinking of Atlantis the physical temple
was destroyed, but the *etheric* counterpart remains
on the *etheric plane*, where she continues to focus
the flame of liberty on the central altar, which is
surrounded by twelve shrines dedicated to the
twelve hierarchies of the Sun. The Goddess of

Liberty (so named for her complete and whole-hearted identification with God's flame of liberty, her God consciousness of liberty) is the Spokesman for the *Karmic Board* and represents the Second *Ray* on that board. Her statue on Liberty Island (formerly Bedloe's Island) in New York Harbor portrays the figure of Longfellow's "Lady with a Lamp," whom he prophesied "shall stand in the great history of the land, a noble type of good, heroic womanhood." She is the archetype of the Woman clothed with the Sun and the new-age woman—inspiring the nations to illumined action by the torch of illumination and the Book of the Law.

(See Mark L. Prophet and Elizabeth Clare Prophet, *The Lost Teachings of Jesus II*, softbound, pp. 181, 251–52, 332, 487; or pocketbooks, Book Three, pp. 144–45, 231–33; Book Four, pp. 46, 237–38.)

Goddess of Mercy. *See* Kuan Yin.

God Flame. The flame of God; the *sacred fire*; the identity, being, and consciousness of God in and as the white fire core of being. Moses declared, "For the LORD thy God is a consuming fire." Wherever the flame of God is or is invoked by his offspring, the sacred fire descends to consume (transmute by its white fire and Seventh *Ray* action, the *violet flame*) all unlike itself. From the sacred fire of Ahura Mazda revealed by Zarathustra, to Jesus' baptism by the Holy Ghost "with fire," to the apostle's perception of the trial by fire, to the eternal flame of the sevenfold lights of the Hebrews, all children of the One who would return to the flame have revered God's flaming Presence and beheld him in the very midst of the Shekinah glory. And in their hearts they accept the reality of his promise unto the *soul*, the waiting Bride, "For I, saith the

LORD, will be unto her a wall of fire round about, and will be the glory in the midst of her."
(Deut. 4:24; Matt. 3:11, 12; I Cor. 3:13–15; I Pet. 1:7; Exod. 25:31–40; 37:17–24; Zech. 2:5.)

Godfré Ray King. *See* Ballard, Guy W.

God Presence. *See* I AM Presence.

God Self. *See* I AM Presence.

Golden age. A cycle of enlightenment, peace, and harmony wherein the *souls* of mankind merge in the *Christ* Flame for the fulfillment of the *divine plan* "as Above, so below." Through the convergence of the *etheric plane* and sheath with the three lower vehicles of the earth body and her evolutions, the heavenly kingdom will come into manifestation on earth as it is even now in the *etheric* octave. *See also* Etheric body.
(See Elizabeth Clare Prophet, "The Golden Age of Jesus Christ on Atlantis," 2 videocassettes; 2 audiocassettes.)

Great Central Sun. *See* Central sun.

Great Divine Director. The *Ascended Master* whose attainment of *cosmic consciousness* qualifies him to ensoul the flame of divine direction on behalf of earth's evolutions and untold lifewaves beyond. Founder of the House of Rakoczy, Teacher of *Saint Germain*, sponsor and *Manu* of the incoming *seventh root race*, this *Cosmic Being* maintains a focus in the Cave of Light in India and in his retreat in Transylvania, the focus of freedom for Europe. The Great Divine Director represents the First *Ray* on the *Karmic Board*. He is also known as the Master R.
(See the Great Divine Director, "The Mechanization Concept," in *Pearls of Wisdom*, 1965, vol. 8, nos. 3–26, also published as *The Soulless One: Cloning a Counterfeit Creation*.)

Great Hub. *See* Central sun.

Great White Brotherhood. A spiritual order of Western
saints and Eastern *adepts* who have reunited with
the *Spirit* of the living God and who comprise the
heavenly hosts. They have transcended the cycles
of *karma* and rebirth and ascended (accelerated)
into that higher reality which is the eternal abode
of the *soul*. The *Ascended Masters* of the Great
White Brotherhood, united for the highest purposes of the brotherhood of man under the Father-
hood of God, have risen in every age from every
culture and religion to inspire creative achievement
in education, the arts and sciences, God-government and the abundant Life through the economies of the nations. The word "white" refers not to
race but to the *aura* (halo) of white *light* surrounding their forms. The Brotherhood also includes in
its ranks certain unascended *chelas* of the Ascended
Masters. *Jesus* Christ revealed this heavenly order of
saints "robed in white" to his servant John in Revelation. *See also* Cosmic hierarchy.
(Rev. 3:4, 5; 6:9–11; 7:9, 13, 14; 19:14. See Elizabeth Clare
Prophet, *The Great White Brotherhood in the Culture, History
and Religion of America.*)

Hierarchy. *See* Cosmic hierarchy.

Higher Self. The *I AM Presence*; the *Christ Self*; the
exalted aspect of selfhood. Used in contrast to the
term "lower self," or "little self," which indicates
the *soul* that went forth from and may elect by *free
will* to return to the Divine Whole through the
realization of the oneness of the self in God.
Higher consciousness.

Holy Amethyst. *See* Zadkiel, Archangel.

Holy Christ Self. *See* Christ Self.

Holy Spirit. Third Person of the Trinity; the omnipresence of God; the cloven tongues of fire that focus the Father-*Mother* God, also called the *sacred fire*; the energies of Life that infuse a *cosmos*. In the Hindu Trinity of *Brahma, Vishnu, and Shiva*, the Holy Spirit corresponds to Shiva, known as the Destroyer/Deliverer because his all-consuming Love, when invoked in the planes of *Matter*, binds the forces of *evil* and transmutes the cause and effect of man's miscreations, thus delivering him from the prison house of *karma* and its dark denizens. Prana is the essence of the Holy Spirit that we take in by the sacred fire breath through the *chakras* to nourish the *four lower bodies*. The Holy Spirit focuses the balance of the Father-Mother God in the white fire core of being. The exorcism of foul spirits and unclean entities is accomplished by the sacred fire of the Holy Spirit in the name of *Christ* and the I AM THAT I AM. The nine gifts of the Spirit are powers conveyed to the Lord's servants to bind death and hell and work his works on earth.

The Person and the Flame of the Holy Spirit is the Comforter whom *Jesus* promised would come when our Lord took his leave—to enlighten us, to teach us, and to bring all things to our remembrance that beloved Jesus has taught us, both in heaven and on earth. Each time a *son or daughter of God* ascends into the Presence of the I AM THAT I AM, the Holy Spirit descends to fill the void and to magnify the Lord's Presence on earth. This is the ritual of the descent of the Holy Ghost promised by Jesus to his disciples when the Master said, "Tarry ye in the city of Jerusalem, until ye be endued with power from on high," which took place on Pentecost.

The representative of the flame of the Holy Spirit to earth's evolutions is the *Ascended Master* who occupies the office of *Maha Chohan*. The Holy Spirit is the Personal Impersonality (see pp. 74–75) of the Godhead and is positioned on the west side of the *City Foursquare*. *See also* Chart of Your Divine Self. (I Cor. 12:4–11; John 14:16, 26; 16:7; Luke 24:49, 51; Mark 16:19; Acts 2:1–4. See Mark L. Prophet and Elizabeth Clare Prophet, *Climb the Highest Mountain*, 2d ed., pp. 386–88, 408–44, 555–62; *The Lost Teachings of Jesus II*, softbound, pp. 158–63; or pocketbook, Book Three, pp. 116–22; *Lords of the Seven Rays*, Book One, pp. 15–20; Book Two, pp. 277–97.)

Human consciousness. That consciousness which is aware of the self as human—limited, mortal, fallen, sinful, subject to error and the passions of the senses—and therefore declares with the Son of man: "I of mine own (human) self can do nothing. It is the Father (the *I AM Presence*) in me that doeth the Work of the LORD." (John 5:30; 14:10.)

Human ego. That point of the personality which embraces the *human consciousness* and all that it stands for as true selfhood; the anti-self, the *synthetic image*. Nevertheless, the positive ego, successful and having a healthy self-image, is the very vital ingredient that enables the human to fearlessly reach for the *Divine Ego*, step by step letting go of itself, forsaking the past until that human mask is no longer a vice or device. And pure joy as radiant being becomes one's new definition of selfhood and perspective on Reality. It is proverbial that a healthy ego is essential to a healthy surrender unto God—the true and only Ego of us all.

Human monad. The entire forcefield of self, the interconnecting spheres of influences—hereditary, environmental, karmic—which make up that self-awareness which identifies itself as human. The reference point of lesser- or non-awareness out of which all mankind must evolve to the realization of the Real Self as the *Christ Self*.

I AM Presence. The I AM THAT I AM; the individualized Presence of God focused for each individual *soul*. The God-identity of the individual; the Divine Monad; the individual Source. The origin of the soul focused in the planes of *Spirit* just above the physical form; the personification of the God Flame for the individual. *See also* Chart of Your Divine Self.
(Exod. 3:13–15.)

Immaculate concept. The pure concept or image of the *soul* held in the Mind of God; any pure thought held by one part of life for and on behalf of another part of life. The essential ingredient to every alchemical experiment without which it will not succeed. The ability to hold the image of the perfect pattern to be precipitated, to see the vision of a project complete, to draw a mental picture, to retain it and to fill it in with *light* and love and joy—these are keys to the science of the immaculate concept taught by *Mother Mary* as well as the Master Alchemist. The exercise of the inner sight through the third eye is a process of purification whereby, as *Jesus* said, "If thine eye be single—and singly, one-pointedly focused upon the Beloved God—thy whole body shall be full of Light"—i.e., of Christ's illumining Presence.

"God is the supreme practitioner of the science of the immaculate concept. No matter how far *man* might wander from his individuality, God ever beholds man in the image of Reality in which He created him.... This science of the immaculate concept is practiced by every *angel* in heaven. It is that law which is written in the inward parts of man, known by his very heart of hearts, yet dim in the memory of his outer mind. It is based on the visualization of a perfect idea which then becomes a magnet that attracts the creative energies of the *Holy Spirit* to his being to fulfill the pattern held in mind."

(Matt. 6:22; Jer. 31:33; Heb. 8:10. See Mark L. Prophet and Elizabeth Clare Prophet, *Climb the Highest Mountain*, 2d ed., pp. 48–50, 155.)

Jesus. The *Ascended Master* Jesus *Christ*. The *avatar* of the Piscean age; the incarnation of the *Word*, the Universal Christ; the example of the *Christ consciousness* that was to have been outpictured by the children of God in the two-thousand-year dispensation of the Piscean age; one who realized the fullness of the *Christ Self* and was therefore called Jesus, the Christ. He came to reveal the individual Christ Self to all mankind and to show the works of the Father (the *I AM Presence*) that can be accomplished by his sons and daughters in and through the flame of the individual Christ Self. Jesus holds the office in *hierarchy* of *World Teacher*, which he shares with the Ascended Master *Kuthumi*, who was embodied as Saint Francis. Jesus' *retreat* is the Resurrection Temple, located in the *etheric* realm over the Holy Land. He also serves in the Arabian Retreat in the Arabian Desert northeast of the Red Sea. *See also* "Jesus Christ and Saint Germain: Wayshowers of the Aquarian Age," pp. 253–63 of this book.

(See Jesus and Kuthumi, *Prayer and Meditation*; *Corona Class Lessons*. Mark L. Prophet and Elizabeth Clare Prophet, *The*

Lost Teachings of Jesus. The following by Elizabeth Clare Prophet: *The Lost Years of Jesus.* "The Lost Years and the Lost Teachings of Jesus," 1-hr. TV show on video. "The Golden Age of Jesus Christ on Atlantis," 2 videocassettes; 2 audiocassettes. "Jesus Christ, Avatar of the Ages," 1 videocassette; 2 audiocassettes. "Roots of Christian Mysticism," five 1-hr. TV shows on video; 6 audiocassettes. For additional lectures on the lost years and lost teachings of Jesus, including teachings on Gnostic texts, send for a Summit University Press catalog.)

Jophiel. *See* Archangel.

Karma. (Skt. *karman,* nominative *karma,* 'act', 'deed', 'work'.) Karma is energy/consciousness in action; the law of cause and effect and retribution. Also called the law of the circle, which decrees that whatever we do comes full circle to our doorstep for resolution. Paul said, "Whatsoever a man soweth, that shall he also reap." Newton observed, "For every action there is an equal and opposite reaction." The law of karma necessitates the *soul's* reincarnation until all karmic cycles are balanced. Thus, from lifetime to lifetime man determines his fate by his actions, including his thoughts, feelings, words, and deeds. *Saint Germain* teaches the accelerated path of transmutation of karma by the *violet flame* of the *Holy Spirit* and the transcending of the rounds of rebirth through the path of individual Christhood leading to the ascension demonstrated by *Jesus.*

(Gal. 6:7. See Mark L. Prophet and Elizabeth Clare Prophet, *The Lost Teachings of Jesus I,* softbound, pp. 129–33; or pocketbook, Book One, pp. 173–77. *The Lost Teachings of Jesus II,* softbound, pp. 44–50; or pocketbook, Book Two, pp. 240–47. The following by Elizabeth Clare Prophet: *The Astrology of the Four Horsemen,* pp. 3–19, 65–71, 491–98. "Prophecy for the 1990s," in *Pearls of Wisdom,* 1988, vol. 31, Book I, pp. 1–91; Book II, pp. 1–123. "Prophecy for the 1990s III," in *Pearls of Wisdom,* 1990, vol. 33, nos. 4–12. "Karma,

Reincarnation and Christianity," in *Pearls of Wisdom*, 1992, vol. 35, nos. 11–14, 17, 22; 2 videocassettes; 3 audiocassettes.)

Karmic Board. *See* Lords of Karma.

Karmic Lords. *See* Lords of Karma.

Keeper of the Scrolls. The *angel* in charge of the *recording angels* assigned to every *lifestream*. The Keeper of the Scrolls is the custodian of the archives containing every *man's* book of life. It is his responsibility to provide the *Ascended Masters* and the *Karmic Board* with the life record of any or all incarnations of an evolving *soul* about which they may inquire. This information is used not only in the soul's final judgment, but also for the purposes of counseling and assigning the soul her duties and mission from lifetime to lifetime. This life record is also used in granting dispensations (of mercy or talents), initiations, or appointment to an office in the ascended or unascended *hierarchy* of the *Great White Brotherhood:* "And at that time thy people shall be delivered, every one that shall be found written in the Book. . . . And the books were opened: and another book was opened, which is the Book of Life." *See* Recording angel.
(Dan. 12:1; Rev. 20:12.)

Keepers of the Flame Fraternity. Founded in 1961 by *Saint Germain*, an organization of *Ascended Masters* and their *chelas* who vow to keep the flame of Life on earth and support the activities of the *Great White Brotherhood* in the establishment of their Community and *Mystery School* and in the dissemination of their Teachings. Keepers of the Flame receive graded lessons in *cosmic law* dictated by the Ascended Masters to their *Messengers* Mark and Elizabeth Prophet.

Kuan Yin. The *Ascended* Lady *Master.* Known as the Goddess of Mercy for her ensoulment of the God flames of mercy and compassion, she keeps the flame of the Divine *Mother* on behalf of the people of China, Asia, and the world. As the representative of the Seventh *Ray* on the *Karmic Board*, she radiates the qualities of mercy, forgiveness, and compassion to the evolutions of earth from her *etheric* temple over Peking, China. Kuan Yin held the office of *Chohan* of the Seventh Ray for two thousand years until *Saint Germain* assumed that office in the late 1700s. In Chinese Buddhism Kuan Yin is the feminine form of the Indian and Tibetan Avalokiteśvara, emanation of Amitābha Buddha. She has been identified with Tara, the White Goddess of Tibet. Kuan Yin ascended thousands of years ago. She has taken the vow of the *Bodhisattva* to serve planet earth until all children of the Light are free.

(See *Kuan Yin Opens the Door to the Golden Age: The Path of the Mystics East and West, Pearls of Wisdom,* 1982, vol. 25, Book I, pp. 1–80, 1–14, 229–34; Book II, pp. 81–140. *Kuan Yin's Crystal Rosary: Devotions to the Divine Mother East and West,* 3-audiocassette album and booklet. Lectures by Elizabeth Clare Prophet: "The Path of the Divine Mother East and West: Mother Mary and Kuan Yin," 3 audiocassettes, A88059, San Francisco. "Teachings, Meditations and Mantras of Kuan Yin and Mother Mary," 3 videocassettes; 3 audiocassettes. "Kuan Yin's Miracle," 4 audiocassettes.)

Kuthumi. The *Ascended Master.* Serves with *Jesus* in the office of *World Teacher;* formerly *Chohan* of the Second *Ray;* master psychologist; sponsor of youth; head of the Order of the *Brothers and Sisters of the Golden Robe* and of the *etheric* Temple of Illumination in Kashmir, also known as the Cathedral of Nature. The Master maintains a focus at Shigatse, Tibet, where he plays his grand organ—drawing the harmony of *cosmos* by the *sacred fires* of his heart. With this celestial music, he sends healing and peace throughout the planetary body to *souls* in transition (especially at the hour of death) and guides them to the etheric *retreats* of the *Great White Brotherhood* for tutoring in preparation for their next earthly life. He inspires architects, poets, and scientists with the mystical remembrance of their own soul's harmony in the celestial geometry and the rhythm of the stars. In his soul's evolution on the path of self-mastery, Kuthumi was embodied as:

Thutmose III, reigned c. 1503–1450 B.C., Egypt. Greatest of pharaohs; an adept ruler, military conqueror, and patron of the arts. He is considered the architect of the Egyptian empire.

Pythagoras, c. 582–c. 507 B.C., Greek philosopher and mathematician. Established the *mystery school* at Crotona, Italy, where he taught his community of initiates. His doctrines influenced many great philosophers.

Balthazar, first century, one of the three Magi (astronomer/adepts) who calculated the time and place of birth and journeyed from the East to pay homage to the Christ Child.

Saint Francis of Assisi, 1182–1226, Italy. Founder of the Franciscan order, the "divine poverello" who embraced "Lady Poverty," first saint known to have received the stigmata.

Shah Jahan, 1592–1666, India. Mogul emperor who brought India to a golden age of art and architecture, exemplified in the magnificent Taj Mahal, built at Agra, his capital, a shrine to his twin flame.

Koot Hoomi Lal Singh, nineteenth-century Kashmiri Brahman, Shigatse, Tibet; also called K.H. In 1875 he founded with *El Morya* the Theosophical

Society to reacquaint mankind with the ancient wisdom that underlies all the world's religions. (See Kuthumi, *Studies of the Human Aura,* also published in *The Human Aura.* Jesus and Kuthumi, *Prayer and Meditation; Corona Class Lessons.* Kuthumi, Lanto, and Meru, *Understanding Yourself,* also published in *Kuthumi On Selfhood—Consciousness: The Doorway to Reality, Pearls of Wisdom,* 1969, vol. 12, nos. 25–40.)

Lemuria. Mu, the lost continent of the Pacific, which, according to the findings of James Churchward, archaeologist and author of *The Lost Continent of Mu,* extended from north of Hawaii three thousand miles south to Easter Island and the Fijis and was made up of three areas of land stretching more than five thousand miles from east to west. Churchward's history of the ancient Motherland is based on records inscribed on sacred tablets he claims to have discovered in India. With the help of the high priest of an Indian temple, he deciphered the tablets. During fifty years of research he confirmed their contents in further writings, inscriptions, and legends he came upon in Southeast Asia, the Yucatan, Central America, the Pacific islands, Mexico, North America, ancient Egypt and other civilizations. He estimates that Mu was destroyed approximately twelve thousand years ago by the collapse of the gas chambers that upheld the continent. (*The Lost Continent of Mu* [1931; reprint, New York: Paperback Library Edition, 1968].)

Lifestream. The stream of life that comes forth from the one Source, from the *I AM Presence* in the planes of *Spirit,* and descends to the planes of *Matter* where it manifests as the *threefold flame* anchored in the heart *chakra* for the sustainment of the *soul* in Matter and the nourishment of the *four lower bodies.* Used to denote souls evolving as individual "lifestreams" and hence synonymous with the term "individual." Denotes the ongoing nature of the individual through its cycles of individualization.

Light. Spiritual light is the energy of God, the potential of the *Christ*. As the personification of *Spirit*, the term "Light" can be used synonymously with the terms "God" and "Christ." As the essence of Spirit it is synonymous with *"sacred fire."* It is the emanation of the Great *Central Sun* and the individualized *I AM Presence*—and the Source of all life. It is that which kindles the divine spark, for the true Light lights every *man*ifestation of God who must descend into a darkened world. The *Lightbearer* is the dispeller of Darkness and the Light of his I AM Presence is from the realms of the Eternal Day. (John 1:7–9.)

Lightbearer. Lightbearer means Christbearer, one who bears the *Light* which is *Christ*, one who bears the responsibility for Christhood in himself and others by defending the truth and honor of God; one who is anointed with the *Christ consciousness* and bears this enlightenment to all. The Lightbearer is the Keeper of the Flame whose motto must be "I AM my brother's keeper—I AM the keeper of the Light who is Christ in my brother."

Lord Maitreya. The *Ascended Master*. Together with Gautama, Maitreya followed the disciplines of the *Buddha* under *Sanat Kumara*. He holds the office of Cosmic *Christ* and Planetary Buddha, serving in *hierarchy* under Lord Gautama, directing the office of the *World Teachers*. He demonstrates on behalf of an evolving humanity the *cosmic consciousness* of the Christ in all areas of human endeavor and its universality throughout *cosmos*. He is known as the

Great Initiator and was, in fact, the initiator of
Jesus in his individualization of the Christ Flame in
his final embodiment as world saviour and exemplar of the Way, the Truth, and the Life to all
aspirants on the path of personal Christhood. Beloved Maitreya was the LORD God in Eden, Guru
of *twin flames*. The long-awaited "Coming Buddha," he has indeed come to reopen his *Mystery
School* to assist *Saint Germain* and *Portia*, twin
flames of the Seventh *Ray* and hierarchs of Aquarius, to usher in the new age. On May 31, 1984, he
dedicated the Heart of the Inner Retreat and the
entire Royal Teton Ranch to the Path and Teaching
of the Cosmic Christ in order that those who
departed from his tutelage, going the way of Serpents (the fallen *angels* who led Eve astray), might
be restored and the children of the *Light* follow the
Son of God in the regeneration. As the sponsor of
twin flames he is the friend of all initiates of the
sacred fire. When called upon, he will give the
illumination of the Christ and the strength of
the *Word* to pass the initiations that come under his
sponsorship. *See also* Mystery schools, Buddha.
(See Lord Maitreya, "On Initiation," in *Pearls of Wisdom*, 1975,
vol. 18, nos. 49–53; *Maitreya On the Image of God: A Study
in Christhood by the Great Initiator, Pearls of Wisdom*, 1984,
vol. 27, Books I and II. Elizabeth Clare Prophet, "Darshan with
the Cosmic Christ," 2 audiocassettes; "The Path of the Bodhisattva: The Historical Maitreya," 2 audiocassettes; "The Age of
Maitreya," 1 videocassette; 2 audiocassettes.)

Lord of the World. Gautama *Buddha* holds the office
of Lord of the World (referred to as "God of the
Earth" in Rev. 11:4), having recently succeeded
Sanat Kumara, who had held the office for tens
of thousands of years. His is the highest governing office of the spiritual *hierarchy* for the planet—

and yet Lord Gautama is truly the most humble amongst the *Ascended Masters*. At inner levels, he sustains the *threefold flame*, the divine spark, for those *lifestreams* who have lost the direct contact with their *I AM Presence* and who have made so much negative *karma* as to be unable to magnetize sufficient *Light* from the Godhead to sustain their *souls'* physical incarnation on Earth. Through a filigree thread of light connecting his heart with the hearts of all God's children, Lord Gautama nourishes the flickering flame of Life that ought to burn upon the altar of each heart with a greater magnitude of love, wisdom, and power, fed by each one's own *Christ consciousness*.

Gautama Buddha received the mantle of Lord of the World on January 1, 1956, from Sanat Kumara, hierarch of the planet Venus, who had held the position of Lord of the World since the darkest hours of Earth's history. Known as the Ancient of Days, Sanat Kumara volunteered to come to Earth thousands of years ago, when cosmic councils had decreed the dissolution of the planet. So great was mankind's departure from *cosmic law*, that the Solar Lords had determined that no further opportunity should be granted humanity, who had willfully ignored and forgotten the *God Flame* within their hearts. The requirement of the Law for the saving of Terra was that one who qualified as the embodied 'Lamb' be present in the physical octave to hold the balance and keep the threefold flame of Life for and on behalf of every living soul. Sanat Kumara offered to be that one.

In his April 8, 1979, *Pearl of Wisdom*, Sanat Kumara told the story of how Venusian devotees volunteered to accompany him and embody among mankind to assist in keeping the flame: "The joy of opportunity was mingled with the sorrow that the sense of separation brings. I had chosen a voluntary exile upon a dark star. And though it was destined to be Freedom's Star, all knew it would be for me a long dark night of the soul. Then all at once from the valleys and the mountains there appeared a great gathering of my children. It was the souls of the hundred and forty and four thousand approaching our palace of light. They spiraled nearer and nearer as twelve companies singing the song of freedom, of love, and of victory....As we watched from the balcony, Venus and I, we saw the thirteenth company robed in white. It was the royal priesthood of the Order of Melchizedek....When all of their numbers had assembled, ring upon ring upon ring surrounding our home, and their hymn of praise and adoration to me was concluded, their spokesman stood before the balcony to address us on behalf of the great multitude. It was the soul of the one you know and love today as the Lord of the World, Gautama Buddha. And he addressed us, saying, 'O Ancient of Days, we have heard of the covenant which God hath made with thee this day and of thy commitment to keep the flame of Life until some among Earth's evolutions should be quickened and once again renew their vow to be bearers of the flame. O Ancient of Days, thou art to us our Guru, our very life, our God. We will not leave thee comfortless. We will go with thee.'"

Thus, they came to Earth with Sanat Kumara and legions of *angels*, preceded by another retinue of *Lightbearers* who prepared the way and established the *retreat* of *Shamballa*—the City of White—on an island in the Gobi Sea (now the Gobi Desert). There Sanat Kumara anchored the focus of the threefold flame, establishing the initial thread of contact with all on Earth by extending *rays* of light from his heart to their own. And there the volunteers from Venus embodied in dense veils of flesh to see Earth's evolutions through unto the victory of their vow. The first from among these unascended Lightbearers to respond to the call of the Lord of the World from the physical octave was, understandably, Gautama and close with him was *Maitreya*. Both pursued the path of the *Bodhisattva* unto Buddhahood, Gautama finishing the course 'first' and Maitreya 'second'. Thus the two became Sanat Kumara's foremost disciples, the one ultimately succeeding him in the office of Lord of the World, the other as Cosmic Christ and Planetary Buddha.

At the moment of the transfer of the mantle of Lord of the World on January 1, 1956, Gautama Buddha assumed the responsibility for sustaining the lifeline to Earth's evolutions through his own heart flame, and Sanat Kumara, as Regent Lord of the World, returned to his home star, Venus, where he maintains an intense activity of involvement with the *Great White Brotherhood*'s service on planet Earth. Gautama's former office of Cosmic Christ and Planetary Buddha was simultaneously filled by Lord Maitreya. In the same ceremony, which took place at the Royal Teton Retreat, the office of *World Teacher*, formerly held by Maitreya, was passed to Lord *Jesus* and his dear friend and disciple Saint Francis *(Kuthumi)*. Lord Lanto took the chohanship of the Second Ray July 1958, which had been held by Kuthumi, and beloved Nada assumed the office of chohan of the Sixth

Ray, which had been held by Jesus during the Piscean age of which he was also the hierarch. *Saint Germain* with *Portia* assumed the rulership of Aquarius on May 1, 1954. While Maitreya represents the Cosmic Christ and Planetary Buddha, Jesus holds the office of the personal Christ as the great exemplar of each one's own Holy *Christ Self*.

Lord Gautama presides as Hierarch of Shamballa, now on the *etheric plane*, to which the physical retreat has been withdrawn. Throughout the ages, the *Messengers* of the Brotherhood, known and unknown, have held the balance in the physical octave for the flame and the Buddha of Shamballa. Thus Jesus, as the anointed Messenger of Lord Maitreya, the Cosmic Christ, was the open door through his Sacred Heart for the light of the Father represented in the persons of Maitreya, Gautama, and Sanat Kumára to be anchored in the hearts of the multitudes of Earth's people. The Lord Jesus Christ defined his office in the physical octave according to cosmic law when he said: "As long as I AM in the world, the I AM that I AM, the Word which I incarnate, is the Light of the world." It was this anchoring of the Light of the I AM Presence in his heart *chakra* that enabled Jesus to take upon himself planetary *karma*, "the *sins* of the world," in order that souls of Light might follow him on the path of Christhood until they, too, should bear in their body temples the Light of the Son of God. (John 9:5. See *Sanat Kumara On the Path of the Ruby Ray: The Opening of the Seventh Seal, Pearls of Wisdom*, 1979, vol. 22, Book I, no. 14.)

Lords of Karma. The *ascended beings* who comprise the Karmic Board. Their names and the *rays* that they represent on the board are as follows: First

Ray, the *Great Divine Director;* Second Ray, the *Goddess of Liberty;* Third Ray, the Ascended Lady Master Nada; Fourth Ray, the Elohim Cyclopea; Fifth Ray, **Pallas Athena**, Goddess of Truth; Sixth Ray, *Portia,* the Goddess of Justice; Seventh Ray, *Kuan Yin,* Goddess of Mercy. The Lords of Karma dispense justice to this system of worlds, adjudicating *karma*, mercy, and judgment on behalf of every *lifestream.* All *souls* must pass before the Karmic Board before and after each incarnation on earth, receiving their assignment and karmic allotment for each lifetime beforehand and the review of their performance at its conclusion. Through the *Keeper of the Scrolls* and the *recording angels,* the Lords of Karma have access to the complete records of every lifestream's incarnations on earth. They determine who shall embody, as well as when and where. They assign souls to families and communities, measuring out the weights of karma that must be balanced as the "jot and tittle" of the law. The Karmic Board, acting in consonance with the individual *I AM Presence* and *Christ Self,* determines when the soul has earned the right to be free from the wheel of karma and the round of rebirth. The Lords of Karma meet at the Royal Teton Retreat twice yearly, at winter and summer solstice, to review petitions from unascended mankind and to grant dispensations for their assistance.

(See Mark L. Prophet and Elizabeth Clare Prophet, *Climb the Highest Mountain,* 2d ed., pp. 529–35.)

Lords of the Seven Rays. *See* Chohan.

Lucifer. (From the Lat., meaning "light-bearer.") One who attained to the rank of *Archangel* and fell from grace through pride, ambition, and the desire to be above the Stars of God (Sons of God and *Elohim*), above the Shekinah glory to rival the Most High. "How art thou fallen from heaven, O Lucifer, son of the morning!..." Archetype of the planetary *dweller-on-the-threshold*. *Antichrist*. The *angels* who followed this archdeceiver, named by *Jesus* "the father of lies" and "a murderer from the beginning," are the fallen ones, also called Luciferians, Satanists or sons of Belial (after their various lieutenants). More than disobedient, these rebels against First Cause were blasphemous and contemptuous of the Father and his children amongst whom they embodied (see the parable of the tares among the wheat, Matt. 13), having been brought low—to the lowly estate of physical incarnation—by the LORD's hosts. Lucifer was bound "on earth" by *Michael* the Archangel on April 16, 1975 (even as he and his angels had been bound "in heaven" by the same Defender of the Faith and his angels) and taken to the Court of the Sacred Fire on Sirius where he stood trial before the Four and Twenty Elders and the four 'beasts' in the final judgment at the great white throne. He went through the second death on April 26, 1975. Many who followed the Fallen One in the Great Rebellion against the Son of God have also been brought to trial. His seed, still "wroth with the Woman" and her *Manchild*, are making war with the heirs of *Sanat Kumara's Light* on planet earth. Daily they are being bound by Archangel Michael and the LORD's hosts and remanded to stand trial in the final judgment as one by one their time is up—*and they are being judged:* "every man according to their works," as Jesus' angel showed it in a vision of the last days of the Piscean age to John the Revelator. *See also* Angel, Satan.

(Read Isa. 14:12–17 for the scriptural account of Lucifer's declaration of war against Almighty God and his Christ; John 8:44; Matt. 13:24–30, 36–43; Rev. 12; 19:4; 20:11–15. See Elizabeth Clare Prophet, *Forbidden Mysteries of Enoch: Fallen Angels and the Origins of Evil*, containing all the Enoch texts, including the Book of Enoch and the Book of the Secrets of Enoch.)

Luciferian. *See* Lucifer.

Macrocosm. (From the Gk., meaning "great world.") The larger *cosmos*; the entire warp and woof of creation, which we call the *Cosmic Egg*. Also used to contrast *man* as the *microcosm*, "the little world," against the backdrop of the larger world in which he lives. *See also* Microcosm.

Maha Chohan. "Great Lord" of the *seven rays*. The representative of the *Holy Spirit* to a planet and its evolutions. One who embodies the Trinity and the *Mother* Flame of the seven rays and *chakras* and is qualified to be *Chohan*, "Lord," of each or all of the seven rays. Hence he is called the Maha Chohan, the Great Lord, as he presides over the Seven Chohans who embody the Law, the *Word*, and the *Christ consciousness* of their respective *rays*. The *Ascended Master* who currently holds the office of Maha Chohan over the Seven Lords (Chohans) of the rays was embodied as the poet Homer. In his final incarnation as a shepherd on the hillsides of India, the *Light* (Christ consciousness) that he drew forth was a mantle of comfort to millions. The Maha Chohan maintains an etheric *retreat* with a physical focus on the island of Sri Lanka (Ceylon) where the flame of the Holy Spirit is anchored. *See also* Chohan.

(See the following by Mark L. Prophet and Elizabeth Clare Prophet: *Climb the Highest Mountain*, 2d ed., pp. 386–88, 411–44, 555–62. *The Lost Teachings of Jesus II*, softbound, pp. 48, 50, 154, 157, 159–61, 163; or pocketbooks, Book Two, pp. 245, 247; Book Three, pp. 111, 114, 117–19, 122. *Lords of the Seven Rays*, Book One, pp. 11, 13, 15–18; Book Two, pp. 277–97.)

Maitreya. *See* Lord Maitreya.

Man. The *man*ifestation of God; male and female made in the image and likeness of God *(Elohim)*. Mankind or the human race; Homo sapiens.

Manchild. *See* Divine Manchild.

Mantra. A mystical formula or invocation; a word or formula, often in Sanskrit, to be recited or sung for the purpose of intensifying the action of the *Spirit* of God in *man*. A form of prayer consisting of a word or a group of words that is chanted over and over again to magnetize a particular aspect of the Deity or of a being who has actualized that aspect of the Deity. *See also* Decree.

(See Mark L. Prophet and Elizabeth Clare Prophet, *The Lost Teachings of Jesus II*, softbound, pp. 141–46, 450–51; or pocketbooks, Book Three, pp. 79–85; Book Four, pp. 192–93; "The Efficacy of Decrees," with instruction on Indian mantras and bhajans, 1 audiocassette. Elizabeth Clare Prophet, *The Liberating Power of the Word*, album 1, 6 audiocassettes. *Devotions to Lord Krishna: The Maha Mantra and Bhajans*, audiocassette and booklet.)

Manu. Sanskrit for the progenitor and lawgiver of the evolutions of God on earth. The Manu and his divine complement are ascended *twin flames* assigned by the Father-*Mother* God to sponsor and ensoul the Christic image for a certain evolution or lifewave that is known as a **root race**—*souls* who embody as a group and have a unique archetypal pattern, *divine plan*, and mission to fulfill on earth. According to esoteric tradition, there are seven primary aggregations of souls, i.e., the first

to the seventh root races. The first three root races
lived in purity and innocence upon earth in three
golden ages before the Fall of Adam and Eve.
Through obedience to *cosmic law* and total identification with the *Real Self*, these three root races
won their immortal freedom and ascended from
earth. It was during the time of the fourth root
race, on the continent of *Lemuria*, that the allegorical Fall took place under the influence of the
fallen *angels* known as Serpents (because they used
the serpentine spinal energies to beguile the soul,
or female principle in mankind, as a means to their
end of lowering the masculine potential, thereby
emasculating the Sons of God). The fourth, fifth,
and sixth root races (the latter soul group not
having entirely descended into physical incarnation) remain in embodiment on earth today. The
seventh root race is destined to incarnate on the
continent of South America in the Aquarian age
under their Manus, the *Great Divine Director* and
his divine complement. The God and Goddess
Meru are the Manus for the sixth root race,
Vaivasvata Manu with his consort is the Manu of
the fifth root race, and Lord Himalaya with his
Beloved is the Manu for the fourth. The Manus are
beloved God-parents who respond instantaneously
to the call of their children with the comforting
presence of their Light endued with such great
Power/Wisdom/Love as to quiver the ethers and
make each little one feel at Home in the arms of
God even in the darkest hour.

Mary. *See* Mother Mary.

Mass consciousness. The collective consciousness of
humanity; the collective unconscious of the race;

the lowest common denominator of mankind's collective awareness vibrating at the level of the *astral plane*. The mass mind is the collective, computerized, programmed mind of humanity.

Mater. (Lat. for "mother.") Mater is the *mater*-ialization of the *God Flame*, the means whereby *Spirit* acquires, 'physically', fourfold dimension and form through the feminine, or negative, polarity of the Godhead. The term used interchangeably with "Matter" to describe the planes of being that conform to and comprise the universal chalice, or matrix, for the descent of that *Light* of God which is perceived as *Mother*. It is through this Mother aspect of himself that the Spirit of God, the Father, evolves the consciousness of the *Christ*, the only begotten Son of God, in his children as a developing Christ-Self awareness through the *threefold flame*—divine spark and signet of their joint-heirship to be. The *soul* that descends from the plane of Spirit abides in time and space in Mater for the purpose of its spiritual/physical evolution that necessitates self-mastery of the energies of God through the judicious exercise of *free will*. The four lower *bodies of man*, of a planet, and of systems of worlds—as the four planes, quadrants and cosmic forces—occupy and make up the frequencies of Matter. *See also* Spirit.

Matter. *See* Mater.

Mental body. One of the four lower *bodies of man*, corresponding to the air element and the second quadrant of *Matter*; the body that is intended to be the vehicle, or vessel, for the Mind of God or the *Christ* Mind. "Let this [Universal] Mind be in you which was also in Christ *Jesus*." Until quickened,

this body remains the vehicle for the *carnal mind*, often called the lower mental body in contrast to the Higher Mental Body, a synonym for the *Christ Self* or *Christ consciousness*.
(Phil. 2:5.)

Messenger. Evangelist. One who goes before the angels bearing to the people of earth the good news of the gospel of *Jesus* Christ and, at the appointed time, the Everlasting Gospel. The Messengers of the *Great White Brotherhood* are anointed by the *hierarchy* as their apostles ("one sent on a mission"). They deliver through the dictations (prophecies) of the *Ascended Masters* the testimony and lost teachings of Jesus Christ in the power of the *Holy Spirit* to the seed of *Christ*, the lost sheep of the house of Israel, and to every nation. A Messenger is one who is trained by an Ascended Master to receive by various methods the words, concepts, teachings, and messages of the Great White Brotherhood; one who delivers the law, the prophecies, and the dispensations of God for a people and an age.
(Rev. 14:6; Matt. 10:6; 15:24. El Morya, *The Chela and the Path*, pp. 115–22. Jesus and Kuthumi, *Prayer and Meditation*, pp. 246–53. Elizabeth Clare Prophet, *The Astrology of the Four Horsemen*, pp. 52–53, 58–61.)

Michael, Archangel. *Archangel* of the First *Ray*, Prince of the Archangels, the first among equals unto whom all other Archangels and their legions defer. Known as the Defender of the Faith, Champion of the Woman and Her Seed, and Leader in the Battle of Armageddon who stands as the defender of the *Christ consciousness* in all children of God. His name means "who is as God." His intercession on behalf of God's people in this age is prophesied in Daniel 12:1: "And at that time shall Michael stand up, the great prince which standeth for the children of thy people: and there shall be a time of trouble, such as never was since there was a nation even to that same time: and at that time thy people shall be delivered, every one that shall be found written in the book."

Archangel Michael is the *Angel of the LORD* who comes to quicken the elect of God with the lost teachings of *Jesus* Christ and to deliver the true and righteous judgments of God upon the seed of the Wicked One. This deliverer sent to us by the LORD has figured as the greatest and most revered of angels in Jewish, Christian, and Islamic scripture and tradition. In the Old Testament he appears as the guardian of Israel and is identified in Jewish mystical literature as the *angel* who wrestled with Jacob, guided Israel through the wilderness, destroyed the army of Sennacherib, and saved the three Hebrew boys from Nebuchadnezzar's fiery furnace. Standing mighty in the LORD's presence, sword drawn, Archangel Michael appeared to Joshua as he prepared to lead the Israelites into battle at Jericho, revealing himself as Captain of the Host of the LORD—impartial defender of all who espouse Truth and Righteousness.
(Josh. 5:13–15.)

It is recorded in Jewish legend that "the fire that Moses saw in the bush was the appearance of Michael, who had descended as the forerunner of the Shekinah." Indeed, wherever the term "Angel of the LORD" is given in scripture it is a reference to this *messenger* of God—the divine figure of His appearing. The Book of Enoch describes Archangel Michael as "the merciful, the patient," "one of the holy angels, who, presiding over human virtue, commands the nations." In *The War of the Sons of Light and the Sons of Darkness*, one of the Dead Sea Scrolls, Michael is the "mighty, ministering angel" through whom God promises to "send perpetual help" to the sons of *Light*. Called Mika'il in Muslim lore, he is the angel of nature, providing both food and knowledge to man.

Saint Michael, venerated by Catholics as patron and protector of the Church, was also the heavenly physician revered in the early Christian community for the miraculous cures wrought by his intercession. Moreover, the beloved Archangel was among the three heavenly visitors who revealed to the young peasant girl Joan of Arc her mission to deliver France. Revelation 12 tells of Archangel Michael's key role as the defender of the Woman clothed with the Sun as he casts the adversary of her *Manchild* out of the courts of heaven: "And there was war in heaven: Michael and his angels fought against the dragon, and the dragon fought and his angels, and prevailed not; neither was their place found any more in heaven." In Revelation 16:1, he is the first of the seven angels to "pour out the vials of the wrath of God upon the earth"—marking the descending woes of mankind's *karma* returning to their doorstep their misuses of God's Light.

As the Archangel of the First Ray, Archangel Michael embodies God's consciousness of faith, protection, perfection, and the will of God. From his *retreat* on the *etheric plane* at Banff in Alberta, Canada, he goes forth into all the world with his legions of blue-lightning angels to protect the children of the Light and preserve freedom on earth.

With his hosts he descends into the pits of Death and Hell to bind the adversaries of the Christ consciousness, remanding them to the Court of the Sacred Fire for their final judgment. He sweeps through the *astral plane*, binding demons and discarnates that prey upon unsuspecting *souls*, rendering incomparable assistance to those beset by the dark forces. His keynote is "The Navy Hymn," "Eternal Father, Strong to Save." The keynote of his retreat is "The Soldiers' Chorus" from *Faust*, by Charles Gounod. The name of his feminine complement is Faith.

At this end of the Piscean age, with two thousand years and more of unbalanced karma falling due paralleled by a period of accelerated initiation—when the *Lightbearers* are facing greater challenges on the path of personal Christhood in order to enter the Aquarian age—the Father has accorded the Lightbearers unprecedented opportunity to invoke the comforting presence and intercession of this Angel of the LORD. As they offer prayers, invocations, hymns and dynamic decrees in the science of the *spoken Word*—such as those included in *Archangel Michael's Rosary for Armageddon* released through the Messenger Elizabeth Clare Prophet—the armor and shield of Archangel Michael is immediately theirs. Responding to the needs of mankind, they give the impelling call for the saving of the nations in this cycle marking the return of personal and planetary karma delivered by the Four Horsemen. Surely, in the midst of this time of troubles the Lightbearers are daily proving the law: "The Call compels the answer." If you are in trouble, shout unto the Angel of the LORD this dynamic decree until he responds: "Lord Michael before! Lord Michael behind! Lord Michael to the right! Lord Michael to the left! Lord Michael above! Lord Michael below! Lord Michael, Lord Michael wherever I go! I AM his Love protecting here! I AM his Love protecting here! I AM his Love protecting here!" *See also* Archangel.

(See Elizabeth Clare Prophet, "Archangel Michael's Rosary for Armageddon," in *Pearls of Wisdom*, 1985, vol. 28, Book I, no. 19; *Archangel Michael's Rosary for Armageddon*, audiocassette and booklet; "Putting on the Armour and Shield of Archangel Michael," audiocassette. *Decrees and Songs to Archangel Michael*, audiocassette. *Hail Light Victorious! A Salute to Archangel Michael, Captain of the LORD's Host*, songs on CD and audiocassette.)

Microcosm. (From the Gk., meaning "small world.") (1) The world of the individual, his *four lower bodies*, his *aura*, and the forcefield of his *karma*. (2) The planet. *See also* Macrocosm.

Misqualification (of energy). The "mist" qualification of fallen man and woman; the spawning of *evil*, or the energy *veil*, through the misuse of *free will* by *souls* evolving in time and space. The misapplication of God's energy. The negative qualification of God's consciousness and life-force to multiply darkness, doubt, disease, degeneracy, and death instead of Light, Love, Divine Wholeness, Peace, and Freedom. The **misqualified energies** that burden the *aura* and electronic belt of the people and their planet are the direct result of this perversion of alchemy, the all-chemistry of God, the science of creation that the Father and Son invite us to "TRY" as co-creators with the Great Alchemist himself.

Monad. *See* Divine Monad, Human monad.

Morya. *See* El Morya.

Mother. "Divine Mother," "Universal Mother," and "*Cosmic Virgin*" are alternate terms for the feminine polarity of the Godhead, the manifestation of God as Mother. *Matter* is the feminine polarity of *Spirit*, and the term is used interchangeably with *Mater* (Lat. meaning "mother"). In this context, the entire material *cosmos* becomes the womb of creation into which Spirit projects the energies of Life. Matter, then, is the womb of the Cosmic Virgin, who, as the other half of the Divine Whole, also exists in Spirit as the spiritual polarity of God.

Jesus himself recognized *Alpha and Omega* as the highest representatives of the Father-Mother God and often referred to Alpha as Father and to Omega as Mother. Those who assume the feminine polarity of consciousness after the *ascension* are known as *Ascended* Lady *Masters*. Together with all feminine (femininely polarized) beings in the octaves of *light*, they focus the flame of the Divine Mother on behalf of the evolutions of mankind evolving in many systems of worlds. However, being androgynous, all of the heavenly host focus any of the masculine or feminine attributes of the Godhead at will, for they have entered the spheres of the Divine Wholeness. *See also* Mother of the Flame.

(See the following by Elizabeth Clare Prophet: "The Path of the Divine Mother East and West: Mother Mary and Kuan Yin," 3 audiocassettes, A88055, Toronto. "The Path of the Divine Mother," 3 videocassettes; 3 audiocassettes. "The Worship of the Goddess—the Path of the Divine Mother," two 1-hr. TV shows on video; 3 audiocassettes.)

Mother Mary. *Archeia* of the Fifth *Ray*, divine complement of *Archangel* Raphael, Queen of Angels, and the Blessed Mother of *Jesus* Christ. Her name means Mother Ray (Ma ray). Called by the Father to embody on earth to give birth to the *Christ* who would save those souls that had been led astray by *Luciferian* rebels, Mary is one of the LORD's hosts who throughout her incarnations on earth has ardently exemplified the Motherhood of God. From the earliest days of *Atlantis* she prepared for her final embodiment, when she would nurture in the Bethlehem babe the 'son' *(soul)* of David, born again to be the Saviour *(avatar)* of the Piscean age. Mary served as a priestess on Atlantis in the Temple of Truth, teaching and studying the healing arts and directing, through her Immaculate Heart, the light of the ineffable Word to the teeming millions of that continent. She was also the mother of David, king of Israel. It was her masterful development on Atlantis of the science of the *immaculate concept*, which she had practiced in heaven, that enabled her to be the LORD's handmaid, preparing her *four lower bodies* for the incarnation of the Word in Christ Jesus, her son. At the conclusion of that blessed life, her *divine plan* fulfilled, Mary ascended to the heart of the Father. Today she serves humanity and the 'living Church' from inner levels, very close at hand with the *hierarchies* of *angels* and *Ascended Masters* who comprise the *Great White Brotherhood*. Mother Mary's intercession is immediate through the giving of her New Age Rosary, which she dictated to the Messenger in 1972.

(See Mark L. Prophet and Elizabeth Clare Prophet, *My Soul Doth Magnify the Lord! Mother Mary's New Age Teachings and Rosary with a Challenge to Christendom. Mary the Mother On the Temple of Understanding: A Challenge to the Christian World, Pearls of Wisdom*, 1972, vol. 15, nos. 29–41. The following lectures by Elizabeth Clare Prophet: "Prophecy: Fátima and Medjugorje," 1-hr. TV show on videocassette. "The Path of the Divine Mother East and West: Mother Mary and Kuan Yin," 3 audiocassettes, A88059, San Francisco. "Mother

Mary's Twentieth-Century Prophecies," 1 audiocassette. "The Divine Mother and World Karma: Mother Mary Intercedes for Mankind," 1 videocassette. *Mother Mary's Scriptural Rosary for the New Age,* 8 audiocassettes. *A Child's Rosary to Mother Mary,* 4 albums, 3 audiocassettes each. *Sanctissima: Music for World Peace,* on CD and audiocassette.)

Mother of the Flame. World Mother. An office of *hierarchy* held successively by those unascended feminine devotees appointed by the *Great White Brotherhood* to nourish, or mother, the flame of Life in all mankind. In 1961 Clara Louise Kieninger was named the first Mother of the Flame of the *Keepers of the Flame Fraternity* by *Saint Germain.* On April 9, 1966, that mantle was transferred to the *Messenger* Elizabeth Clare Prophet. At that time Clara Louise Kieninger became the Regent Mother of the Flame. She made her *ascension* on October 25, 1970, in Berkeley, Calif., and continues to hold that office from the ascended level. *See also* Mother.

Mystery schools. Since the expulsion of *man* and woman from the Garden of Eden (the Mystery School of *Lord Maitreya,* symbolizing the pure consciousness of God: E-Don, meaning divine wisdom, or *Elohim* Dominion) because of the misuse of the *sacred fire* in the incorrect application of *free will,* the *Great White Brotherhood* has maintained mystery schools, or *retreats.* These have served as repositories for the knowledge of the *sacred fire* that is vouchsafed to *twin flames* when they have demonstrated the discipline necessary to keep the way of the *Tree of Life.* After the Fall (the willful descent into lower planes of consciousness), the Great White Brotherhood sponsored mystery schools on *Lemuria* and *Atlantis,* where the higher spiritual truths were taught to those who were willing to keep the disciplines of the adepts. The Sangha of the Buddha, the Essene community at Qumran, and Pythagoras' school at Crotona were among the more recent mystery schools. Other schools were located in the Himalayas, the Far East and Egypt, as well as in Europe and South America. One by one, these mystery schools were destroyed or disbanded.

Wherever these schools have been destroyed, the *Ascended Masters* who sponsored them withdrew their flames and sacred shrines to their retreats on the *etheric plane*. Here their disciples are trained between embodiments and in their finer bodies (during sleep or samadhi) in order that they might attain that Divine Self-knowledge which, until *Saint Germain* once again advanced it in this century, has not been available to mankind en masse in the physical plane for centuries. In 1984, Lord Maitreya reestablished his mystery school at the Royal Teton Ranch in southwestern Montana.

Occult. That which is hidden. The "occult" mysteries of the *Great White Brotherhood* held in their *retreats* for thousands of years are currently being brought forth by the *Ascended Masters* through their *Messengers*. There is evidence in scripture and other writings not included in the Bible—such as the Gnostic gospels, especially the Gospel of Thomas and the Secret Gospel of Mark—that the apostles kept a secret and advanced teaching given by *Jesus* to his inner circle. Did Paul allude to this when he said, "We speak the wisdom of God in a mystery, even the hidden wisdom, which God ordained before the world unto our glory"?

(I Cor. 2:7. See James M. Robinson, ed., *The Nag Hammadi Library in English* [New York: Harper and Row, 1977]; Elaine Pagels, *The Gnostic Gospels* [New York: Random House, 1979]; Morton Smith, *The Secret Gospel* [New York: Harper and Row, 1973]. For a list of lectures by Elizabeth Clare Prophet on the Lost Teachings of Jesus and Gnostic texts, send for a Summit University Press catalog.)

Omega. *See* Alpha and Omega.

Path. The strait gate and narrow way that leadeth unto Life. The path of initiation whereby the disciple who pursues the *Christ consciousness* overcomes step by step the limitations of selfhood in time and space and attains reunion with Reality through the ritual of the *ascension*.
(Matt. 7:14. See El Morya, *The Chela and the Path*.)

Pearls of Wisdom. Weekly letters of instruction dictated by the *Ascended Masters* to their *Messengers* Mark and Elizabeth Prophet for students of the sacred mysteries throughout the world. The *Pearls of Wisdom* have been published by *The Summit Lighthouse* continuously since 1958. They contain both fundamental and advanced teachings on *cosmic law* with a practical application of spiritual truths to personal and planetary problems.
(For introductory 12-week series, send $5.00. These priceless, very personal messages are also available in bound volumes.)

Physical body. The most dense of the four lower *bodies of man*, corresponding to the earth element and the fourth quadrant of *Matter*; the body that is the vehicle for the *soul's* sojourn on earth and the focus for the crystallization in form of the energies of the *etheric*, *mental*, and *emotional bodies*.

Portia. The *Ascended* Lady *Master*. Through thousands of years of service to God on the Seventh *Ray* of justice, freedom, mercy, forgiveness, alchemy, and sacred ritual, beloved Portia attained to the embodiment of the *God Flame* and *God consciousness* of divine Justice as divine Opportunity. Hence, she is called the Goddess of Justice or the Goddess of Opportunity. Representing the Sixth Ray of service and ministration on the *Karmic Board*, Portia keeps the flame of justice and opportunity on behalf of the evolutions of earth. Beloved Portia is the *twin flame* and divine consort of *Saint Germain*. Together they direct the next two-thousand-year cycle, the seventh dispensation known as the Aquarian age.

Power, Wisdom, and Love. The trinity of the *threefold flame*—Power representing the Father, Wisdom the Son, and Love the *Holy Spirit*. The balanced manifestation of these God-qualities in and as the flame within the heart is the prerequisite to personal Christhood. Attributes of the Hindu conception of the Trinity as (1) Brahma, the Creator, (2) Vishnu, the Preserver, and (3) Shiva, the Destroyer of *evil*/Deliverer of *souls*. According to the Eastern tradition, the Divine *Mother* is the universal force, Shakti, who releases the light/action, energy/consciousness of this threefold flame of *Spirit* into the *Matter cosmos* through the precious hearts of her children. *See also* Threefold flame.

Presence. *See* I AM Presence.

Psychic. (From Gk. *psyche* 'soul'.) One who has developed his *soul*, or solar, faculties for heightened awareness of the physical, *astral*, mental, and sometimes the *etheric* belts of earth and her evolutions. A psychic, or one who is psychic, has, in this or previous embodiments, developed faculties of sensitivity or extrasensory perception not generally accessed by mankind. This may include altered states above or below the normal threshold of awareness and the tapping of the computer of the subconscious or the superconscious mind. Although some use these faculties constructively with a respectable degree of accuracy, in many cases the information as well as the discrimination thereof is unreliable.

The term "psychic" has come to be used synonymously with the term "astral" in its negative context and pertains to the penetration and manipulation of energy at the level of the *astral plane*. According to the *Ascended Masters*, one who has involved his energies in the psychic, psychicism, or psychic phenomena is functioning on the lower astral plane. Thus, by the strong ties established with entities of the lower octaves, he postpones the day of his true spiritual development and oneness with the penetrability of the Godhead. Conversely, through oneness with God and direct apprehension of the higher octaves, he may derive spiritual benefit for his soul in the *etheric plane* (heaven world), journeying in his etheric sheath to the *retreats* of the Ascended Masters of the *Great White Brotherhood* and the cities and temples of *light* located in that plane. True spiritual God-mastery is not measured by clairvoyance or psychic phenomena but by the God-control of the *sacred fires* of the heart and adeptship on the path of Love.

Raphael. *See* Archangel.

Rays. Beams of *light* or other radiant energy. The light emanations of the Godhead which, when invoked in the name of God or in the name of the *Christ*, burst forth as a flame in the world of the individual. Rays may be projected by the *God consciousness* of *ascended* or *unascended beings* through the *chakras* and the third eye as a concentration of energy taking on numerous God-qualities, such as love, truth, wisdom, healing, etc. Through the misuse of God's energy, practitioners of black magic project rays having negative qualities, such as death rays, sleep rays, hypnotic rays, disease rays, psychotronic rays, the evil eye, etc. *See also* Seven rays. (See Mark L. Prophet and Elizabeth Clare Prophet, *Lords of the Seven Rays.*)

Readings. Probings of the records and *soul* memory of past, present, and future and of planes of consciousness beyond the physical. If readings are done by a *psychic* or through regression by hypnosis, they may be a probe of or an accessing of the *astral body* and astral belt of the earth, hence the *human consciousness* in all its personal and planetary astrological aspects. Since this takes into account experiences of the lower self without benefit of the soul's ongoing integration with the *Higher Self* and its point of perspective—looking down upon herself from the plane of causation to the plane of effect—such a reading is at best one dimensional. It may be a rerun that evokes deep emotions, but it will fail to re-create the rapture of the soul's self-transcendence in Higher Consciousness—the victorious denouement of her passage through the dark night.

Readings by an *Ascended Master* on behalf of a *chela* are given in order that lessons may be learned, goals set, and right choices made based on the totality of the life picture, involving the *karma* of the scene, the priorities of self-mastery, service with one's *twin flame,* and a vision of future freedom.

The realization of this freedom may depend on a commitment to sacrifice in the present—to willingly embrace obligations and debts in a one-pointed striving for the mark. When the Ascended Masters give a reading, they give it for the disciple who wants to know not for curiosity or self-importance but that he may pay the price for the soul's separation from the Law of the One, balance karma, get off the treadmill of reembodiment, serve the I AM Race and their endeavors on behalf of humanity, reunite with his twin flame, and ascend to God. The Ascended Masters present an accurate assessment of the soul's integration with the *Christ Self* in the four planes of *Matter*. They quicken the memory of the *divine plan* for this life and tell their students what is their progress on the *Path*. On the basis of the evaluation of the *Lords of Karma*, the Masters reveal what is most essential to the soul's salvation, drawing from the Book of Life and the hall of records maintained by the *Keeper of the Scrolls*.

Since a reading taken from the subconscious opens the records that have been sealed in wisdom's name by the Christ Self for this lifetime, the Ascended Masters recommend that instead of a reading the *violet flame* be invoked to "clear," i.e., transmute, these records without prior probe in order that the soul may daily ascend to God, transcending the past, living in the Eternal Now, strengthened by Higher Consciousness. The violet flame itself may reveal to soul and mind flashes of the past as these pass into the flame for transmutation. Transmutation by the violet flame frees us to be who we really are by our victories in God, unencumbered by the mésalliances of our yesterdays.

Real Image. (1) The true image of God after which *man* (male and female) was made in the beginning. The Real Image is the likeness of God, the *Christ*, or *Light*-emanation of God; it is the blueprint of the true identity of the *sons and daughters of God*. (2) The face of God mirrored by his *angels* and innocent *souls*.
(Gen. 1:26, 27.)

Real Self. The *Christ Self*; the *I AM Presence*; immortal *Spirit* that is the animating principle of all manifestation. *See also* Chart of Your Divine Self.

Recording angel. The *angel* assigned to the *soul* to record all her actions, words, deeds, feelings, thoughts—in short, her comings and goings in the planes of *Mater*. The recording angel records each day's events and turns them over to the *Keeper of the Scrolls*, who is the head of the band of angels known as the angels of record and of all recording angels assigned to the lifewaves evolving in time and space.

Retreats. Focuses of the *Great White Brotherhood* chiefly on the *etheric plane* where the *Ascended Masters* preside. Retreats anchor one or more flames of the Godhead as well as the momentum of the Masters' service and attainment for the balance of *light* in the *four lower bodies* of a planet and its evolutions. Retreats serve many functions for the councils of the *hierarchy* ministering to the lifewaves of earth. Some retreats are open to unascended mankind, whose *souls* may journey to these focuses in their *etheric body* between their incarnations on earth and in their finer bodies (during sleep or samadhi).

Many of the Masters' retreats, including their *mystery schools*, were anchored in the physical plane during earth's earlier *golden ages* and even after the Great Rebellion of the fallen *angels* and the Fall. In the face of desecration and destruction of their shrines, the Masters withdrew their centers and their flames to the etheric plane, hence the term "retreat." Following the *ascension* of the *Messenger* Mark L. Prophet on February 26, 1973, the children of God were given renewed opportunity from the *Lords of Karma* to balance their *karma* by attending classes at the retreats of the Seven *Chohans*, the *Maha Chohan*, and the *World Teachers*. On January 1, 1986, Gautama Buddha and the Lords of Karma granted a petition of the Lords of the Seven Rays to open universities of the Spirit in their etheric retreats for tens of thousands of students to systematically pursue the path of self-mastery on the seven rays. Traveling in their finer bodies during sleep, students spend fourteen days at each of the retreats of the Chohans and the Maha Chohan.

(See "The Opening of the Temple Doors," in *Pearls of Wisdom*, 1973, vol. 26, nos. 10–19. El Morya, *The Chela and the Path*, chap. 5. Mark L. Prophet and Elizabeth Clare Prophet, *Lords of the Seven Rays*, Book Two, pp. 302–9. Elizabeth Clare Prophet, "The Message of the Inner Buddha," in *Pearls of Wisdom*, 1989, vol. 32, pp. 419–28.)

Root race. *See* Manu.

Sacred fire. The Kundalini fire that lies as the coiled serpent in the base-of-the-spine *chakra* (the Mūlā-dhāra) and rises through spiritual purity and self-mastery to the crown chakra, quickening the spiritual centers on the way. God, *light*, life, energy, the I AM THAT I AM. "Our God is a consuming fire." The sacred fire is the precipitation of the Holy Ghost for the baptism of *souls*, for purification, for alchemy and transmutation, and

for the realization of the *ascension*, the sacred
ritual of the return to the One.
(Heb. 12:29.)

Sacred labor. That particular calling, livelihood, or
profession whereby one establishes his *soul's* worth
both to himself and to his fellowman. One perfects
his sacred labor by developing his God-given talents as well as the gifts and graces of the *Holy
Spirit* and laying these upon the altar of service to
humanity. The sacred labor is not only one's contribution to one's community but it is the means
whereby the soul can balance the *threefold flame* and
pass the tests of the *seven rays*. It is an indispensable
component of the path to reunion *with* God through
the giving of oneself in practical living *for* God.

Saint Germain. The *Ascended Master. Chohan* (Lord)
of the Seventh *Ray* of Freedom, Hierarch of the
Aquarian Age, sponsor of the United States of
America; initiator of *souls* in the science and ritual
of alchemy and transmutation through the *violet
flame* by the power of the *spoken Word*, meditation,
and visualization. His *retreat* in North America is
the *Cave of Symbols* at Table Mountain, Wyoming.
He also uses the Royal Teton Retreat at the Grand
Teton, Jackson Hole, Wyoming; the retreat of his
Guru, the *Great Divine Director*, the Cave of
Light in India; and the Rakoczy Mansion, his
focus in Transylvania. The keynotes of the
Rakoczy Mansion are "Tales from the Vienna
Woods" and "Rakoczy March." Following are his
soul's incarnations as revealed in various dispensa-
tions/activities:
Ruler of a *golden-age* civilization in the area of the
Sahara Desert 50,000 years ago.
High priest on *Atlantis* 13,000 years ago. Served in

the Order of Lord *Zadkiel* in the Temple of Purification, located where the island of Cuba now is.

The Prophet Samuel, eleventh century B.C., Israel. Great religious leader who figured as prophet, priest, and last of the Hebrew judges.

Saint Joseph, first century A.D., Nazareth. Protector of *Jesus* and *Mary.*

Saint Alban, late third or early fourth century, town of Verulamium, renamed St. Albans, Hertfordshire, England. First British martyr. Sheltered a fugitive priest, became a devout convert, and was put to death for disguising himself as the priest so he could die in his place.

Teacher of Proclus. The last major Greek Neoplatonic philosopher, Proclus (c. 410–485, Athens) headed the Platonic Academy and wrote extensively on philosophy, astronomy, mathematics, and grammar.

Merlin, c. fifth or sixth century, Britain. Magician, seer, and counsellor at King Arthur's court who inspired the founding of the Order of the Knights of the Round Table.

Roger Bacon, c. 1220–1292, England. Philosopher, educational reformer, and experimental scientist; forerunner of modern science renowned for his exhaustive investigations into alchemy, optics, mathematics, and languages.

Christopher Columbus, 1451–1506, probably born Genoa, Italy, settled in Portugal. Discovered America in 1492 during first of four voyages to the New World sponsored by King Ferdinand and Queen Isabella of Spain.

Francis Bacon, 1561–1626, England. Philosopher, statesman, essayist and literary master, author of the Shakespearean plays, father of inductive science and herald of the scientific revolution. Took the initiation of the ascension May 1, 1684, then reappeared as:

Le Comte de Saint Germain, the "Wonderman of Europe," eighteenth and nineteenth centuries. According to Prince Karl of Hesse, the Count revealed himself as the son of Prince Ferenc Rakoczy II of Transylvania; others have speculated he was a Portuguese Jew or son of the king of Portugal. Outstanding alchemist, scholar, linguist, musician, artist and diplomat; worked behind the scenes to bring about a United States of Europe and to forestall the bloodshed of violent revolution. His powers included bilocation, appearing at court and then dissolving his form at will, removing flaws from diamonds and other precious stones, and precipitating an elixir that prevented aging. He was also ambidextrous and could compose simultaneously a letter with one hand and poetry with the other, or two identical pieces of writing with each hand. He visited Marie Antoinette and her intimate friend, Madame d'Adhémar, who later wrote the story of his adeptship and warning of the coming debacle and death of the king and queen.
(See Madame d'Adhémar, *Souvenirs de Marie Antoinette*, excerpted in Isabel Cooper-Oakley, *The Count of Saint-Germain* [Blauvelt, N.Y.: Rudolph Steiner Publications, 1970]. "Saint Germain on Freedom," in *Pearls of Wisdom*, 1977, vol. 20, nos. 31–52; 1978, vol. 21. nos, 1–7; *Saint Germain On Alchemy*; *Saint Germain On Prophecy*. Mark L. Prophet and Elizabeth Clare Prophet, *Lords of the Seven Rays*, Book One, chap. 7; Book Two, chap. 7. *Saint Germain: Chohan of the Seventh Ray of Freedom*, 2-audiocassette album. Lectures by Elizabeth Clare Prophet: *The Golden Age Prince: A Lecture on Francis Bacon*, 2-audiocassette album. "Saint Germain: 'The Man Who Never Dies and Who Knows Everything,'" 1-hour TV show on video. *Saint Germain On Alchemy*, 2-videocassette album; 3 audiocassettes. "Christopher Columbus: The Man and the Myth," three 1-hr. TV shows on video; 2 audiocassettes.)

Sanat Kumara. Great Guru of the seed of *Christ* throughout *cosmos*; Hierarch of Venus; the Ancient of Days spoken of in Daniel 7:9, 13, 22. Sanat Kumara (from the Skt., meaning "always a youth") is one of the Seven Holy Kumaras. Long ago he came to Earth in her darkest hour when all light had gone out in her evolutions, for there was not a single individual on the planet who gave adoration to the God Presence. Sanat Kumara and the band of 144,000 souls of Light who accompanied him volunteered to keep the flame of Life on behalf of Earth's people. This they vowed to do until the children of God would respond to the love of God and turn once again to serve their Mighty I AM Presence. Sanat Kumara's *retreat, Shamballa,* was established on an island in the Gobi Sea, now the Gobi Desert. The first to respond to his flame was Gautama *Buddha,* followed by *Lord Maitreya* and *Jesus.*

Sanat Kumara is revered in Hinduism as one of the four or seven sons of Brahma. They are portrayed as youths who have remained ever pure. He is said to be one of the oldest progenitors of mankind. Sanat Kumara has revealed his fourfold identity as champion of the Cosmic Christ in the four quadrants of *Matter* and in his own *Lightbearers* as (1) Kārttikeya, the god of war and commander-in-chief of the army of gods. Legends say Kārttikeya was born specifically to slay the demon Tāraka, who symbolizes the lower mind, or ignorance. (2) Kumāra, "the holy youth." (3) Skanda, the son of Shiva. (4) Guha, "cave"; so called because he lives in the cave of the heart.

Sanat Kumara held the position of *Lord of the World* until his disciple Gautama Buddha reached sufficient attainment to hold that office. On January 1, 1956, Gautama Buddha was crowned Lord of the World and Sanat Kumara, as Regent Lord of the World, returned to Venus and to his twin flame, the Lady Master Venus. There, in another dimension of the 'physical/*etheric*' octave—together with the other Holy Kumaras, Mighty *Victory* and his legions, many *Ascended Masters* and the Lightbearers of Venus—he continues his service with the *Great White Brotherhood* on behalf of planet Earth. On May 25, 1975, Lady Master Venus announced that she had come to "tarry for a time on Terra" to dedicate anew the fires of the *Mother* as Sanat Kumara keeps the flame on Venus. Sanat Kumara frequently dictates through the *Messenger* and envelops the Earth in the swaddling garment of his auric field. *See also* Lord of the World.

(See *Sanat Kumara On the Path of the Ruby Ray: The Opening of the Seventh Seal, Pearls of Wisdom*, 1979, vol. 22, Book I.)

Satan. (From Gk., Heb. 'adversary'.) A lieutenant of the fallen Archangel *Lucifer* and ranking member of his false *hierarchy*, mistakenly thought to be the archdeceiver himself. However, before his fall Satan had never attained to the rank of *Archangel*. Thus in the hierarchy of fallen *angels*, neither he nor any other ever exceeded Lucifer. The "Devil" was Lucifer and the surviving fallen angels that were under him are all called devils, Lucifer's seed still outranking the seed of the lesser powers and principalities of Darkness. Even so, in their personification of *Evil*, or the Energy *Veil*, those who deified and were the embodiment of Absolute Evil were referred to by the generic term "devil." Both Lucifer and Satan and their various lieutenants have been referred to in scripture as the adversary, the accuser of the brethren, the tempter, the *Antichrist*, the personification of the *carnal mind* of mankind, i.e., the planetary *dweller-on-the-threshold*, Serpent, the beast, the dragon, etc. On January 27, 1982, Satan was remanded to the Court of the Sacred Fire, resulting in his final judgment and second death.

(See Jesus Christ, "The Final Judgment of Satan," in *Pearls of Wisdom*, 1982, vol. 25, Book I, no. 16.)

Science of the spoken Word. *See* Spoken Word.

Seraphim. Also known as the seraphic hosts. The order of *angels* dedicated to the focusing of the flame of purity and the consciousness of purity before the throne of God, in the electronic fire rings of the Great *Central Sun*, and throughout the *cosmos* in the planes of *Spirit* and *Matter*. Justinius is the Captain of Seraphic Bands. Under his direction they serve at the altar of God in the Great Central Sun and at the *ascension* flame and the Ascension Temple at Luxor. *Serapis Bey*, the Hierarch of the Ascension Temple and *Chohan* of the Fourth *Ray*, was originally of the order of the seraphim. Isaiah saw "seraphims" (Heb. 'burners', 'burning ones') standing above the LORD's throne, each one having six wings: "With twain he covered his face (before the LORD's glory), and with twain he covered his feet (in reverence before the holiness of the LORD), and with twain he did fly (accelerate his vibration to the planes of the Great Central Sun, decelerate to the planes of physicality and form)." The seraphim are initiators of the LORD's servants on earth, purging and purifying the ones chosen to be his ministering servants—priests, prophets, *messengers*, etc. Isaiah himself received the seraphic initiation, which he vividly describes: "Then flew one of the seraphims unto me, having a live coal in his hand, which he had taken with the tongs from off the altar: and he laid it upon my mouth, and said, Lo, this hath touched thy lips; and thine iniquity is taken away, and thy *sin* purged."

Serapis Bey describes his vision of the seraphim in his *Dossier on the Ascension:* "The seraphim came and they were as flaming streaks of fire passing through the atmosphere, and I knew that they possessed the quality of cosmic penetrability. Like cosmic rays they could pass through the flesh form of man, through his thoughts and feelings. When penetration occurred and the seraphim flew through human consciousness, what residue was left behind or what absorption was accomplished?

"I saw clearly that absorption was accomplished and that residue was left behind—absorption by reason of instantaneous transmutation of all substance that came nigh unto their trajectory. I noted also that the residue left behind was of intense white-fire devotion, charged with a yearning for purity. I perceived that this quality lingered within the consciousness of many; and yet, unless it was fed or accepted by them, its decay rate in their consciousness would be of relatively short term, for a disassociation of these ideas would cause the lingering sparks of the seraphim to pursue the parent body and leave their temporarily unwelcome home. Affinitizing with the consciousness of the seraphim is tantamount to retaining the benefits of the seraphic hosts.

"I know of no power more valiantly capable of assisting anyone into his own ascension in the light than the transmutative efforts toward Cosmic

Christ purity that are emitted by the seraphic hosts. In our *retreat* at Luxor, the meditations upon the seraphim are a very important part of our spiritual instruction. *Jesus* himself spent a great deal of time in communion with the seraphic hosts. This developed in him the superior power whereby he could cast out demons and take dominion over the outer world of form." The *mantra* of the seraphim that they chant without ceasing before the throne of the LORD is: "Holy, holy, holy is the LORD of hosts: the whole earth is full of his glory."
(Isa. 6:2, 3, 6, 7. See Serapis Bey, *Dossier on the Ascension*, pp. 115–40.)

Serapis Bey. The *Ascended Master.* Lord (*Chohan*) of the Fourth *Ray*; Hierarch of the Ascension Temple at Luxor, Egypt; keeper of the *ascension* flame. Known as the great disciplinarian, Serapis reviews and trains candidates for the ascension. In the nineteenth century, he worked closely with *El Morya*, *Kuthumi*, Djwal Kul, and other Masters to found the Theosophical Society. The keynote of Serapis Bey is "Celeste Aïda" by Verdi and the keynote of his retreat is "Liebestraum" by Liszt. Serapis Bey's embodiments include:
High priest on *Atlantis* more than 11,500 years ago, served in the Ascension Temple.
Amenhotep III, c. 1417–1379 B.C., Egyptian pharaoh, called "the Magnificent." Brought Egypt to its height of diplomatic prestige, prosperity, and peace. His extensive building of monuments, palaces, and temples included construction of the temple of Luxor.
Leonidas, c. 480 B.C., king of Sparta. With only 300 soldiers he resisted the advance of Xerxes' vast Persian army in a herculean effort at Thermopylae.

Though finally defeated, their fight to the last man is celebrated in literature as the epitome of heroism in the face of overwhelming odds. *See also* Chohan. (See Serapis Bey, *Dossier on the Ascension: The Story of the Soul's Acceleration into Higher Consciousness on the Path of Initiation.* Mark L. Prophet and Elizabeth Clare Prophet, *Lords of the Seven Rays*, Book One, chap. 4; Book Two, chap. 4. Elizabeth Clare Prophet, *A Retreat on the Ascension—an Experience with God*, 8-audiocassette album.)

Seven rays. The *light* emanations of the Godhead, e.g., the seven rays of the white light, which emerge through the prism of the *Christ consciousness*. The seven rays are (1) blue, (2) yellow, (3) pink, (4) white, (5) green, (6) purple and gold, and (7) violet. There are also five "secret *rays*," which originate in the white fire core of being, and numerous cosmic rays personally qualified by the heavenly hosts that radiate through the sacred hearts of the Father's emissaries to lesser evolved *lifestreams*.

Seventh root race. An evolution of *souls* sponsored by the *Great Divine Director* and destined to embody on the continent of South America under the seventh dispensation, the Aquarian age, and the Seventh *Ray. See also* Root race.

Shamballa. Shamballa, the *etheric* "City of White," ancient *retreat* of *Sanat Kumara*, was originally a physical replica of the Venusian City of the Kumaras. Shamballa was built on an island in the brilliant blue Gobi Sea (now the Gobi Desert) by volunteers who preceded Sanat Kumara to Terra. From the mainland, Shamballa was approached by a beautiful marble bridge. The main temple there, where Sanat Kumara established the focus of the *threefold flame* thousands of years ago, was marked by a golden dome and was surrounded by terraces, flame-fountains, and seven temples—one for each of the *seven rays*. Each year the people would come from many miles to witness the visible, physical *sacred fire* and to take home a piece of wood consecrated by Sanat Kumara to light their fires through the coming year. Thus began the tradition of the Yule log, commemorating the return to the fire of Christhood. The physical retreat of Shamballa was withdrawn to the etheric octave in subsequent dark ages.

On December 31, 1976, Gautama *Buddha*, Hierarch of Shamballa and successor of Sanat Kumara, announced that America is the place where "we will transfer Shamballa." He said, "Here we will transfer that city of *light* one day. It will be the implementation now of a secondary forcefield, the Omega aspect of Shamballa, as the Alpha aspect remains positioned where it is . . . in the Gobi Sea of light over the Gobi Desert." Lord Gautama recently established his **Western Shamballa** in the etheric octave over the Inner Retreat near Yellowstone National Park. On April 18, 1981, he announced: "From Shamballa I arc a light. I would establish the ground of the Ancient of Days . . . . In this hour I contemplate— note it well—the arcing of the flame of Shamballa to the Inner Retreat as the Western abode of the Buddhas and the *Bodhisattvas* and the Bodhisattvas-to-Be who are devotees of the *Mother* light."
(See Elizabeth Clare Prophet, "The Message of the Inner Buddha," in *Pearls of Wisdom*, 1989, vol. 32, pp. 419–23.)

Shiva. *See* Brahma/Vishnu/Shiva.

Sin. Broadly, any departure from *cosmic law* that is the result of the exercise of *free will*.

Sons and daughters of God. (1) Those who come forth as the fruit of the divine union of the spirals of

Alpha and Omega; those who have the *Christ* with them as the Immanuel. The creation of the Father-*Mother* God *(Elohim)* made in the image and likeness of the Divine Us, identified by the *threefold flame* of Life anchored within the heart. (2) On the *Path,* the term "sons and daughters of God" denotes a level of initiation and a rank in *hierarchy* that is above those who are called the children of God—children in the sense that they have not passed the initiations of the *sacred fire* that would warrant their being called joint-heirs with Christ, hence sons and daughters of God.

Soul. God is a *Spirit* and the soul is the living potential of God. The soul's demand for *free will* and her separation from God resulted in the descent of this potential into the lowly estate of the flesh. Sown in dishonor, the soul is destined to be raised in honor to the fullness of that God-estate which is the one Spirit of all Life. The soul can be lost; Spirit can never die.

The soul remains a fallen potential that must be imbued with the reality of Spirit, purified through prayer and supplication, and returned to the glory from which it descended and to the unity of the Whole. This rejoining of soul to Spirit is the alchemical marriage that determines the destiny of the self and makes it one with immortal Truth. When this ritual is fulfilled, the highest Self is enthroned as the Lord of Life and the potential of God, realized in man, is found to be the All-in-all. (See Mark L. Prophet and Elizabeth Clare Prophet, *Climb the Highest Mountain,* 2d ed., pp. 8–13.)

Spirit. The masculine polarity of the Godhead; the co-ordinate of *Matter;* God as Father, who of necessity

includes within the polarity of himself God as
Mother and hence is known as the Father-Mother
God. The plane of the *I AM Presence,* of perfection;
the dwelling place of the *Ascended Masters*
in the kingdom of God. (When lowercased, as in
"spirits," the term is synonymous with discarnates,
or *astral* entities; "spirit," singular and lowercased,
is used interchangeably with soul.)

Spoken Word. The Word of the LORD God released in
the original fiats of creation. The release of the
energies of the *Word,* or the Logos, through the
throat *chakra* by the Sons of God in confirmation of
that lost Word. It is written, "By thy words thou shalt
be justified, and by thy words thou shalt be con-
demned." When man and woman reconsecrate the
throat chakra in the affirmation of the Word of God,
they become the instruments of God's own commandments that fulfill the law of their re-creation
after the image of the Son.

Invocations offered by priests and priestesses of the
sacred fire on *Lemuria* in this power of the spoken
Word were originally given according to the science
of the Logos. The perversion of this science in the
practice of black magic occurred later, in the last
days of Lemuria, bringing about the destruction of
the temples of the *Cosmic Virgin* and the cataclysm
that sank the continent. The Easter Island images
are the remains, marking the site of the wars of the
gods that shook the earth in those terrible days. By
contrast, this science of the spoken Word was used
in its pure form by the Israelites to fell the walls of
Jericho. Today disciples use the power of the Word
in *decrees,* affirmations, prayers, and *mantras* to
draw the essence of the sacred fire from the *I AM*

Presence, the *Christ Self,* and *Cosmic Beings* to channel God's *light* into matrices of transmutation and transformation for constructive change in the planes of *Matter.*

The science of the spoken Word (together with that of the *immaculate concept*) is the essential and key ingredient in all alchemy. Without the Word spoken, there is no alchemy, no creation, no change or interchange in any part of Life. It is the alchemist's white stone which, when successfully applied by the secrets of the heart flame, reveals the "new name written, which no man knoweth saving he that receiveth it." Blessed is he that overcometh the *carnal mind's* opposition to the exercise—the practice that makes perfect—of the science of the spoken Word in the offering of daily dynamic decrees unto the LORD, for unto him shall the *Holy Spirit* "give to eat of the hidden manna."

The Master of the Aquarian age, *Saint Germain,* teaches his disciples to invoke by the power of the spoken Word the *violet flame* for forgiveness of *sins* and for the baptism of the sacred fire in preparation for transition into the Higher Consciousness of God. *See also* Decree, Mantra.

(Matt. 12:37; Rev. 2:17. See Mark L. Prophet and Elizabeth Clare Prophet, *The Science of the Spoken Word.* Jesus and Kuthumi, *Prayer and Meditation. Prayers, Meditations, and Dynamic Decrees for the Coming Revolution in Higher Consciousness,* Sections I and II. Mark L. Prophet and Elizabeth Clare Prophet, *The Science of the Spoken Word: Why and How to Decree Effectively,* 4-audiocassette album. Elizabeth Clare Prophet, *"I'm Stumping for the Coming Revolution in Higher Consciousness!"* 3-audiocassette album; *The Liberating Power of the Word,* album 1, 6 audiocassettes. For audiocassettes of decrees, songs, mantras and rosaries, including decrees to Archangel Michael, El Morya, and Lord Lanto and violet flame decrees, see pp. 465–66.)

The Summit Lighthouse. An outer organization of the *Great White Brotherhood* founded by Mark L. Prophet in 1958 in Washington, D.C., under the direction of the *Ascended Master El Morya*, Chief of the *Darjeeling Council*, for the purpose of publishing and disseminating the Teachings of the Ascended Masters.

Synthetic image. That aspect of man or woman which is the counterfeit of true selfhood. The synthetic image is diametrically opposed to the *Real Image* of the *Christ Self*, which is the true identity of the *sons and daughters of God*.
(See Mark L. Prophet and Elizabeth Clare Prophet, *Climb the Highest Mountain*, chap. 1.)

Threefold flame. The flame of the *Christ* that is the spark of Life anchored in the secret chamber of the heart of the *sons and daughters of God* and the children of God. The sacred trinity of *Power, Wisdom, and Love* that is the manifestation of the *sacred fire. See also* Chart of Your Divine Self.
(See "A Trilogy on the Threefold Flame of Life," in *Saint Germain On Alchemy*, pp. 265–352.)

Transfiguration. An initiation on the path of the *ascension* that takes place when the initiate has attained a certain balance and expansion of the *threefold flame.*
(Matt. 17:1–8. See Jesus and Kuthumi, *Corona Class Lessons*, pp. 113–43.)

Tree of Life. The Tree of Life is symbolical of the *I AM Presence* and *Causal Body* of each individual and of the connection, depicted in the *Chart of Your Divine Self*, of *Light's* children with their immortal Source. It is referred to in Genesis and Revelation: "Out of the ground made the LORD God to grow every tree that is pleasant to the sight and good for food; the Tree of Life also in the midst of the garden, and the tree of knowledge of good and *evil*." "In the midst of the street of it and on either side of the river was there the Tree of Life, which bare twelve manner of fruits and yielded her fruit every month: and the leaves of the tree were for the healing of the nations." The twelve manner of fruits thereof are the twelve qualities of the *God consciousness* that man and woman are intended to realize as they follow the initiations on the path of the *ascension*. These are God-power, God-love, and God-mastery, God-control, God-obedience, and God-wisdom, God-harmony, God-gratitude, and God-justice, God-reality, God-vision, and God-victory.

(Gen. 2:9; Rev. 22:2. See Elizabeth Clare Prophet, "Keys from Judaism: The Kabbalah and the Temple of Man," Part 2: "The Creation of the Tree of Life," 1-hr. TV show on video.)

Tube of light. The white *light* that descends from the heart of the *I AM Presence* in answer to the call of man as a shield of protection for his *four lower bodies* and his *soul* evolution. *See also* Chart of Your Divine Self.

Twin flame. The *spirit's* masculine or feminine counterpart conceived out of the same white fire body, the fiery ovoid of the *I AM Presence*.

(See "Twin Flames in Love," in *Pearls of Wisdom*, 1978, vol. 21, nos. 34–47; 8-audiocassette album. *The Ascended Masters On Soul Mates and Twin Flames*, *Pearls of Wisdom*, 1985, vol. 28, Books I and II. *The Coming Revolution: The Magazine for Higher Consciousness*, Summer 1986. Elizabeth Clare Prophet, *Twin Flames in Love II*, 3-audiocassette album; condensed in 1-audiocassette album *Twin Flames and Soul Mates: A New Look at Love, Karma and Relationships*.)

Unascended being. One who has not passed through the ritual of the *ascension*: (1) One abiding in time and space who has not yet overcome the limitations of the planes of *Mater* (as opposed to an *ascended being,* who has ascended into the Presence of God). (2) One who has overcome all limitations of Matter yet chooses to remain in time and space to focus the consciousness of God for lesser evolutions.

The Universal. God, the One, the Divine Whole; energy that pervades the *cosmos* in the planes of *Spirit* and *Matter* as the universal presence of the *Holy Spirit.*

Uriel. *See* Archangel.

Victory. The *Ascended Master.* A Venusian Master whose devotion to the flame of victory for more than a hundred thousand years has given him the authority over that flame through vast reaches of the *cosmos.* Mighty Victory was one of the *Cosmic Beings* who responded to *Saint Germain's* call for cosmic assistance to the earth in the 1930s. He has twelve cosmic Masters serving with him in addition to legions of *angels* and *ascended beings* who focus the consciousness of God's victory and the victorious sense to every *soul* evolving in the planes of *Matter.*

Violet flame. Seventh *Ray* aspect of the *Holy Spirit.* The *sacred fire* that transmutes the cause, effect, record, and memory of *sin,* or negative *karma.* Also called the flame of transmutation, of freedom, and of forgiveness. *See also* Chart of Your Divine Self, Decrees.

(See Mark L. Prophet and Elizabeth Clare Prophet, *Climb the Highest Mountain,* 2d ed., pp. 359–62; *The Lost Teachings of Jesus II,* softbound, chap. 13; or pocketbook, Book Four, chap. 13. *The Science of the Spoken Word.* Elizabeth Clare Prophet, *The Astrology of the Four Horsemen,* chaps. 39, 40; "Saint

Germain and Violet Flame Decrees," 1 videocassette; "On the Violet Flame and the Chakras," 1 videocassette. *Save the World with Violet Flame! by Saint Germain 1–4*, audiocassettes of decrees and songs. *Violet Flame for Elemental Life—Fire, Air, Water and Earth 1* and *2*, audiocassettes of decrees and songs.)

Vishnu. *See* Brahma/Vishnu/Shiva.

Western Shamballa. *See* Shamballa.

Word. The Word is the Logos; it is the power of God and the realization of that power incarnate in and as the *Christ*. The energies of the Word are released by devotees of the Logos in the ritual of the science of the *spoken Word*. It is through the Word that the Father-*Mother* God communicates with mankind. The Christ is the personification of the Word. *See also* Christ, Decree.

World Teacher. Office in *hierarchy* held by those *ascended beings* whose attainment qualifies them to represent the universal and personal *Christ* to unascended mankind. The office of World Teacher, formerly held by *Maitreya*, was passed to *Jesus* and his disciple Saint Francis (*Kuthumi*) on January 1, 1956, when the mantle of *Lord of the World* was transferred from *Sanat Kumara* to Gautama *Buddha* and the office of Cosmic Christ and Planetary Buddha (formerly held by Gautama) was simultaneously filled by Lord Maitreya. Serving under Lord Maitreya, Jesus and Kuthumi are responsible for setting forth the Teachings in this two-thousand-year cycle leading to individual self-mastery and the *Christ consciousness*. They sponsor all *souls* seeking union with God, tutoring them in the fundamental laws governing the cause/effect sequences of their own *karma* and teaching them how to come to grips with the day-to-day challenges of their individual dharma, one's duty to fulfill the Christ potential through the sacred labor.

The World Teachers have sponsored the education of souls in the Christ *light* at every level, from preschool through primary and secondary education to college and university levels. In every nation on earth, they have inspired teachers, philosophers, scientists, artists, professional and nonprofessional people with the wisdom of the ages as it applies to each particular culture, even as the many cultures of the world serve to bring forth the many facets of the Christ consciousness.

The term "world teacher," lowercased, refers to the embodied disciple who dedicates himself to the lifetime calling of planetary enlightenment under the Universal Christ. This appellation is descriptive of the disciple's chosen *sacred labor* and dedication to it. It is not an indication of his attainment or that he has necessarily qualified himself to share the office or mantle of Jesus and Kuthumi.

Zadkiel, Archangel. *Archangel* of the Seventh *Ray;* focuses the consciousness of God-freedom on behalf of *souls* evolving in the *Spirit-Matter* planes. Together with his *twin flame,* the *Archeia* Holy Amethyst, Zadkiel teaches the children of the *Light* the mastery of the freedom flame and the Seventh Ray in the governments and economies of the nations, in the science of alchemy, and in the ritual of invocation. Zadkiel prepares them for the priesthood in the Order of Melchizedek. *Retreat:* Temple of Purification on the *etheric plane* over Cuba and the Caribbean islands.

**Publications and Tapes Listed in the Glossary
Available from Summit University Press**

Books and Magazines:

Ashram Notes, $19.95, #2675.

Ashram Rituals booklet, $4.95, #2687.

*The Astrology of the Four Horsemen: How You Can Heal
Yourself and Planet Earth,* $6.99, #2698.

The Chela and the Path, $7.95, #420.

Climb the Highest Mountain: The Path of the Higher Self,
2d ed., softbound $16.95, #642.

*The Coming Revolution: The Magazine for Higher Conscious-
ness,* Summer 1986, $3.00, #2001.

*Corona Class Lessons . . . for those who would teach men the
Way,* $12.95, #1654.

Dossier on the Ascension, $7.95, #1038.

*Forbidden Mysteries of Enoch: Fallen Angels and the Origins
of Evil,* $14.95, #1592.

*The Great White Brotherhood in the Culture, History and
Religion of America,* $10.95, #422.

The Human Aura, $5.99, #1483.

Intermediate Studies of the Human Aura, $9.95, #266.

Lords of the Seven Rays, $5.95, #2079.

The Lost Teachings of Jesus I, hardbound $19.95, #2075;
softbound $14.95, #2040; pocketbooks (Books 1 and 2
contain Volume I), $5.99 ea., #2157, #2158.

The Lost Teachings of Jesus II, hardbound $21.95, #2077;
softbound $16.95, #2076; pocketbooks (Books 2, 3 and 4
contain Volume II), $5.99 ea., #2158, #2159, #2160.

The Lost Years of Jesus, hardbound $19.95, #2080; softbound
$14.95, #1593; pocketbook $6.99, #2156.

*My Soul Doth Magnify the Lord! Mother Mary's New Age
Teachings and Rosary with a Challenge to Christendom,*
$7.95, #1001.

Prayer and Meditation, $12.95, #569.

*Prayers, Meditations and Dynamic Decrees for the Coming
Revolution in Higher Consciousness,* Sections I and II,
$2.95 ea., #105, #1657.

The Sacred Adventure, $7.95, #1479.
Saint Germain On Alchemy: Formulas for Self-Transformation, $6.99, #1835.
The Science of the Spoken Word, $9.95, #104.
Studies of the Human Aura, $8.95, #116.
Understanding Yourself, $4.99, #1484.
Pearls of Wisdom hardbound volumes:
　　1981 (vol. 24), Books I and II, $19.95 ea., #1481, #1482.
　　1982 (vol. 25), Books I and II, $19.95 ea., #1655, #1656.
　　1984 (vol. 27), Books I and II, $24.95 ea., #2646, #2647.
　　1985 (vol. 28), Books I and II, $19.95 ea., #2316, #2317.
　　1986 (vol. 29), Books I and II, $19.95 ea., #2163, #2164.
　　1987 (vol. 30), $24.95, #2605.
　　1988 (vol. 31), Books I and II, $24.95 ea., #2670, #2671.

Audiotapes and CDs of Decrees, Songs, Mantras, and Rosaries:

Archangel Michael's Rosary for Armageddon with booklet, $6.95, beginning pace, A85108.
A Child's Rosary to Mother Mary, 15-minute scriptural rosaries for all ages, 4 audiotape albums, 3 tapes ea., $15.95 ea. album, beginning pace. Album 1, A7864. Album 2, A7905. Album 3, A7934. Album 4, A8045.
Decrees and Songs by the Messenger Mark L. Prophet, 2 audiotapes, $14.95, beginning pace, A8202.
Decrees and Songs to Archangel Michael, $6.95, intermediate pace, B89092.
Devotions to Lord Krishna: The Maha Mantra and Bhajans, $8.95, A92070.
El Morya, Lord of the First Ray: Dynamic Decrees with Prayers and Ballads for Chelas of the Will of God 1–4, $6.95 ea. Tape 1, intermediate pace, B88125. Tape 2, intermediate pace, B88126. Tape 3, advanced pace, B88127. Tape 4, advanced pace, B91102.
Hail Light Victorious! A Salute to Archangel Michael, Captain of the LORD's Host, CD, $11.95, D92045; audiotape, $8.95, A92045.
Hail to the Chief! A Salute to El Morya, CD, $11.95, D92044; audiotape, $8.95, A92044.
Kuan Yin's Crystal Rosary: Devotions to the Divine Mother

East and West, 3 audiotapes, $15.95, beginning pace, A88084.

Lanto, Lord of the Second Ray: Dynamic Decrees with Prayers and New Age Songs for Chelas of the Wisdom of God, $6.95, intermediate pace, B89052.

Mantras of the Ascended Masters for the Initiation of the Chakras, 5 audiotapes, $37.50, intermediate pace, B85135–39.

Mother Mary's Scriptural Rosary for the New Age, 8 rosaries, $6.95 ea. audiotape, beginning pace: The Teaching Mysteries, Sunday Morning, the Second Ray, A93024. The Masterful Mysteries, Sunday Evening, the Eighth Ray, A92049. The Love Mysteries, Monday, the Third Ray, A93025. The Joyful Mysteries, Tuesday, the First Ray, A93023. The Healing Mysteries, Wednesday, the Fifth Ray, A92047. The Initiatic Mysteries, Thursday, the Sixth Ray, A92048. The Glorious Mysteries, Friday, the Fourth Ray, A92046. The Miracle Mysteries, Saturday, the Seventh Ray, A93026.

Sanctissima: Music for World Peace, CD, $14.95, D92020; audiotape, $8.95, A92020.

Save the World with Violet Flame! by Saint Germain 1–4, $6.95 ea. Tape 1, beginning pace, B88019. Tape 2, advanced pace, B88034. Tape 3, intermediate pace, B88083. Tape 4, advanced pace, B88117.

Violet Flame for Elemental Life 1 and *2*, $6.95 ea. Tape 1, intermediate pace, B91114. Tape 2, intermediate pace, B91115.

Other Audio- and Videotapes:

The ABC's of Your Psychology on the Cosmic Clock: Charting the Cycles of Karma and Initiation, 8 audiotapes, $59.95, A85056.

The Age of Maitreya, 1 video, $14.95, HP90113; 2 audiotapes, $14.95, A90038.

Ashram Rituals, 2 audiotapes with booklet, $18.90, A90028.

The Buddha and the Mother, 6 audiotapes, $44.95, A7532.

The Buddhas in Winter, 16 audiotapes, $99.95, A83002.

The Buddhic Essence, 2 videos, $14.95; 4 audiotapes, $29.95, A93007.

The Chalice of Elohim, 5 audiotapes, $36.95, A87082.

Christopher Columbus: The Man and the Myth, 3 videos, $27.50, GL92070; 2 audiotapes, $15.00, A92081.

The Class of the Archangels, 8 audiotapes, $59.95, A8100.

The Control of the Human Aura through the Science of the Spoken Word, 2 audiotapes, $14.95, A8075.

Darshan with the Cosmic Christ, 2 audiotapes, $14.95, A88092.

The Divine Mother and World Karma: Mother Mary Intercedes for Mankind, 1 video, $14.95, V8614-1.

The Efficacy of Decrees, 1 audiotape, $7.50, B89067.

El Morya: Chohan of the First Ray, 2 audiotapes, $14.95, A7626.

The Golden Age of Jesus Christ on Atlantis, 2 videos, $22.50, GP91107; 2 audiotapes, $14.95, A91074.

The Golden Age Prince: A Lecture on Francis Bacon, 2 audiotapes, $14.95, A83176.

The Healing Power of Angels, 2 video albums, 2 tapes ea.: album 1, $33.95, V8609-0; album 2, $39.95, V8616-0; 2 audiotape albums, 12 tapes ea., $79.95 ea. album, A86055, A86040.

"I'm Stumping for the Coming Revolution in Higher Consciousness!" 3 audiotapes, $21.95, A7917.

Insatiable Desire: The Enemy Within and *The Eightfold Path of Self-Mastery*, 2 videos, $21.90, HL92031–32; 2 audiotapes, $14.95, A92034.

Jesus Christ, Avatar of the Ages, 1 video, $14.95, HP91060; 2 audiotapes, $14.95, A91063.

Karma, Reincarnation and Christianity, 2 videos, $29.95, GP92001; 3 audiotapes, $21.95, A92006.

Keys from Judaism: The Kabbalah and the Temple of Man: Part 1: *The Big Bang and Jewish Mysticism*, 1 video, HL92056; Part 2: *The Creation of the Tree of Life*, 1 video, HL92057; Part 3: *The Sefirot: Emanations of God*, 1 video, HL92058; Part 4: *The Origin of Evil*, 1 video, HL92059, $10.95 ea. Complete lecture, 4 videos, $29.95, GL92056; 4 audiotapes, $29.95, A92050.

Kuan Yin's Miracle, 4 audiotapes, $29.95, A88068.

The Liberating Power of the Word, audiotape, album 1, 6 tapes, $44.95, A84035.

Lords of the Seven Rays: Find the Perfect Master and Crystal for You, 2 videos, $21.90, HL88027–28.

Lords of the Seven Rays on Crystals, with Chakra Initiations, 4 audiotapes, $29.95, A88078.

The Lost Teachings of Jesus: "On the Enemy Within," 2 audiotapes, $14.95, A87097.

The Lost Years and the Lost Teachings of Jesus, 1 video, $10.95, HL88002.

A Message of Perfect Love from the Heart of Gautama Buddha, 3 audiotapes, $21.95, A8134.

Mother Mary's Twentieth-Century Prophecies, 1 audiotape, $7.50, A91136.

Mother's Chakra Meditations, 8 audiotapes, $59.95, A82162.

On Dealing with Death, Discarnates and Malevolent Spirits, Part III, 4 audiotapes, $29.95, A91110.

On the Healing Power of Angels: Christ Wholeness—the Seven Rays of God, 2 videos, $33.95, GP87089; 3 audiotapes, $21.95, A87100.

On the Violet Flame and the Chakras, 1 video, $10.95, HL88063.

The Path of the Bodhisattva: Confession, 1 video, $16.95, HP88086; 2 audiotapes, $14.95, A88133.

The Path of the Bodhisattva: The Guru-Chela Relationship— Marpa and Milarepa, 3 audiotapes, $21.95, A88142.

The Path of the Bodhisattva: The Historical Maitreya, 2 audiotapes, $14.95, A88135.

The Path of the Divine Mother, 3 videos, $33.95, GP92043; 3 audiotapes, $21.95, A91116.

The Path of the Divine Mother East and West: Mother Mary and Kuan Yin, 3 audiotapes, $21.95, A88055 (Toronto); 3 audiotapes, $21.95, A88059 (San Francisco).

Peace in the Flame of Buddha, 2 audiotapes, $14.95, A7658.

Prophecy: Fátima and Medjugorje, 1 video, $10.95, HL87012.

Putting on the Armour and Shield of Archangel Michael, 1 audiotape, $7.50, B89059.

A Retreat on the Ascension, 8 audiotapes, $59.95, A7953.

Roots of Christian Mysticism, 5 videos, $37.50, GL92060; 6 audiotapes, $44.95, A92054.

Saint Germain and Violet Flame Decrees, 1 video, $9.95, 3105-06.

Saint Germain: Chohan of the Seventh Ray of Freedom, 2 audiotapes, $14.95, A7648.

Saint Germain On Alchemy, 2 videos, $26.50, V8607-0; 3 audiotapes, $21.95, S86096.

Saint Germain: "The Man Who Never Dies and Who Knows Everything," 1 video, $10.95, HL89008.

Saint Germain's Heart Meditation I, audiotape, $7.50, A87027.

The Science of the Spoken Word: Why and How to Decree Effectively, 4 audiotapes, $29.95, A7736.

Self-Healing Workshop with the Healing Power of Angels, 3 audiotapes, $21.95, A87023.

Seminar on the Cosmic Clock: Charting the Cycles of Your Karma, Psychology and Spiritual Powers on the Cosmic Clock, 2 audiotapes, $14.95, A88087; accompanying packet of study materials, $1.00, #2368A.

The Seven Elohim in the Power of the Spoken Word, 4 audiotapes, $29.95, A7636.

Teachings, Meditations and Mantras of Kuan Yin and Mother Mary, 3 videos, $33.95, GP88042; 3 audiotapes, $21.95, A88052.

Twin Flames and Soul Mates: A New Look at Love, Karma and Relationships, 1 audiotape, $9.95, S86005.

Twin Flames in Love I, 8 audiotapes, $59.95, A7856.

Twin Flames in Love II, 3 audiotapes, $21.95, A82155.

The Worship of the Goddess—the Path of the Divine Mother, 2 videos, $14.95, GL92065; 3 audiotapes, $21.95, A92073.

Notes

BOOK ONE
Studies in Alchemy

CHAPTER 1
1. Matt. 5:45.
2. Matt. 11:12.

CHAPTER 2
1. John 2:1–11.
2. I Pet. 4:18.

CHAPTER 3
1. Matt. 5:13.
2. Gen. 19:26.
3. II Tim. 2:15.

CHAPTER 4
1. Heb. 13:2.
2. Heb. 12:1.
3. Heb. 11:6.
4. Amos 5:4.
5. Matt. 19:26.

CHAPTER 5
1. Matt. 11:2–5.
2. Exod. 5:6–19.
3. Matt. 16:19; 18:18.
4. Luke 22:42.

CHAPTER 6
1. *mowlde:* Middle English
   for mold.

2. I Cor. 15:52.
3. Mark 8:22–26.
4. Rev. 22:17.
5. Matt. 9:16, 17.

CHAPTER 7
1. Gen. 1:3.
2. Luke 10:37.
3. John 14:17; 15:26; 16:13.
4. John 2:1–11.
5. Matt. 14:15–21.
6. II Chron. 7:1–3; II Kings
   1:10, 12.
7. Matt. 4:3, 4.
8. Matt. 6:33.
9. Heb. 11:1.

CHAPTER 8
1. Luke 22:42.
2. Matt. 10:34–36.
3. Matt. 19:26.
4. Rev. 10:9.
5. Rev. 22:19.

CHAPTER 9
1. Francis Bacon, *Essays
   or Counsels, Civil and
   Moral* (1625).
2. II Cor. 5:1.
3. I Cor. 15:31.
4. Eph. 4:22–24; Col. 3:9,
   10.

5. Julia Ward Howe, "Battle Hymn of the Republic," st. 5.
6. II Cor. 5:17.
7. Isa. 35:1.
8. John 14:2.
9. Hosea 8:7.
10. John 1:9.
11. Matt. 5:14; John 8:12; 9:5.
12. I John 1:7.
13. John 8:11.
14. Matt. 5:18.
15. Heb. 10:27.
16. Luke 7:47.
17. Ps. 136.
18. II Cor. 6:2.
19. Gen. 4:7.
20. John 14:16, 26; 15:26.
21. Ps. 2:7.
22. Ps. 37:1, 2.
23. Jer. 33:3.
24. Matt. 6:6.

BOOK TWO
Intermediate Studies in Alchemy

CHAPTER *1*

1. Rev. 3:15, 16.
2. Ps. 136.
3. Ps. 2:7; Acts 13:33; Heb. 1:5; 5:5.
4. Rom. 4; James 2:23.
5. Zech. 4:6.
6. John 14:12.
7. Acts 10:15.
8. Matt. 21:42.
9. Heb. 9:23.
10. Matt. 6:33; Luke 12:31.

CHAPTER 2

1. Gen. 1:26, 28.
2. Luke 21:19.
3. Eph. 5:26.

CHAPTER 3

1. *Destiny:* Deity established *in* you.
2. Prov. 22:6.
3. The establishment of a fountain of cosmic light over the city of Los Angeles was announced by the Great Silent Watcher at the Class of the Angels on September 21, 1963, "for a period of one hundred years or as long as the Great Law will permit." This tripartite etheric fountain extends thirty miles in diameter. The outer ring is composed of a blue fountain of cosmic faith rising one mile high above the city; the next ring, one mile within the blue, is a golden fountain of cosmic illumination twenty-eight miles wide and one mile and a half high; and in the center there is a pink fountain of cosmic love twenty-six miles across and two miles high. After the announcement, Mighty

Victory said, "We are laying the foundation stone here tonight for mankind's cosmic victory." Such a fountain of cosmic light may be established by the hierarchy with the assistance of the angel devas and builders of form wherever students faithfully invoke and visualize the fountain described.

4. Ps. 23:1.
5. Matt. 23:24.
6. I Cor. 15:54.

CHAPTER 4

1. Gen. 2:9; 3:24; Rev. 2:7; 22:2.
2. Heb. 13:8.
3. Matt. 6:33.
4. Alfred Lord Tennyson, "Sir Galahad," stanza 1.

CHAPTER 5

1. Gen. 3:22, 23
2. Exod. 7:8–12
3. Heb. 12:1.

CHAPTER 6

1. Matt. 4:3.
2. *Webster's Seventh New Collegiate Dictionary* defines noblesse oblige (literally, nobility obligates) as "the obligation of honorable, generous, and responsible behavior associated with high rank or birth"; that is, the sons of God, because of their high birth and heritage, are obliged to invoke the will of God and to practice the science of alchemy selflessly on behalf of all mankind.
3. See the Great Divine Director, "The Mechanization Concept," in *Pearls of Wisdom*, vol. 8 (1965), pp. 9–142, also available in paperback, *The Soulless One* (Los Angeles: Summit University Press, 1981).
4. John 10:10.
5. I Cor. 15:51, 52.

CHAPTER 7

1. Matt. 5:1.
2. Gen. 30:25–43.
3. Matt. 6:1.
4. Heb. 13:2.
5. II Cor. 3:18.
6. Matt. 21:1–7.
7. Mark 11:1–7.

CHAPTER 8

1. Rev. 12:1.
2. Rev. 4:6; 15:2.
3. I Cor. 14:8.
4. Matt. 3:17.
5. Matt. 16:26.
6. Matt. 10:16.
7. Isa. 11:9.

8. Acts 1:9, 11.
9. Matt. 24:40.
10. II Cor. 12:2.
11. Exod. 13:21.

CHAPTER 9

1. Saint Germain is using the term in its broad interpretation, "any pleasure in being abused or dominated" (*Webster's Seventh New Collegiate Dictionary*, s.v. "masochism").
2. Matt. 6:28, 29.
3. I Cor. 9:26.

CHAPTER 10

1. Luke 18:17.
2. Gen. 2:17.
3. Matt. 23:37.
4. I Cor. 2:9.
5. Matt. 28:18.
6. Gen. 3:24.
7. I Cor. 15:47–50.
8. Matt. 5:13.
9. Saint Germain uses the term "senile" here to mean approaching the end of an age.
10. *Innocence*: inner sense.

CHAPTER 11

1. John 3:17.
2. John 5:17.
3. Matt. 5:48.
4. Mark 10:32–34.
5. Luke 1:52.

CHAPTER 12

1. Matt. 24:22.
2. Mark 16:17.
3. *Ideation*: I AM Deity in action.
4. Isa. 40:6–8.
5. Matt. 14:15–21.
6. John 6:19.

Jesus Christ and Saint Germain

1. Dan. 7:9, 13, 22.
2. Exod. 3:13–15.
3. John 1:9.
4. Jer. 23:5, 6; 33:15, 16; Zech. 3:8; 6:12; Jer. 31:33, 34; Mic. 4:4.
5. Rev. 3:4, 5; 6:9–11; 7:9, 13, 14; 19:14.
6. Hab. 2:3; John 8:32.
7. Rev. 12:17; 19:10.
8. Rev. 14:6.
9. Matt. 5:17.
10. John 14:6.
11. Isa. 11:9; Hab. 2:14.

BOOK THREE

A Trilogy On the Threefold Flame of Life

CHAPTER 1

1. Prov. 16:32.
2. Luke 21:19.
3. Lord Acton to Bishop Mandell Creighton, 5 April 1887, quoted in

John Bartlett, comp., and Emily Morison Beck, ed., *Familiar Quotations: A Collection of Passages, Phrases and Proverbs Traced to Their Sources in Ancient and Modern Literature,* 14th ed., rev. and enl. (Boston: Little, Brown and Co., 1968), p. 750.
4. II Pet. 1:19.
5. Gen. 1:16.
6. Col. 3:11; I Cor. 15:28; Gen. 1:26, 27.

CHAPTER 2

1. Prov. 4:7.
2. Isa. 22:13; Luke 12:19; I Cor. 15:32.
3. Matt. 6:20.
4. Rev. 6:1–8.
5. Matt. 11:12.
6. Gen. 2:9; 3:24; Rev. 2:7; 22:2, 14.
7. Send for *Prayers, Meditations, and Dynamic Decrees for the Coming Revolution in Higher Consciousness*—a handbook of daily invocations to the sacred fire you can use to command the flow of God's Power, Wisdom and Love through your heart for the alchemy of positive change. Use precise formulas of the Word to balance and expand your threefold flame, transmute the records of past lives that are often the cause of current physical and emotional burdens, free yourself from unwanted habits, and direct God's healing light into the cause and core of community, national, and world problems. Sections I, II, and III, $2.95 each.
8. Matt. 10:36.
9. Matt. 13:24–30, 36–43.
10. Refers to George Orwell's book *1984,* published in 1949 and made into a movie in 1955 (produced by N. Peter Rathvon) and in 1984 (produced by Simon Perry).
11. Matt. 7:20.
12. Luke 6:39.

CHAPTER 3

1. John 15:13.
2. Rev. 3:16.
3. James 1:8; 4:8.
4. Rev. 3:12.
5. Luke 23:34.
6. Gen. 3:24.
7. Isa. 55:8.

8. Ps. 61:2.
9. I John 4:20.
10. I John 4:21.
11. II Cor. 5:6.
12. I John 4:18.
13. I John 4:18.
14. Heb. 11:6.
15. John 21:6.
16. I John 5:7.
17. John 3:16.
18. I John 4:7.
19. James 1:21.
20. Exod. 28:36; Zech. 14: 20, 21.
21. I John 4:16.
22. I John 4:17.
23. Matt. 25:21, 23.
24. Gen. 17; 18:9–15; 21:1–8; Judges 13; I Sam. 1; Luke 1.
25. Luke 16:8.
26. Heb. 13:1.
27. Gen. 2:18.
28. Gen. 22:17.
29. I Cor. 12:4–11.
30. John 13:34, 35.
31. John 15:13, 14.
32. Luke 23:34.
33. John 8:32.
34. Matt. 9:27–31.
35. Mark 5:25–34; Luke 8: 43–48.
36. Heb. 12:6.
37. Rev. 21:2, 9-27.

Index
for Books One, Two and Three

SUMMIT ❧ UNIVERSITY®

Apply the teachings of the saints and sages of East and West to the challenges of modern-day living

Summit University has everything you could ask for in a spiritual retreat. Located at the beautiful Royal Teton Ranch in southwestern Montana in the heart of the Northern Rockies, Summit University offers you a chance to get away from noise and pollution, daily cares and worries. Here people of all ages and walks of life come apart to commune with God. They experience the joy of physical, mental and spiritual renewal through study, prayer, meditation, a balanced diet of whole foods and communion with nature.

But Summit University is more than just a spiritual retreat. It is an unprecedented opportunity to study the mystical paths of the world's religions as taught by the Ascended Masters and their Messenger. Here you can learn how to apply the principles demonstrated by the prophets, saints and adepts of East and West to unfold the inner potential of your Creative Self and effectively deal with the challenges of modern-day living.

The Ascended Masters are part of a spiritual order of Western saints and Eastern Masters known as the Great White Brotherhood. (The term "white" refers not to race but to the aura of white light that surrounds these immortals.) They are our elder brothers and sisters on the path of personal Christhood who have graduated from earth's schoolroom, ascending as Jesus did at the conclusion of his earthly mission. At Summit University the Ascended Masters offer the living Teaching to those who would follow in their footsteps to the Source of that reality they have become.

Founded in 1971 under the direction of the Messengers Mark L. Prophet and Elizabeth Clare Prophet, Summit University holds an eight-week retreat each summer. It begins with you as self-awareness and ends with you as God Self-awareness. Day by day you can experience rebirth as, in the words of the apostle Paul, you "put off the old man," being "renewed in the spirit of your mind," and "put on the new man, which after God is created in righteousness and true holiness."

Summit University prepares you to walk the path of reunion with God. Working toward this goal, you will learn how to apply the sacred scriptures of East and West to your own path of discipleship. And you will explore the teachings of Jesus Christ, Gautama Buddha, Lao Tzu and Confucius as well as the teachings of Hinduism, the Kabbalah and other spiritual traditions.

Learn how to purify the aura and use prayers, mantras and meditations to solve personal and planetary problems

The curriculum at Summit University is unique. Here you will study techniques for self-transformation that you can use to live life to its fullest. You will learn exercises to purify and protect the aura and the chakras. You will study how to use astrology and the Cosmic Clock to chart the cycles of personal psychology and karma. Through a study of karma and reincarnation, you will gain profound insights into the karmic testings everyone must face on their chosen path.

Courses also include step-by-step instruction in how to use the science of the spoken Word and the violet flame of the Holy Spirit to transmute negative karma, the causes of disease and environmental pollution. And you will learn how to use prayers, mantras, meditations, dynamic decrees and visualizations to invoke God's intercession to solve personal, community and planetary problems.

Summit University also offers the teachings of the Divine Mother East and West, including Kuan Yin and Mary, with instruction on twin flames and how to use the teachings of the Ascended Masters to meet the practical needs of self and society. Teachings and meditations of the Buddha taught by Gautama, Maitreya and the Bodhisattvas of East and West are a highlight of the Summit University experience.

Tutored by professionals in the medical and health

fields, you will learn to put into practice some of the lost arts of healing that can help the soul reintegrate with her inner blueprint. These include realignment through balanced nutrition, macrobiotic cooking and natural alternatives to achieve wholeness. Classes in hatha yoga are also offered.

At weekend services you will hear lectures and dictations from the Masters delivered through the Messengers (in person or on videotape). At a midweek healing service, the Messenger or ministers offer invocations for the infirm and the healing of the nations. Other services include songs and hymns to the Blessed Mother for world peace.

The academic standards of Summit University emphasize mastering the basic skills of both oral and written communication. Summit University prepares students to enroll in undergraduate and graduate programs in accredited schools and to pursue careers as constructive members of the international community.

Summit University also offers training for "the Literacy Army," the Ascended Master El Morya's solution to the alarming rise in illiteracy. You will study effective phonics-based reading programs that teach you how to help children and adults of any age learn how to read, write and spell.

A spiritual community at the Royal Teton Ranch

Summit University is an integral part of the Community of the Holy Spirit located on the Royal Teton Ranch in southwest Montana. At this spiritual community ancient truths become the joy of everyday living in a fellowship of kindred souls drawn together for the fulfillment of their mission.

The Royal Teton Ranch is the international headquarters of Church Universal and Triumphant, The Summit Lighthouse, Montessori International, Henry Wadsworth Longfellow Academy and Summit University Press. Elizabeth Clare Prophet makes the Royal Teton Ranch her home and base of operations. Seekers of truth come to the ranch to retreat, meditate, commune with nature or participate in community life with the 600 permanent residents. Activities include organic farming and ranching, publishing the Ascended Masters' teachings and learning the art of macrobiotic cooking.

Montessori International is the place prepared at the Royal Teton Ranch for the tutoring of the souls of younger seekers on the Path. This private school for infants through grade six was founded in 1970 by Mark and Elizabeth Prophet. The faculty upholds the standards of academic excellence as well as the true education of the heart for the child's unfoldment of his Inner Self. Montessori International is dedicated to the educational principles set forth by Dr. Maria Montessori and the Ascended Masters. Montessori International programs also incorporate effective techniques developed by Glenn Doman, Romalda Spalding, and Anna Ingham.

For those aspiring to become Montessori teachers of children age two and a half through seven, Summit University sponsors a Montessori Teacher Training Course that offers an in-depth study of these principles and their application at home and in the classroom. This course is taught by Master Teachers trained by Dr. Elisabeth Caspari, a student of Dr. Montessori.

Those attending Summit University Level II focus on the education of the heart, the soul, the mind and the spirit as well as healing the inner child. To facilitate soul healing, they combine their spiritual studies with a study of the methods of Maria Montessori and other pioneers in education. Through a study of early childhood education, they learn to teach as well as to pick up the dropped stitches in their own development.

For information on Summit University, Montessori International, conferences and seminars, and the Ascended Masters' library and study center nearest you, call or write the Royal Teton Ranch, Box 5000, Livingston, MT 59047-5000. Telephone: (406) 222-8300.

FOR MORE INFORMATION

Mark L. Prophet and Elizabeth Clare Prophet have written over fifty books on the teachings of the Ascended Masters, the immortal saints and sages of East and West. Setting the highest standards of metaphysical writing, the Prophets have published such classics of esoteric literature as *The Lost Years of Jesus, The Lost Teachings of Jesus, Climb the Highest Mountain, The Human Aura, Saint Germain On Alchemy, The Science of the Spoken Word,* and *Forbidden Mysteries of Enoch* as well as annual volumes of *Pearls of Wisdom* published weekly since 1958.

In addition, the Prophets have lectured internationally and founded Summit University. Mark Prophet passed on in 1973 and Mrs. Prophet has carried on their work. She is based at the Royal Teton Ranch in southwestern Montana. The ranch is the home of a spiritual community where seekers for truth come to retreat, meditate, commune with nature, attend Summit University seminars, or participate in community life.

Mrs. Prophet conducts workshops and retreats on the practical application of the mystical paths of the world's religions. She explores the teachings of Jesus Christ, Gautama Buddha, Lao Tzu, and the great lights of Hinduism as well as teachings on the path of the Divine Mother, East and West. Cable TV shows based on these teachings air weekly.

For a free catalog of books and tapes or for information about Summit University retreats, weekend seminars and quarterly conferences, Mrs. Prophet's cable TV shows, the Keepers of the Flame Fraternity, or the Ascended Masters' library and study center nearest you, write or call:

Summit University Press, Box 5000, Livingston, Montana 59047-5000 Telephone: (406) 222-8300

All in our community send you our hearts' love and a joyful welcome to the Royal Teton Ranch!

Reach out for the **LIFELINE TO THE PRESENCE.**
Let us pray with you!
To all who are beset by depression, suicide, difficulties or insurmountable problems, we say
MAKE THE CALL! (406) 848-7441